American Murder

American Murder

Volume 2

Homicide in the Late 20th Century

Gini Graham Scott

PRAEGER

Westport, Connecticut
London

Library of Congress Cataloging-in-Publication Data

Scott, Gini Graham.
American murder / Gini Graham Scott.
p. cm.
Includes bibliographical references and index.
ISBN 978-0-275-98388-8 (set : alk. paper) — ISBN 978-0-275-99977-3 (v. 1 : alk. paper) — ISBN 978-0-275-99978-0 (v. 2 : alk. paper)
1. Murder—United States—History—20th century. 2. Murder—United States—History—20th century—Case studies. 3. Murder—Investigation—United States—History—20th century. 4. Murder in mass media—History—20th century. I. Title.
HV6524.S35 2007
364.15209730904—dc22 2007028409

British Library Cataloguing in Publication Data is available.

Library of Congress Catalog Card Number: 2007028409
ISBN-13: 978-0-275-98388-8 (set)
ISBN-13: 978-0-275-99977-3 (vol. 1)
ISBN-13: 978-0-275-99978-0 (vol. 2)

First published in 2007

Praeger Publishers, 88 Post Road West, Westport, CT 06881
An imprint of Greenwood Publishing Group, Inc.
www.praeger.com

Printed in the United States of America

The paper used in this book complies with the Permanent Paper Standard issued by the National Information Standards Organization (Z39.48–1984).

10 9 8 7 6 5 4 3 2 1

Contents

	Preface	vii
1	The 1960s	1
	The Case of Charles Schmid	*12*
	The Case of Jerry Brudos	*25*
2	The 1970s	39
	The Case of Ed Kemper	*48*
	The Case of Juan Corona	*59*
	The Case of David Berkowitz	*71*
3	The 1980s	85
	The Case of Wayne B. Williams	*98*
	The Case of Dorothea Puente	*113*
	The Case of David Brown	*128*
4	The 1990s	147
	The Case of Charles Stuart	*153*
	The Case of Pamela Smart	*168*
	The Murder of Tupac Shakur	*182*
	Notes	193
	Selected Bibliography	209
	Index	211

Preface

In many ways, the first half of the twentieth century seems like an age of innocence compared with the massive upheavals and changes in society since the 1960s. New developments in computers, communications, biometrics, forensics, and other sciences and technologies have not only revolutionized the way we live but have given today's homicide investigator an arsenal of new techniques for investigating murder. Among them are DNA analysis, informational tracking systems, internationally linked crime databases, telephone records, and credit reports, not to mention the global sharing of information by police, FBI, and other law enforcement personnel.

The pattern of crime also changed. There continued to be the typical homicides due to everyday conflicts, jealousies, and killings for revenge or money. Increasingly, the news pages and TV programs became filled with stories of serial killers and mass murderers—a trend that seemed to gather steam after the 1950s, driven by a number of factors, including the growing atomization and alienation of society, the loosening of traditional codes of morality, the increasing expression of sexuality in popular culture, and the fascination with crime in the media, turning some killers into celebrities. Less restrained by modern mores and fueled by images of sex and success (or rage if they weren't able to succeed in obtaining sex, money, or power), serial killers plotted and mass murderers acted on a media-saturated stage. The audience for these crimes as morality plays eagerly followed the latest criminal case as entertainment, and the smaller number of actual or potential victims experienced devastated lives or fears of being next.

This fascination was captured by the most influential, best-selling book of 1965—Truman Capote's *In Cold Blood,* based on his years of research in Kansas after two cold-blooded killers came to the farmhouse of wealthy farmer Herb Clutter and his family, searching for money. The killers were parolees, and had heard from another inmate who claimed he had money in a safe at the Clutter home. They weren't able to get any money, so they tied up the family members (Herb, his wife, and two children) and shot them in cold blood. In recounting the tale, Capote applied the techniques of fiction to telling a factual story, creating what was then considered the first nonfiction novel. He not only interviewed the local police and citizens, but became a close companion of the two killers until the day of their execution by hanging. His book was considered a masterpiece and he became the most famous writer in America as a result—a kind of harbinger of the kind of interest that continued through the 1960s and 1970s, leading to the true crime boom of the 1980s and 1990s. This renewed interest later showed up on TV, such as in the "you are there, blow-by-blow" criminal cases featured on the Court TV channel and the murder-of-the-week movie specials and on programs like *48 Hours* and *60 Minutes*. Capote's legacy in initiating this trend is still celebrated today, as witnessed by the release of two films about him—*Capote* (2005) and *Infamous* (2006), describing how he journeyed to Kansas with his friend, writer Harper Lee, after seeing a short article about the murders in the *New York Times* and became obsessed with the case.

This volume of *American Murder* explores developments in murder since the 1960s. As in Volume 1, the book looks at the changing nature of homicide and the investigative techniques used by the police, but it includes some of the most mysterious and baffling cases that have captured the public imagination. Using the same format as in Volume 1, which featured cases from the 1900s through the 1950s, each chapter begins with a discussion of homicide and investigative trends and then highlights a few of the most interesting cases of each decade. Most of the time, investigators were able to solve the case, but some remain unsolved.

In the 1960s, 1970s and 1980s, a growing number of serial killers appeared on the scene—some writers began to refer to these decades as the "age of the serial killer." In turn, homicide investigators increasingly began using psychological techniques to help them figure out who did it and why. Such techniques were initially developed by FBI profilers at the Behavioral Sciences Unit in the 1970s. The police began to turn to the FBI for help in some of their cases or learned to use these techniques themselves. At the same time, FBI help was often needed because a growing number of serial killers moved from state to state.

In the mid-1990s, DNA analysis came into use to help identify the killer. The 1994 O. J. Simpson trial was the first widely known use of the technique. Now that DNA evidence has gained widespread acceptance, it has been used to help solve previously closed or dropped cases.

The volume ends with the still unsolved murder of Tupac Shakur, in which a prominent rap star was shot in the middle of a busy Las Vegas intersection by a hail of bullets from a car that sped away. Despite hundreds of witnesses and the most scientific of investigative techniques, detectives still haven't solved the case. On the other end of the spectrum, without any witnesses to the murder and the most rudimentary of investigative methods 100 years ago, in the Cordelia Botkin case, they did find the killer. Developments since the 1990s will be the subject of future work looking at homicide and investigative techniques in the twenty-first century.

American Murder

Chapter 1

The 1960s

THE 1960S WERE a time of major social upheaval, protest, and change in America, and patterns of crime and investigation were impacted by these developments. Apart from the usual run-of-the-mill killings that developed out of personal conflicts, bar brawls, and robberies gone bad, many homicides were driven by ideology and erupted from anger about society. Some were expressions of violent anger from individuals who were alienated, took out their frustrations in a burst of gunfire, and were quickly caught.

In fact, murder historian Roger Lane suggests that the assassination of John F. Kennedy on November 22, 1963, marked a watershed in the history of the United States—signaling the transition into a more violent, angry decade. As he points out, there had already been some killings arising out of the beginnings of the civil rights movement during the decade—most notably the murder of black activist Medgar Evers in 1963.[1] The protests and killings for political reasons took center stage. As Lane writes, "As television replaced newsprint as the major source of information, new and heinous kinds of murder, including assassinations and killings for ideological reasons . . . were publicized more graphically than ever before."[2]

This social upheaval contributed to an overall rise in the homicide rate. Up to this point, the increasing urbanization of America, as well as the rest of the world, had contributed to a decline in homicide rates, due to civilizing effects of city living, despite the popular image of crime and violence in the cities. The protests against traditional institutions and social norms helped disrupt the usual rules and common courtesies that kept violence in check—there was more hostility and murder than ever. Meanwhile, contributing to this development was the growing movement of African Americans to the cities, accompanied by white middle-class flight to the suburbs, leading to the growth of an impoverished inner city—which led to more big-city homicides, too.[3] Yet another factor was the growing distrust of the police on the part of both African Americans who had learned to distrust the Southern justice system and students who began to flock to the civil rights cause and then turned their attentions to protesting U.S. involvement in the Vietnam conflict.

Thus, for various reasons from 1963 on until the beginning of the 1970s, a growing number of conflicts and homicides riveted the nation, turning popular attention from the more sensational individual and personal killings that were more like local and national soap operas to more serious murders for social reasons. In turn, the political outrage that followed some of these cases resulted in further strengthening the role of the Federal Bureau of Investigation (FBI) in dealing with homicides, particularly when local officials were sometimes involved in these cases—or when local investigators ignored key facts to protect their own.

One early example was the murders by the Ku Klux Klan of three Congress of Racial Equality activists, James Chaney, Michael Schwerner, and Andrew Goodman, in the summer of 1964 in Mississippi. When the authorities of Neshoba County failed to prosecute the crime as a murder, and civil right protests grew, the Justice Department stepped in. Eventually, FBI informants provided information to a federal grand jury, which arrested nineteen men, including Klansmen and law officers, for depriving the three men of their civil rights by killing them. In 1967 eight of them were finally sentenced to terms of three to ten years.[4]

Two defendants, E. G. Barnett, a Democratic candidate for sheriff, and Edgar Ray Killen, a local minister, were strongly implicated in the murder by witnesses, but they were set free by a deadlocked jury. Nearly three decades later, on January 6, 2005, Killen was indicted by a Neshoba County grand jury on three counts of murder and on June 21, 2005, he was convicted on three counts of manslaughter.[5]

Over the next few years, protests on the city streets turned increasingly violent, as anger against President Lyndon Johnson's involvement in the war in Vietnam and race riots and clashes with the police erupted in city after city—including New York, Philadelphia, St. Louis, Rochester, and many smaller cities. In some areas, small cadres of black activists, like the Black Panthers in Oakland, entered into an escalating war with the local police and FBI. At the same time, advocates of hippie and counterculture lifestyles on the college campuses and in major cities, especially in San Francisco's Haight-Ashbury area, promoted a general attitude of anti-authoritarian defiance and illegal drug use that contributed to the clashes with authorities that sometimes led to homicide. Lane describes this increasingly volatile atmosphere:

> Resentment of American actions in Vietnam and fear of the draft contributed to a collegiate counterculture, greatly expanded drug use, and hostility to authority in all

> forms. The civil rights coalition blew up as young militants turned on old white allies in the name of "Black Power" . . .
>
> Trouble almost always began (in the urban ghettos) as a conflict between police and local residents, maybe a "justifiable homicide" or even a minor arrest that sparked a fight and drew a crowd. The officers were then surrounded, jeered, and stoned. . . . When the National Guard was sent in serious killing began.[6]

Mostly the killings were of the rioters themselves, including some women and children, which only further increased the hostility toward authority and tension in the cities. However, by the end of the 1960s, the inner-city rioting cooled as residents began to realize they were the biggest victims. Not only were they more likely to be killed and injured, but the riots left the city area around them in smoky ruins.[7]

In the late 1960s, at a time when Americans were still debating who really killed Kennedy (many did not believe the 1964 Warren Commission report that Lee Harvey Oswald acted alone), two more assassinations shocked the nation and led to more questions about mysterious conspiracies. One was the killing of Dr, Martin Luther King Jr. in Memphis, Tennessee, on April 4, 1968. Though the presumed killer, James Earl Ray, was soon identified by his prints on the gun discarded on the scene, the mystery was how a hand-to-mouth petty thief and robber suddenly managed to become an international traveler able to escape with a false passport to Canada and then to London, where he was finally captured after an international search spurred by the FBI. The mystery deepened when Ray recanted his original confession that he acted alone and spoke of a mysterious "Raoul" who helped organize the plan to kill King and helped him escape. It is, in fact, still questioned today, with the support of the King family trying to find out who really planned the assassination.

On June 5, 1968, the killing of Robert F. Kennedy by Sirhan Sirhan in Los Angeles, at a time when Kennedy was just starting a run for the presidency, also raised questions about conspiracy. Though Sirhan protested he had killed Kennedy with no outside help but to call attention to the liberation of his native Palestine from Israeli rule, many questioned whether he had acted alone, especially when Sirhan, like Ray, repudiated his confession once in prison.[8]

Apart from these most famous assassinations of the 1960s, there were other politically motivated killings that generated their own mysteries—such as the killing of Black Muslim leader Malcolm X in February 1965, and the killing of Black Panthers leader Fred Hampton in December 1969 when the police stormed into his apartment in an illegal raid after several years of growing conflict between the police and Panthers.[9]

Such socially and politically motivated homicides contributed to pushing other types of more personal homicides with the more frequent motives of love, revenge, greed, and sex out of more general popular attention. The focus was on social movements and social protest. There was one especially notable exception that grew out of the other big social development of the 1960s—the rise of the hippies and counterculture.

For the most part, hippies and counterculture life did not spark homicides, since their entire ethos was one of love and personal freedom. The popular slogan was "make love, not war," and 1960s guru Timothy Leary spoke of "Turn on, tune in, drop out." The ideal was living in peace and harmony with others who shared similar values. Instead of striving for money and possessions, hippies urged peaceful communal living in a world where people helped one another and shared good vibes and good grass. It was also a world where conflict was discouraged, as were feelings of personal possessiveness and jealousy. Instead, people were encouraged to be open and sharing of one another in relationships. Should any personal conflict develop, people should feel free to simply move on. It was an atmosphere of "do your own thing," and presumably people would just enjoy and groove together in a peaceful environment, made even more harmonious by the use of feel-good drugs like marijuana, mushrooms, and LSD. Violence and killing would presumably be unlikely.

But at the end of the 1960s, the hippie scene turned ugly and led to one of the most highly publicized killings of the decade in August 1969. The sense of a failed hippie dream was already in the air. After the euphoria of Woodstock in New York in 1969, the widely publicized concert at Altamont in 1969 in northern California had turned violent, with the killing of a concertgoer by the Hells Angels, called on by the Rolling Stones to keep the peace at the concert. The 1967 Summer of Love in San Francisco had turned into growing crowds of tourists and money-hungry gangsters eager to turn a subculture built on love into a financial windfall. The easy, "let it happen" promotions of free concerts in Golden Gate Park by Chet Helms and the Family Dog had turned into a big business led by Bill Graham and his Fillmore concerts.

In this context, Charles Manson inspired a team of his followers, led by Tex Watson, to go to the Beverly Hills estate occupied by Roman Polanski's pregnant wife, Sharon Tate, on August 9, 1969. After an orgy of killing, they left her repeatedly stabbed body, along with those of four other victims in the mansion and on the grounds. Especially disturbing, they had written the word "pig" in Tate's blood on the living room door. The next day, Manson and his followers committed two more gruesome murders in the Los Feliz district of Los Angeles, stabbing the body of Rosemary La Bianca forty-one times and her husband twelve times. This time, they had left their statement in the form of the word "war" scratched on LaBianca's stomach, and the phrases "Death to Pigs," "Rise," and "Helter Skelter" written in blood on the walls. The killings terrified the rich and famous—including Frank Sinatra, who went into hiding—and mesmerized America. Two months later, in mid-October, the investigation led to a hippie cult known as the Manson Family living on a ranch in Death Valley. As investigators and the world soon discovered, Manson, a thirty-five-year-old petty crook with a long criminal record, had been able to entice a group of alienated teenagers and young adults to become part of a communal family that enjoyed a lifestyle full of sex and drugs, including LSD.[10] It was like a symbol of what the dream of the 1960s had become—the ideal of love and freedom turned inside out into violence. Though the crime was quickly solved and Manson and his followers were sentenced to long terms or life in prison, the case was riveting because of the mystery of *why* it happened. The killings seemed senseless—just done for the sport of it on a grand scale.

This apparent senselessness was also a harbinger of something new that came to characterize more and more of the homicides in the decades ahead—the rise of the mass murderers and serial killers. These kinds of killers felt no qualms about killing and were typically either motivated by a high level of anger against particular people or society in general or by a powerful sex drive that they felt free to express, given the breakdown in traditional social restraints. There were in fact a number of such killings in the 1960s—by serial killers such as Jerry Brudos of Oregon and Charles Schmid of Arizona, who targeted young women or girls; Albert DeSalvo of Boston, who went after women; John Collins of Michigan who targeted women at college; and the mysterious Zodiac killer of California, who seemed to go after anyone and sent cryptic messages to the papers about his latest crimes.[11] Mostly such killings were not given too much attention in the press, because the focus was more on the political turmoil and ideological killings of the period. Yet the stage was set for the big explosion that came in the 1970s, 1980s, and 1990s, as growing social alienation and breakdown of traditional social institutions led to a growth of homicides, as well as other types of crime.

Paradoxically, even as serious crime was growing, the social climate of the day led to changes in the law making it even more difficult for police officers and detectives to go after criminals—which perhaps contributed to the growth of crime. Besides effectively suspending the death penalty for any offense for the next few decades by trying to clarify the rights of criminal defendants, the U.S. Supreme Court limited the rights of police to use evidence in criminal trials. One famous ruling was *Mapp v. Ohio* in 1961, in which the court ruled based on the Fourth Amendment that the evidence found by police without a proper search warrant couldn't be used in a criminal trial. Another important ruling was *Gideon v. Wainright* in 1963, based on the Seventh Amendment, which required that any defendant in a felony trial had the right to a lawyer at state expense. In 1966, the Court decided the case of *Miranda v. Arizona*, based on both the Seventh and Fifth Amendments, and established that a person who was arrested had a right to be informed of the right to remain silent and have a lawyer.[12]

These and other rulings of the day not only helped defendants but contributed to the growing lawlessness and rising homicide rates of the day. They made it harder to obtain evidence that could be used in court and harder to convict. They contributed to reversing some convictions, including one of the most famous cases of the previous decade—the trial of Sam Sheppard, whose case is still in the news today, as the DNA on Sheppard's recently exhumed body is tested to determine maybe once and for all if he really killed his wife, Marilyn, or if, as he claimed, a "bushy-haired intruder" did it. In 1954, he was arrested after telling the police that he had struggled with this intruder and when he woke up, he discovered his pregnant wife lying bloody and dead in their bedroom from about thirty-five wounds with a heavy instrument, as investigators later determined. There had been no apparent physical evidence of an intruder, and neither the police nor the first jury believed him. In 1966, the Supreme Court agreed that he could be retried because there was so much publicity about his case in the 1950s that he couldn't get a fair trial. This time, with the help of defense attorney F. Lee Bailey, Sheppard was acquitted after a forensic expert testified for the defense that blood samples found in the house belonged to neither Sam nor Marilyn.[13] It was part of a continuing trend for well-connected defendants in high-profile cases to defeat any evidence against them with powerful attorneys. The new legislation made it even more easy for them to do so—plus, there was a growing number of such cases in the 1960s and on into the 1970s, 1980s, and 1990s as people felt freer to act out their criminal impulses, which sometimes led to murder.

By contrast, lower income killers were more likely to be convicted and sent off to prison or an insane asylum if convicted—and now there were a growing number of them. Their murders were more violent or their methods more devious and bizarre, as if in this "attack the establishment and authority" decade, they were trying to flaunt their ability to do so to the public. The press gladly accommodated them in their headlines and on the news.

One who did so in grand fashion was the Boston Strangler, who for a year and a half between 1962 and 1964 raped, killed, and sometimes sadistically mutilated thirteen women. His approach was to break into the locked apartments of his victims, who ranged in age from nineteen-year-old Mary Sullivan to eighty-five-year-old Mary Mullen. He got his name because of the way he left many of his victims—with a nylon stocking or cord around her neck. In some cases, he added bizarre calling card touches, such as when he left Sullivan with a broom handle in her vagina and a "Happy New Year!" card wedged between her toes.[14] He turned out to be a mentally deranged individual named Albert DeSalvo, who was then at the Bridgewater State Hospital. After being arrested for breaking and entering into an apartment, he reported hearing voices. Though he was never actually put on trial as the Boston Strangler, he was transferred to the Walpole State Prison and remained there for life. Though many people were disturbed that he was never tried, it was a way to effectively convict him for murder at a time when it was becoming more difficult to use evidence to try cases and secure convictions.

In July 1966 came another case that was dubbed the "Trial of the Century" because it was murder on such a grand scale. This occurred when Richard Speck, a drifting petty criminal who often worked as a ship hand or longshoreman killed eight student nurses from the South Chicago Community Hospital. They were living together in a nearby dormitory, and he originally went there intending to rob them to get enough money to get a place for the night before he shipped out the next day. Somehow, he got sexually excited as he bound one of the nurses to prevent her from running away to report him. He raped her, and then, shocked by what he had done, went on to kill her and seven other nurses, missing just one of them, who hid under a bed. Though he was soon caught and sentenced to death, the 1967 Supreme Court ruling invalidated that sentence, resulting in his resentencing to life in prison.[15] Though many were outraged that he had gotten away with murder, it was another sign of the "help and understand the defendant" times.

In short, as Lane describes it, the 1960s were a time when there was widespread anti-establishment political process, and the same spirit of rebellion contributed to rising crime generally and to increasingly violent bizarre and impulsive homicides—and lesser chances of convictions and penalties as well. In turn, these impulses were given support by the rapid growth of TV, which made people want more however they could get it, and the media helped glamorize the criminal as an ideological protester. As Lane observes:

> Homicide in the modern world has been mostly an irrationally impulsive crime, committed by young men, especially poor and aimless young men energized by frustration and anger. And in the 1960s . . . both consumption and employment combined to heighten frustration, release the curbs on irrationally impulsive behavior, and fill the streets with aimless young men. . . .
>
> The urban industrial revolution worked to curb impulsive behavior, as the hard discipline of mass schooling, backed up by cops and courts and moral lessons, reinforced the basic requirements of the new kinds of work itself. . . .
>
> But by the 1960s, the very abundance of the post industrial economy was creating whole new layers of frustration. Modern marketing techniques, such as mass advertising and open shelves, virtually cried "Take!" to all comers . . . [while] television greatly magnified "relative deprivation" . . . and so created demands for "More!" that were almost impossible to satisfy legitimately. And at the same time, it grew harder for many to satisfy more basic needs through ordinary work.[16]

As Lane goes on to explain, this volatile mix of forces might lead to murder, especially with the decline of traditional institutions, the restraints of traditional morality, and the appeal of alcohol and drugs.

> Once there was a clearly apparent reward for putting up with the boredom and frustration of mass education, for obeying the cops, staying out of trouble, learning to curb the appetite for mind-altering drugs. But once the decay of the urban industrial revolution diluted these payoffs, the moral lessons came to seem irrelevant and the institutions of social control simply tyrannical.[17]

More people were drawn to crime, including murder. More of these were of the serial angry man or sex killer variety, as well as killers who gave into an impulse for simply getting their name in the papers. Why? According to crime historians Colin and Damon Wilson, this new breed of killers was suffering from low self-esteem, and killings were a way to assert power over others, get attention from the national public, and basically assert that "they exist."[18] As Wilson and Wilson write, "In most cases of serial murder there is an element of this kind of self-assertion. Many such killers are naturally 'dominant'—members of what zoologists call 'the dominant' 5 percent—but find themselves in a situation in which they feel passive and impotent."[19]

Generally, such seeds for serial murder were planted in childhood due to neglect or abuse, according to the Wilsons, most particularly in lower income and working-class families, where physical abuse was most common, though in the upper income groups, a child might be more likely to feel emotionally deprived.[20] In the teenage years, when the hormones kick in, the individual—all of them male—would feel a compulsion to act out, leading to escalating attacks, including rapes; in some cases, the person would ultimately begin to kill. The process could go on quietly over time, until the killer was finally caught; in other cases, the killer might act out in a blaze of glory, seeking quick attention.

For instance, in one Mesa, Arizona, case in November 1966, an eighteen-year old student, Robert Smith, walked into a hairdressing parlor, ordered four young women and a three-year-old girl to lie face down on the floor, and began blasting away with a shotgun, killing them all. Afterward, when he was led away by police, he proclaimed to a bewildered press why he did it. "I wanted to get known, to get myself a name. . . . I knew I had to kill a lot of people to get my name in the newspapers all over the world."[21]

Cases like Smith's suggested that a new type of crime was beginning to emerge—the crime of self-esteem. Wilson and Wilson suggested this might correspond to the hierarchy of needs proposed by psychologist Abraham Maslow. Initially, humans at the bottom of the scale would want to simply survive; any killings at this level would be motivated by this urge. Once this need is satisfied, the next is for security, which would include crimes for financial gain. On the next level is a need for sex, love, and companionship, triggering the kinds of killings motivated by love triangles, jealousies, and romantic passion. Then comes the need to be "recognized and respected: in other words, the need for self-esteem." If this level is satisfied, a final level that sometimes emerges is the need for "self-actualization," expressed through various creative means.[22]

In Wilson and Wilson's view, the higher level of prosperity led to the rise of second-level crimes for domestic security, such as Belle Gunness killing prospective suitors for not only cash but a good home and social security. By the second half of the nineteenth century, the age of the sex crime—symbolized by Jack the Ripper in England—began as individuals sought to satisfy sexual needs. Starting in the late 1950s and flowering in the early 1960s was the rise of the crimes for self-esteem, with killers like Melvin Rees,[23] motivated not just by a desire for sex but a need for self-esteem and power. Whereas the earlier generation of sex killers like Earle Nelson or Ed Gein sought sex due to a powerful compulsion, while recognizing their urge was wrong, the new type of self-esteem killers no longer felt what they were doing was wrong. Instead, the blame should be on society itself, or perhaps on God or nature.[24]

> The typical rapist killer is suffering from a kind of sexual starvation, and he "steals" sex as a starving man might steal food. He recognizes it as wrong, but the compulsion is overwhelming. The self-esteem killer denies that what he is doing is wrong. Like some bomb-throwing revolutionary, he feels that society is somehow to blame—or God, or the laws of nature. It is true that he is a sex criminal, but sex is no longer the basic driving force. What such men are really interested in is power, self-esteem.[25]

In fact, Wilson and Wilson describe Charles Manson as a kind of self-esteem or even self-actualizing type of killer, who saw the murders as a kind of "violent protest against a society that denied him self-actualization."[26]

In turn, in the 1960s society seemed more supportive than ever of trying to understand these "abused," "misunderstood," or "low self-esteem killers," and they were not only supported by the ideological underpinnings of rebellion but by the attention of the media to the most bizarre and outrageous of the crimes. Meanwhile, due to all of these developments, the police and detectives found it more difficult to combat such crimes—even with the continuing advances in science.

These advancements were mostly further refinements of methods that were already in place and an expansion of the fingerprinting database kept by the FBI. In the mid-1960s, for example, more sophisticated "blood fingerprinting" techniques were developed. They included new methods of raising latent fingerprints on a porous surface, including cloth and wood, using iodine fumes and spraying the surface with a chemical known as ninhydrin. Additionally, investigators could now see fingerprints on flesh by employing a special X-ray technique to visualize the print.[27]

Unfortunately, the police still needed to have a record of the fingerprints on file somewhere if they didn't already have a suspect, as was the case in the notorious Zodiac killer in San Francisco at the end of the 1960s. The Zodiac started out as a predator on courting couples, and eventually killed five people and left two victims near death. To attract attention, he began sending letters to the press calling himself the Zodiac and threatening more terrible crimes, including commandeering a bus with schoolchildren and killing them all with a machine gun. He left a palm print and some fingerprints in two of his crimes. One occurred in September after he appeared wearing a hood at the popular Lake Berryessa, stabbed two picnicking students repeatedly, and shortly after called the Napa police department to report a double murder (although one victim survived). After the police traced the call to a phone a block away, they took a palm print from the telephone. But they had no way to match the print to anyone. The same problem occurred a few weeks later when someone shot San Francisco cab driver Paul Stine in the back of the head and ran off, leaving three bloody fingerprints on the passenger seat. Again, with no record of the prints on file, the police hit a dead end, although by now a few sightings as he fled had given the police a preliminary portrait of him. He was probably in his early twenties, was overweight, wore horn-rimmed glasses, and seemed to be very familiar with the San Francisco and northern suburbs of Napa and Vallejo. Perhaps some kind of mass fingerprinting might have worked as was once done in the English town of Blackburn twenty years earlier that caught killer Peter Griffiths. But this was never tried to catch the Zodiac, though after the Stine killing, the Zodiac stopped killing,[28] though he subsequently sent one of the police investigators on the case a few taunting notes to crow that he hadn't been caught (though there was some question later whether the police officer himself might have sent some of these notes to keep his own name in the news).

There were also further advances in ballistics. Earlier, the comparison microscope had provided a major step forward in that bullets or bullet fragments could be laid side by side and compared. In addition, other techniques came into wider use, such as making a gelatin cast of the bullet and then splitting it open and spreading it flat to examine one or more bullets more closely. In the mid-1960s, one ballistics investigator brought even greater precision to examining deaths by bullets. Herbert Leon MacDonell was called the Isaac Newton of ballistics by one journalist because of his unique breakthrough methods. When he made his name in ballistics, he was working for the Corning Glass Works in upstate New York and had already gained renown as an expert in porous glass technology. He often spoke to groups on forensic medicine as a Fellow of the American Academy of Forensic Sciences.

In April 1966 MacDonell was invited to apply his bullet examination skills after a fellow Glass Works employee, Robert Ferry, had shot another man, Roy Roxbury, on a deer hunt. Was it an accident in which Ferry had shot at a deer he had seen, or was it negligence in that Ferry was just shooting in the general direction of a noise he had heard? By closely examining the shotgun pellet that killed Roxbury, MacDonell was able to discover that the wadding packed between the explosives and the pellets to drive the pellets forward after firing was stuck to the slug instead of falling away after a few yards as usual. Then he discovered a particular wood fiber clinging to the slug, and the slug was much lighter than it should be. At the trial, MacDonell's theory that the slug had lost 14 percent of its weight and contained the wood fiber because it ricocheted off a tree was proof that the shooting had been an accident. After the jury agreed with him and found Ferry not guilty, he even found the exact tree from which the bullet had ricocheted. It was a masterful, novel use of ballistics. In 1969, MacDonell gained national celebrity in the field when he applied his techniques to the widely publicized killing of Fred Hampton, after he was shot in his Chicago apartment. According to the police version, the police had knocked on the door where Hampton was sleeping, but then had opened fire after a shotgun slug had torn through the door in response. After MacDonell carefully examined the trajectories of the shotgun shells in the door, he was able to determine that there was no evidence that any of the Panthers had fired. Using a piece of string from the impact crater through the hole in the door and opposite wall, he was able to trace the course of the revolver bullets and show conclusively that the bullets had been going in the opposite direction from that claimed by the police.

He even passed straws with thin metal rods inside through the bullet holes to show how the bullet holes in the door were in an exact line with those that had come through the wall, and he showed how the police had concentrated their fire at the bottom section of the bed, where their informant had said Hampton's head would be. As a result of his testimony, the grand jury investigating the case eventually ordered the FBI to turn over its own forensic evidence to the state attorney for Cook County, which supported the conclusion that the police had fired first. Eventually the Panthers won a $1.85 million judgment from Cook County on the grounds that their civil rights had been violated by the raid.[29] It was another illustration of the advances in ballistics during the decade.

Now there were the beginnings of a more psychological approach to understanding killers. A psychiatrist in New York, Dr. James Brussel, who was formerly the assistant commissioner of Mental Hygiene for New York State, started in the mid-1950s as a psychiatric consultant to various police agencies. The press called him the "Sherlock Holmes of the couch" for his novel psychological techniques, and he wrote about his methods in a 1968 book, *Casebook of a Criminal Psychiatrist.* He first started working with the New York Police Department in 1956 to help them figure out who had been planting bombs since November 1940. The bombs had been accompanied by assorted letters and threats that expressed anger directed against Con Edison, such as the note planted beside the first bomb that didn't explode: "Con Edison Crooks—This is for you." In 1955, as the bombs and letters became more frequent, one letter to the New York *Herald Tribune* read "So far 54 bombs placed—these bombings will continue until Con Edison is brought to justice." After a December 1956 bomb blew up seats in the Paramount Theater in Brooklyn, injuring six people, the police began an intensive manhunt and called on Dr. Brussel to help. Brussel soon crafted an uncannily accurate profile of a paranoid, middle-aged man of about forty-five or fifty, who was single, a loner, and had a serious grievance against Con Edison for an earlier injury.

After his profile turned out to be right on target, investigators called on him more in the 1960s to develop profiles of killers in other cases, including the Boston Strangler and Dr. Carl Coppolino, an anesthesiologist who was accused of killing his wife. As Brussel described his methods, which later became used to combat the growing number of hard-to-find serial killers:

> I always start such a deduction with a solid basis of science, but somewhere along the way intuition and imagination begin to take over. When you think about an unknown criminal long enough, when you've assembled all the known facts about him and poked at them and stirred them about in your mind, you begin to *see* the man. You picture his face, hear his voice. . . . You may even see the clothes he wears.[30]

As the 1960s developed, so did more sophisticated methods of both physical and psychological investigation to deal with even more difficult-to-solve crimes—especially those involving strangers killed by serial killers. Among the most baffling were the search for the serial killer of women in Oregon from 1964 to 1966 and the serial killings of women left in the desert of Arizona between 1964 and 1965. Following are these stories, reflecting the trends and developments in investigative techniques for the 1960s.

THE CASE OF CHARLES SCHMID

Tucson, Arizona, 1964–66

In late May 1964, the United States was still reeling from the assassination of John F. Kennedy, just six months before, and it was the beginning of the Beatles craze. Their song "A Hard Day's Night" was just hitting the charts, followed by "Help!" the next year, and the image of the outlaw as hero—or the hero as outlaw—had become very trendy. Even at a time when some films were celebrating old-fashioned virtues, like *Mary Poppins* and *My Fair Lady*, others like the first big James Bond movies and Anthony Quinn's *Zorba the Greek* were paying homage to the larger-than-life individualist, who liked to do things his own way, whether capturing bad guys or celebrating life. One of the rewards was adoring female admirers. At the same time, the usual rules of behavior were being replaced by a more do-your-own-thing ethos being celebrated by a rising counterculture that contemporary writers and filmmakers were already warning about, such as in the Peter Brook film *Lord of the Flies* based on William Golding's 1954 book about boys who run rampant on an island, released from the norms of ordinary civility. It was also a year when there was race riots in Harlem and many other U.S. cities in reaction to the enforcement of civil rights laws; Cassius Clay, who later became Muhammad Ali, had just won the world heavyweight boxing championship from Sonny Liston. A growing number of teenagers were playing out the James Dean image. Even if he had been a rebel star who died in the 1950s, his cult image lived on in the restless teenagers who hung out on the dusty cruising roads of the 1960s, like in Tucson in 1964.

Back then, Tucson was a kind of dead-end dusty stop in the desert where there was little to do, and the teens living there became restless and bored easily. Though the city had grown rapidly after World War II to a population of about 300,000 by the mid-1960s, and most of the jobs were in copper mining, agriculture, and air and missile facilities, unemployment was high and wages were low. Thus, many teenagers and young adults were unemployed, and with overcrowded schools and split shifts, many of them had lots of excess time on their hands to hang out and drift. Jack Gilmore describes those days: "'Tucson is dead,' the kids complain. For most of them—uninterested in school, unemployable—the desert takes nothing and offers nothing, but remains an embarrassing burden. Life is a drag. 'There's nothing to do.'"[31]

As a result, the police found that many restless teenagers and young people simply went missing because they had run away from a place that offered nothing. Those that stayed would typically head to the East Speedway drag through town. "That's where the action is," as one police sergeant described it. In those days, that's what the speedway was—"a long broad unzoned road reaching from downtown Tucson east across the city, fading into the foothills and cactus, crowded with drive-ins, hamburger havens, service stations, used-car lots, laundromats, and rock 'n' roll clubs."[32] The boys would come with their "hot-engine" cars with "bitchin' wheels," and the teenage girls would flock to party with them, either in the desert or in someone's house.

In that kind of world, Charles Schmid Jr. told stories and attracted a small following of loose-end guys and drifting teenage girls. "Smitty," later called the Pied Piper of Tucson, was known for his fascinating stories and the way he attracted a following of young girls when he was a teenager and in his early twenties. He had a compelling presence, almost like a Svengali, even though he was quite short (only five feet, three inches) and had no major job or financial prospects. He managed to attract a bevy of bored young teenagers who hung out at the drive-ins and juke joints along Tucson's East Speedway Boulevard and they thought of him as a happening swinger—someone who always had "wheels, money, tall tales and an inexhaustible supply of available girls' phone numbers," as one article about him in *Time* put it (November 26, 1965, p. 27).

In high school, Schmid had been a gymnast and had even won the state gymnastics championship in 1960. But he was never a very good student and dropped out of school, preferring instead to impress girls by cruising down the street in his red convertible and looking like a pint-sized Elvis Presley lounge lizard in his slick, raven-black dyed hair, pancake makeup, pale cream lipstick, engineer boots stuffed with rags to make himself seem taller, and cowboy-style sleeveless poncho or vest. He got a little money—about $300 a month—to support himself from his adoptive parents, who had once operated a child care center and now operated a nursing home. He was under no real pressure to find a steady job. He dabbled occasionally at putting together a rock band or imagining entrepreneurial ventures that might turn into something, like an idea for a laundry he imagined. But none of these projects ever got off the ground.

Instead, Smitty seemed to find his gift in weaving fascinating, bizarre stories about mythical achievements and outrageous outlaw behavior, imagining himself with unusual psychic powers allowing him to visualize things before they happened, and waxing philosophic about how life was like a cosmic joke with a God who played with people like puppets. He was determined to rebel against these ordinary rules and regulations that held everyday people in check. He intended to be different and stand out from the crowd. As he shared with Gilmore in interviews, diaries, and letters, "Something too powerful inside me drives me and makes me different. I have to wear different shoes that I've designed. I've got to make my car different and I have to be different. . . . I can't be a puppet or do what everybody else does. . . . I want to be an individualist."[33]

This pose attracted a few teens eager for adventure and excitement. Among them was Mary French, a girl who was often a bit out of it, given to lapsing into daydreams before she dropped out of school, and John Saunders, another poor student and dropout who was often beaten, bullied, or teased in school when younger. A third was Smitty's good friend, Richard (Richie) Bruns, who spent a short time in jail for burglary.[34] Smitty had met Mary at a desert beer party, and while he continued to date and propose marriage to other girls, he led Mary to think he might marry her, so she got a job at a local hospital and contributed her earnings to an account in his name. For Smitty, Mary and the other girls helped him feel like a gigolo; they were like playthings to him—and with his smooth talking and fascinating stories, he got them to do things for him or keep his secrets. Mary and John particularly did things for him, which helped confound the police.

That's what happened on the night of May 31, 1964, when Alleen Rowe disappeared. Schmid and Saunders dropped by at Mary's house around 8 p.m., and Schmid began talk about how he wanted to kill someone that night. He had talked about this before, telling Mary, "I want to kill someone. I want to kill a girl," because he wanted to see what it would be like and if he could get away with it. He had previously put together a list of possible candidates, including fifteen-year old Alleen Rowe, who had once stood up Saunders for a date, and he asked Mary to try to talk Alleen into going out with John again. He even told her his plans in advance that he would "hit her with a rock and bury her in the desert."[35] Earlier that afternoon, Mary had tried repeatedly to get Alleen to go out with John, and Alleen said she couldn't go because she had exams the next day at school and had to be there at 6 the next morning. But finally, Alleen agreed. Her mother left at 9 p.m. to go to work, thinking Alleen was shortly going to bed. Mary tapped on the window just after her mother left to let her know Smitty and John were outside in the car waiting. Alleen snuck out wearing just a bathing suit and shift with her hair in curlers, and Alleen jumped in the backseat with John; Mary joined Smitty up front. Outwardly, it seemed like just another double date, and they headed toward a wash at the edge of the desert where Smitty and Mary had gone to drink before.

After they sat around drinking for a while, Smitty asked Mary to get a radio from the car and walked her partway, when Alleen began screaming. "She needs help," Smitty said, and after telling Mary to go to the car and stay there, he returned to where Saunders was trying to kiss a naked and crying Alleen. Smitty handed him a rock, but Saunders couldn't hit Alleen with it, so Smitty hit her on the head himself. Afterward, he returned to the car to get a shovel and asked Mary to follow him down to the wash. He told Mary, "I love you very much." She helped them dig a hole and bury Alleen. Afterward, Smitty took off his blood-stained shirt, buried it and the shovel, wiped the car of fingerprints, and took Mary home. On the way, Smitty reminded both John and Mary to stick to the same story—that John had a date with Alleen that night, but when they went to pick Alleen up, she wasn't home. So they took Mary home and he and John went their own way.[36]

This was the story they stuck with for over a year, despite hours of repeated questioning by police. With no other evidence to show that Alleen was anything but another teenage runaway in a town that knew so many of them, the police felt there was nothing they could do.

Norma Rowe, Alleen's mother, certainly tried the best she could to rouse police interest. When she called the following evening to report Alleen was gone and only her bathing suit was missing, one officer told her, "Girls disappear for a while after disagreements with their parents . . . but usually they return home as soon as they're hungry."[37] He spoke about boyfriends and elopements as possible reasons for leaving home, and though he was surprised that none of Alleen's clothes were missing besides the bathing suit, he kept trying to reassure her mother. He didn't put much stock in a strange story Rowe related about some kind of sex club of local young boys and girls involved in drugs, liquor, and organized prostitution. As Norma explained, Alleen had told her the leaders of the group had tried to get her to join the club but she had repeatedly turned them down. She was now afraid that this group had "tried to force Alleen into their terrible activities," and when Alleen refused again, the leaders had done something to keep her quiet.[38]

"We'll investigate," said the officer, but over the next few days, they found no evidence to show there was any kind of sex club operating—though later news accounts would talk about a "sex club" killing.[39]

Meanwhile, Norma did what she could to keep the police on the case. Besides calling to find out about any new developments, on the day she reported Alleen's disappearance, she wrote up a list of potential suspects, which included the names of Charles Schmid, John Saunders, and Mary French, because Alleen had told her about Mary and her friends in the past and Norma didn't fully approve of them. Since the police had no other leads, they went out to question those on the list. In fact, they questioned Mary French eight or nine times the first day, as well as talking to Schmid and Saunders. Schmid repeatedly called Mary to ask if the police had questioned her yet. Later that night he came over, first alone and later with Saunders, and they drove out to an isolated dirt road, where Schmid went over the story they had agreed to tell the police so they would "all have it straight."[40] Apparently, they convinced the police for the time being.

Norma's accounts to the police were getting wilder. A week after Alleen disappeared, Norma's ex-husband called from Texas to say he had a nightmare in which the girl was murdered in the desert, and Norma was convinced this was the case. When she told the police, they said they needed more "factual evidence," and for now they had no more real leads to pursue. Briefly, Detective Sergeant Robert Wilhelm, heading up the Juvenile Detail, stepped into the case and sent out several detectives who questioned a number of people Alleen had known. But again, nothing turned up.

Norma looked for help to private detectives and reporters, who asked some questions as well. But nobody was talking. In fact, a few teenagers, including Schmid, even sought the assistance of their parents and family lawyers to stop the questions. Their lawyers, among them John Price representing the Schmids, obtained injunctions to prohibit the police from further questioning their children, which further hampered any investigation. As one lawyer commented to reporters, "These kids have no information and are being badgered by the police to cover up for their own lack of information about the missing girl."[41]

The problem was the wall of silence that was created by the power of Schmid to keep those who knew in line. From time to time the police got occasional reports that Alleen had been seen on the streets of various cities in the Southwest, and they duly checked these out. Of course, the leads went nowhere. Almost a year later, in March 1965, Norma spoke to the state attorney general and then to the head of the FBI in Arizona, but they could do little. Finally, she told reporters that the police thought Alleen was a runaway, though she was sure her daughter was dead.

A week later, reading about her frustrations, an anonymous woman called the Rowe residence with a possible lead, telling Norma's fourteen-year-old son, Clint, that she saw a grave near the end of a golf course and that she knew in the past there were some "really rough groups of kids out there, drinking and having wild parties." She told essentially the same story to the police, giving them the name of the golf course at the Rolling Hills Estates.

The call rekindled Mrs. Rowe's hopes that there might be some resolution, and that Saturday, Sergeant Wilhelm led a group of detectives through the golf course and surrounding area. They found nothing remotely resembling a grave; when Mrs. Rowe conducted her own search later, she didn't find anything either. News of the search stirred up more calls and leads that went nowhere. Norma even consulted a psychic from New Jersey and at her request, sent her an item of clothing owned by Alleen, so the psychic could try to sense where she might be now. The psychic didn't have any more luck than the police had.

Meanwhile, Schmid was going on with his life like nothing had happened; Saunders went off to join the navy shortly after Price had gotten the injunction preventing the police from asking Schmid further questions. But then, Schmid couldn't help but brag, though the friends he told at first thought this was just another of his fantastic stories. Then he killed again.

The second murder occurred after Saunders had joined the navy and Smitty started hanging out with his friend Richie Bruns. Smitty enjoyed telling Richie what a "terrible man" he was, while Richie would share his own secrets. The stories involved a mix of truth and fictional bravado. Plus they shared plans for wild schemes, such as when Smitty told Richie he wanted to order a pair of piranha fish from South America that they could breed and dump into a local lake.[42]

In July 1994, Smitty noticed a sixteen-year-old blonde named Gretchen Fritz at a swimming pool near the speedway hangout. Though her father was a leading heart and chest specialist and her mother was active in local society affairs, Gretchen had a wild side and the reputation as being an "easy put-out." She frequently cut classes to cruise along the speedway and was implicated in the attempted hold-up of a liquor store. Smitty soon began dating her, and one time Gretchen brought two of her girlfriends along on a double date with Bruns. But Richie insulted one of them, who he thought was a "fat pig," and after that there was a mutual dislike between Richie and Gretchen.[43]

For a time, Smitty's relationship with Gretchen became wild and furious. One time, for instance, Gretchen's father caught him naked at their house, but he didn't stop them from seeing each other, though they tried to be more discreet after that. Smitty would slip into her window at night and they would make love while her parents were asleep elsewhere in the house.

At the same time, Smitty continued to see other girls, including Mary French. After a few months, Gretchen began fighting with Smitty, often because she was jealous. Also, she sometimes complained about Richie, suggesting he might get Smitty in trouble because he had been in a reformatory and had committed assorted misdeeds, which he had confessed to Smitty, though not all of them were true.[44] The relationship got even more complicated when Smitty began seeing sixteen-year-old Darlene Kirk, in addition to Gretchen and Mary French, offering to get engaged or married to all of them at various times. Though Gretchen wanted Smitty to be loyal to her, she ran around with others as well, and Smitty was very jealous of anyone who showed the slightest interest in her. One time, Smitty even enlisted Richie in a letter-writing campaign to Gretchen's parents so they would keep a closer eye on her. In one such letter, Richie anonymously wrote, "Where was your darling daughter when you were having dinner last night? She was down at Johnnie's seeing Smitty."[45] Smitty even dictated one letter for Richie to type and send to the health department saying that Gretchen had venereal disease; then he told Gretchen that Richie was behind the letters.

One day in the summer of 1964, shortly after Smitty and Richie began fantasizing about and planning possible crimes together—from assaults and mayhem to murder—Smitty, Richie, and another boy actually made a quick foray over to the house of a girl named Mary Tyler they both said they hated. But a few days after a botched attempt to get in her house that was foiled when they heard footsteps, Smitty confided to Richie the story of what happened to Alleen Rowe. By then, Saunders was out of the navy, and while Smitty, Saunders, and another boy were on a hunting trip by the golf course, Smitty bragged about how he had done it and how his lawyer had gotten an injunction against the police so they couldn't question him about it anymore. Richie didn't know whether to take the story seriously, but the following week, he passed the story on to a few local teens who hung around the speedway. Meanwhile, Smitty himself told another longtime friend of his, Paul Graff, who had himself spent some time in an industrial school for boys as a result of a hold-up gone bad. "Do you want to go out and see the grave?" Smitty joked, though at the time, Paul declined to go. While the police and Mrs. Rowe remained in the dark, the story about what may or may not have happened to Alleen Rowe spread.

Possibly Smitty may have told Gretchen about it, too, and may have even taken her to the grave to show her the body, since he later told Richie that Gretchen was "blackmailing" him that she might tell if he "didn't do exactly what she said."[46] Then again, this might have been another one of Smitty's tall tales. In any case, Smitty's relationship with Gretchen was becoming increasingly troubled, and Richie, who never liked Gretchen, was urging him to dump her. At one point, Paul offered to provide a quart of sulfuric acid and Richie offered to throw it at Gretchen, but Smitty hesitated to do anything, still feeling ambivalent about his relationship with her. He decided to dump Darlene and tried to match her up with Richie, though Darlene was much less interested in Richie than he was in her.[47]

This was a kind of odd explosive triangle that would eventually lead to both murder and Schmid getting caught. Gretchen went to San Diego with her parents on a vacation. Smitty had tried a brief fling at starting an upholstery shop, but his partners tried to cut him out of the arrangement, and it collapsed, leaving him feeling discouraged by another failure. He tried to relax with another round of parties for a couple of weeks. Gretchen returned from California, complaining about the parties while she was gone. On top of that, Mary was asking Schmid to marry her because she claimed she was pregnant with his baby. Meanwhile, Richie had started following Darlene around, watching her obsessively, perhaps afraid he might lose her to Schmid.

This was a recipe for disaster. Gretchen called Smitty in early August saying she, too, was pregnant and wanted to know what he would do about it. Their argument was perhaps the last straw. A week later, on August 16, Gretchen drove over to Schmid's, asked him to run away with her to get married, and when he refused, she ran off, calling out, "You rat!" and drove away.

That night was the last time Gretchen's parents saw her. At about 7:30, she left for the Cactus Drive-In Theater with her thirteen-year-old sister, Wendy, to see the currently popular Elvis movie *Tickle Me*. During the intermission, Wendy went to buy some refreshments, but Gretchen and Wendy never returned home. After Wendy left the window, no one seemed to know what happened to the sisters.

The next morning, Mrs. Fritz began calling Gretchen's friends, but no one seemed to know anything, including Schmid, though he offered to check around and actually made a few calls. Mrs. Fritz called the police, who began by checking the neighborhood and the Cactus Drive-In, and then visited the houses of some friends of both girls. After nothing turned up and the police put out an all-points bulletin for Gretchen's car, they first thought maybe Gretchen was kidnapped because of Dr. Fritz's prominence in the community. After several days without a request for ransom, they felt that perhaps the girls had simply run off. When they spoke to Schmid, he suggested that maybe Gretchen had made some new friends in San Diego and had gone there. The police never bothered to check out this possibility, just figuring that Gretchen was one more willful, rebellious teen who had gone away—much like they had thought Alleen

Rowe had done about a year before. That's what Schmid told Richie the day after Gretchen disappeared—"She ran away last night and took Wendy with her and left in the car."[48]

In turn, much like Norma Rowe had a year before, Mrs. Fritz hired a local private eye, William Helig. He managed to turn up a possible lead four days after the girls disappeared—he found Gretchen's Pontiac in a hotel parking lot near the speedway. It looked like the car had been driven about sixty miles to a dirt road, since there was gravel and mud on the floor in front and on the back seats. He also found Gretchen's purse with $20, two movie ticket stubs, Gretchen's keys, and a business card from Smitty's upholstery shop. It was enough for the police to do some more investigating, and the resulting press coverage led to a call to the rangers patrolling south of Tucson that two girls who looked like Gretchen and Wendy were hitchhiking on the Nogales highway, when a car heading toward the Mexican border picked them up. Were they there? After the head of the Rangers Sheriff Burr said he didn't have the authority or the money to send a deputy across the Mexican border, Dr. Fritz volunteered to pay, and Range Deputy John Gammons spent a few days in the border town of Nogales with pictures of the girls asking questions of residents. About a dozen people reported seeing two girls who looked similar, and many thought they saw the girls boarding a bus heading south into Mexico, but the immigration authorities had no record of the girls getting tourist permits. Gammons traveled on, traveling about 500 miles into Mexico to Mazatlán. But nothing. Gammons returned discouraged, though the sheriff's department sent out hundreds of handbills in Spanish and asked a Mexican newspaper to print a notice about the missing girls. That led nowhere, too.

Helig continued to ask questions in Tucson, including contacting Schmid, feeling somehow he must know something since he had gone steady with her for several months. How was it, Helig probed, that Gretchen and her sister would simply leave without giving him some idea or even "an inclination that she wanted to leave, or was planning to go somewhere?"[49]

Still Schmid kept his cool, telling Helig that Gretchen only talked vaguely about her desire to leave but never mentioned any definite plans. The best he could do was suggest that Gretchen had returned to San Diego.

At this point, the whole investigation by both the police and Mrs. Fritz's private eye might have hit a serious dead end, much like the Rowe investigation had the year before. But again Schmid kept on talking—and this time he told the wrong person, who was afraid that maybe he might next kill his own girl, too. About a week after Gretchen disappeared, Smitty was drinking beer with Richie when he began talking about what really happened to Gretchen, saying he had killed her and her sister right there in the living room and then carried them to the trunk of Gretchen's car and put them in the most obvious place where he could get caught, because he just didn't care any more. "And that's three, counting Alleen. Each time it gets easier."[50]

Initially Richie wasn't sure whether to believe Smitty. It could be just idle talk. In any case, Richie didn't say anything right then. Meanwhile, the official investigation went along listlessly. The police seemed to be at a dead end.

Mrs. Fritz continued her own unofficial efforts. Much like Mrs. Rowe had turned to a psychic, Mrs. Fritz turned to an astrologer, who told her the girls were dead. In turn, Helig turned to a kind of underworld group called the Tucson Mafia to put some pressure on Schmid, who he felt knew more than he was telling. Since Schmid had told Helig he believed Gretchen and Wendy had gone back to San Diego, Helig decided to give Schmid the chance to prove it. Two members of the Tucson Mafia would personally escort him to San Diego.

The scene was like something out of a bad detective movie. Schmid got a call that two men would come pick him up and take him to a meeting—a night when Schmid had invited Richie and other friends over for a party. Just before this party was supposed to begin, at about 7 p.m., two well-dressed men arrived in a car to pick up Schmid, and as the friends he invited to party went into his deserted house, the men took Schmid to a small upstairs apartment. After grilling him a little about his San Diego claim, they drove him back to the party at his house, so they could talk to Richie about what he knew. Richie blanched white as a sheet, as Schmid described how they wanted to take him to San Diego to look for Gretchen, since he recalled seeing the men's picture in the papers in connection with the Mafia.[51] But he said he knew nothing. Smitty tried to reassure him that he would just go along with the guys and try to "fake it out as best I can." He could see that Smitty was worried that the Mafia and others were now looking for the girls.

Did Smitty really do something? Even Richie wasn't sure at this point, though the meeting with the Mafia guys unnerved him. As a result, he urged Smitty to call the FBI to report them, and though Smitty claimed he couldn't get through, Richie called himself and left a message. Meanwhile, Richie began getting nervous, because he was known around town for having a feud with Gretchen. Maybe he could get in trouble, too, if the girls' bodies were found, so he suggested going out to the desert to bury them. As he later stated, he just wanted to see the bodies—to see if there really *were* dead bodies. In the past, Smitty had told him so many stories—some of them true, some not. With the Mafia coming around trying to find out what happened, he wanted to be sure.[52]

The day before Schmid left for San Diego, he took Richie to see the bodies. After they dropped by Smitty's parents' house to pick up a shovel, they stopped for hamburgers and drove to a popular drinking and making out spot by the desert. Taking the shovel with them, they began walking. At first, after they walked a ways toward the wash, Schmid couldn't find them and Richie began to have doubts. But then, Schmid announced, "Wait a minute, I smell her." Moments later, Schmid was pointing to a dark black form at the bottom of the wash, and Richie saw bits of hair, a white bra peeking through a blouse, and an old rag tied around the legs. "We better bury the bodies," Schmid said, and Richie helped him do it. On the way back, Schmid commented to Richie, "You are in it as deep as I am now," which left Richie a little shaken. The next day, Schmid headed to California—just missing the FBI, which had stopped at his house looking to talk to him, perhaps because of the message Richie had left at their office.

Schmid's trip was the beginning of the end. Soon after he checked into a motel near the beach with the two men, Schmid went around to places by the beach with photos of Gretchen, asking if anyone had seen her. In doing so, he apparently gave the impression of being an FBI agent, and around 4 p.m., a group of policemen arrested him for impersonating an FBI agent. At the station, the police advised him that he was going to be charged with murdering the Fritz sisters. Oddly, after he was held and questioned for an hour, he was released, and when he returned to the motel, he discovered that the police had just arrested the two Mafia men and taken them away from the motel in handcuffs.[53]

Not knowing what to do or how to get back to Tucson, since he had no money, he called his mother collect, who wired him some money, and he took a bus back to Tucson. As he rode back, his parents contacted Richie to find out if the Mafia guys had tried to take him anywhere, and though he said no, the story shook him up even more. When Schmid returned, there were more questions to him about what happened in San Diego from the Tucson police and the FBI; Helig himself went about questioning again all the teenagers he had spoken to before. Several police officers began questioning them again, too.

The pressure was stepped up, and once more, Schmid's parents and other parents sought and obtained an injunction from the court to stop the interrogations. It was like a replay of what happened after Alleen Rowe disappeared. No one was talking, though many people knew.

If only someone would break. The investigation seemed stalled again, as Smitty, Richie, and the other teenagers who hung out on the strip went on with their lives. In early October, Smitty went on a date with fifteen-year-old Diane Lynch, who had not been getting along too well with a boy she had been going steady with. A friend, Gloria Andrews, fixed her up with Smitty, apparently hoping to get Diane's old boyfriend on the rebound. The date started out with a foursome at a Mexican taco café, and soon after Smitty and Diane hit it off, Gloria and her date dropped them off at a local restaurant where they could talk together. The evening went well, and they weren't even discouraged when an elderly astrologer wearing Indian jewelry stopped by their table saying, "You two must never see one another again. And under no circumstances must you marry one another." She claimed she could see their fortune "as though it's smoke coming off your bodies."[54] If they disobeyed her warning, she saw "hard trouble" ahead.

Smitty and Diane just laughed off the warning. Smitty asked Diane to marry him that night, and about three weeks later, on October 24, in Nogales, just north of the Mexican border, they did. It was perhaps Smitty's last-ditch attempt to bring some sense of stability to his disorganized life—though like the astrologer said—it helped bring about "hard trouble."

When Smitty told Richie soon after they returned that day, Richie could hardly believe he had done it. "How can you do this? What about the dead girls?" he asked. But Smitty just laughed him off, and then he, Diane, and Richie spent the day just driving around Tucson.[55] But the marriage bothered Richie.

Perhaps that's why he spent more time continuing to watch Darlene Kirk, the girl Smitty had once dated and then tried to pass off to him, though Darlene wasn't interested in Richie. He literally sat on the block in his car for hours at a time just watching. Finally, Darlene's father complained, and after the police started watching Richie closely and he made what sounded like a threat against the family, he was charged with disorderly conduct and was scheduled to go to trial on November 3. In fact, the Schmids' lawyer, John Price, was all set to defend him. Then, realizing that the prosecution had lined up numerous witnesses to testify against Richie, Price worked out a deal with the judge. In return for pleading guilty, Richie would be on probation for six months and leave Tucson for ninety days.

As Richie prepared to leave town, an article appeared in the *Arizona Daily Star* about the three missing girls: "Teenage Girls Have Disappeared into Thin Air," it said.[56] It concluded: "But police still have no leads to the girls," and echoed the police belief that perhaps the girls might have run away and changed their appearance. It was an unnerving omen. So was Richie's brief meeting with Smitty the afternoon before he left town. Smitty drove up behind his car, and when he got out, he looked "dirty and unkempt" with old makeup caked all over his face.[57]

When Richie got to Columbus, Ohio, where he was going to be staying with his grandmother, he became more nervous. At first, he felt out of place when he arrived at the airport and started looking for a job and checking out the nightspots in town. He began feeling angry about losing Darlene, and he started worrying about what Smitty might do. Maybe Smitty might go kill someone else. He was worried that Smitty might talk about how he had helped him kill the girls—or even blame the killings on him, since it was well known that he and Gretchen didn't get along.[58]

Finally, Richie began pouring out his story to his grandmother, and then he called his father in Tucson, who called the Tucson police. Within a few minutes, a police officer called, and Richie was telling his story to him as well. "Would you be willing to come back and show us the bodies?" the detective wanted to know. The next day, Detective Wilhelm and a Columbus police detective escorted him to the Columbus police station, where he filled out some papers saying he was returning voluntarily to show the Tucson police where the bodies were.

After that, the story was soon out. The next day, November 10, Richie led a team of detectives, including Wilhelm, to the wash and showed them the bodies of Gretchen and Wendy. At Richie's request, some detectives went to pick up Darlene, because Richie said he had been watching her because he was afraid Smitty would kill her. He told the police about Smitty because he could no longer protect her once he had to leave town. Meanwhile, the police drove Richie to try to find Alleen's grave, though he wasn't able to find it, because he had never been there. The police thought Saunders and French might be able to show them, and they planned to bring them back to guide the search.

Other investigators collected the bones from the skeletons, and the coroner's pathologist examined them at the mortuary, quickly concluding that the bones were in fact the remains of two young girls about the age and height of the Fritz sisters. A few days later, dental records provided absolute identification.

Would Schmid now confess? Richie didn't think he would, but the police arranged for him to confront Schmid while they watched in an adjoining room through a two-way mirror. He agreed in return for the police promise to pick up Darlene.[59]

Schmid played it cool. After the police picked him up and placed him in the room with the two-way mirror, detectives played the tapes in which Richie said Schmid had committed the murders along with Mary French and John Saunders. Schmid acted like this was a real surprise. "What is this? Are you guys for real?" he protested.[60] When Richie was led into the room, Schmid just glared at him, saying, "I know why you're doing this . . . I know why you fingered me." Schmid told the detectives he would prove his innocence at his trial.

He indeed tried to prove his innocence. His lawyer, William Tinney, planned to put on a defense that Richie had in fact killed the girls because he had long hated Gretchen and then tried to frame Schmid. Initially, when Mary French was brought back from Texas, she at first denied even knowing Alleen Rowe or anything about her disappearance. She sat cold as ice when Detective Robles of the Tucson Police Department questioned her. She still loved Schmid and wanted to protect him. Robles said, "You know Smitty got married, you know that?"[61] Mary suddenly poured out everything, describing in detail almost exactly what Bruns had said Smitty told him. She agreed to testify against Schmid in return for pleading guilty to reduced charges of being an accessory to murder and concealing and compounding a felony, making her eligible for parole in four to five years. Meanwhile, Saunders agreed to plead guilty to first-degree murder, in return for a life sentence, which would make him eligible for parole in seven years.

The national press jumped on the story, with one compelling picture in *Time* showing Mary French helping the police search for Alleen Rowe's body, though they were unable to find it.[62]

At the trial, which began on February 21, 1966, when Tinney tried to argue a big frame-up for something Richie did, the jurors apparently decided to believe Richie and Mary. Though Tinney had numerous witnesses who testified about how Richie and Gretchen often fought, the prosecution produced others who described how Schmid told them how Gretchen kept pestering him to continue their relationship and that he was scared because she had taken a diary where he had written about how he previously killed another boy and Alleen

Rowe. She had something on him that provided a motive. Perhaps most damning of all was Mary's testimony supporting Richie's basic story—"that Smitty had told him he had killed the Fritz sisters and had taken him to the graves."[63] The trial ended on March 10, with a little over two hours of deliberations. The jury came back with a guilty verdict, and they set the penalty at death.[64] The astrologer's warning about marrying Diane proved true, because perhaps if Schmid hadn't married her, Mary French might never have testified. Her testimony helped convict him.

Still, Schmid continued protesting his innocence, and Tinney even planned to appeal on the grounds that part of the evidence of his guilt involved bringing in a claim that Schmid was trying to cover up for a previous murder for which he had not been charged and for which there was not even a body recovered. After some discussion back and forth, F. Lee Bailey, then a thirty-three-year-old rising criminal defense attorney, stepped into the case. Bailey was especially drawn to the case after he got the Sheppard murder case overturned on the grounds that Sheppard couldn't receive a fair trial because of all the publicity, and there certainly had been massive damning publicity in Schmid's case. Also, Bailey would assist Tinney in defending in the Rowe case, which was postponed because Bailey was then defending Carl Coppolini.

Finally, on May 10, while Schmid's appeal on the Fritz case was still pending, the Rowe case began—even without the discovery of Alleen's body. It was a kind of odd case because Bailey would be defending Schmid for "a murder that had already been used by the state to convict and sentence him to death for two other murders" as the *Tucson American* reported.[65] Even so, Bailey would be defending Schmid on the grounds that he was appealing his conviction in the previous case and there was no body found in this one.

Suddenly, after the jury had been selected, there was a sudden change of course, perhaps because Bailey saw that the prosecution would be able to bring in the Fritz convictions and the results of the appeal were still uncertain. After a flurry of motions, which Bailey lost, Schmid finally pled guilty to second-degree murder in return for escaping the gas chamber.[66] The prosecution was satisfied, because at least this way, whatever happened in the Fritz appeal, Schmid would be in jail for life.

That's exactly where he remained until his death. Soon after his conviction, he dismissed his lawyers and sought to appeal his convictions himself, arguing that he had not only been framed by others for the crimes but that his attorneys had coerced him into pleading guilty. In fact, he said he could prove his innocence by taking them to the corpse of Alleen Rowe, which would show that she had been strangled by John Saunders and he had just helped him conceal the body. Before his sentencing, on June 23, 1967, the police actually led him there to do just this. Perhaps Schmid had even managed to convince himself this is what happened, because when he led a small search party out to the grave, which included Sheriff Burr, two lawyers as impartial witnesses, and pathologist

Edward Brucker, he excitedly told Brucker that he would find no fractures and this would prove what he was claiming all along. Schmid was sure that finally the body would clear him. By the next day, the results of the autopsy and detailed X-rays were in. There were fractures at the base of the skull, and the dried blood around the fractures, indicated they occurred when Alleen was still alive. Even a rock near thc skull showed blood specks confirming that Alleen had been hit on the head, just like French and Saunders had said. Though Schmid could no longer maintain his innocence, he didn't seem to have any regrets over what he had done, only that he was caught. Or as Burr stated, describing the characteristics of the complete sociopathic personality: "Charlie doesn't have any regrets about anything he's done, he doesn't feel sorrow, not even remorse. . . . He doesn't like anybody, and says that he has no close ties with anybody."[67]

It was over. His wife, Diane, divorced him while he was in prison, and though he never won his appeal in the Fritz case, his death sentence was ultimately nullified and turned into a life sentence along with other death penalty sentences by the courts. In 1972, Schmid made a couple of escape attempts but was quickly caught. In 1975 he was killed in prison by two inmates who felt he tried to be too big in prison. He had bragged his way up from solitary confinement to the Honor Dormitory when two prisoners attacked him, stabbing him several times.[68] He died several days later. It was a fitting end for a man who had always told stories to make himself bigger than he was.

THE CASE OF JERRY BRUDOS

Portland, Salem, and Corvallis, Oregon, 1968–69

The most vicious serial killings ever known in Oregon began with some missing women's underwear taken from backyard clotheslines in the mid-1950s. Most of the time, these occasional thefts of panties and bras weren't even reported, or if they were, the police didn't take them very seriously. But then in 1968, the man taking the underwear turned to murder—and when the first bodies turned up tied with nylon electrical cord to heavy engine parts in the Long Tom River of Oregon's Willamette Valley, the police began to discover a case of gruesome mutilation and cannibalism that easily matched the activities of Albert Fish from the 1930s and Edward Gein.

The first hint of serious foul play began in January 1968, when nineteen-year-old Linda Slawson, who was going door to door selling encyclopedias, turned up missing. She was living in Aloha, Oregon, a Portland suburb, and she had recently signed on as an encyclopedia saleswoman to help pay the rent, buy groceries, and perhaps get some new clothes. But she found it hard going trying to convince the residents to buy a set plus the yearbooks and atlas that went with it. Even when she tried to enthusiastically replay the pitch she had learned from her instructors, the people seemed impatient and said they weren't interested as they closed the door, and she went on to ring the doorbell at the next house.[69]

In one house, a heavy-set, pudgy man invited her in, told her he was interested, and led her to his workshop in the basement so he wouldn't disturb his mother and little girl, who were upstairs. As Slawson bent over to open her case with the brochures, he moved behind her and slammed her on the head. That was the last anyone knew about what happened to Linda Slawson for about a year. The encyclopedia company sales office wasn't particularly worried when she didn't show up or call about her sales, because salespeople came and went, and the office manager figured she had quit. Nobody even knew the sales leads she was supposed to contact the night of January 26, so there was no place to start when her family called the Portland Police Department and reported their daughter missing. They explained that she wasn't the kind of girl to simply take off and move away, although in 1968, there were a growing number of people in her age range doing just that, as the hippie and counterculture movement gathered steam on the West Coast. But the movement hadn't really hit Oregon yet, and in any case, Linda was a young, pretty woman trying to make a living for herself. So the Missing Persons detectives simply added her to their roster. Her case was simply in the files, largely forgotten, until more reports of missing girls and a few bodies began to turn up. Unfortunately, they all involved disappearances in different jurisdictions, so it wasn't until the bodies began appearing that the detectives in different communities in the Willamette Valley began to connect the pieces.

The next girl to go missing (about ten months later) was twenty-three-year-old Jan Whitney, who was finishing her degree at the University of Oregon in Eugene, about sixty miles south of Salem. A part-time student, she lived in McMinnville, about halfway between Portland and Salem, so it was easy to drive back and forth between McMinnville and Eugene along Interstate 5, about a two-hour drive. On November 26, 1968, after visiting friends in Eugene, she headed home to McMinnville, looking forward to the upcoming Thanksgiving with friends and relatives. Somewhere along the way, she simply disappeared. Her worried family called and a description of her car went out on a teletype to Oregon and adjoining states. The police found her red and white Nash Rambler parked in a rest area parking lot near Albany, a short distance from Corvallis. Oddly, it was locked, with no external damage and no evidence of a struggle or injury. It also had a minor mechanical problem that would prevent it from being driven, and the keys were gone. Though the Oregon State Police technicians found a good latent print on a hubcap, at the time the police couldn't do any more than compare it to a suspect (if they had one), because the FBI only collected single-print information on the ten most wanted criminals at the time. The police searched the land and ditches near the freeway, but that provided no clues either. The other curious question was why Jan Whitney had taken a detour off the freeway instead of going straight to McMinnville. For now the police couldn't answer that question either.

A few days after newspaper accounts appeared about Whitney's disappearance, the Oregon State Police received an anonymous letter mailed from Albany in a plain envelope that was carefully printed, as if the author wanted to disguise his handwriting, stating that the writer had been at the rest stop where her car was abandoned and she disappeared. After State Police Lieutenant Robert White made an appeal to the public asking for the letter writer to come forward, he heard nothing, and there was no way to tell if this was really from someone who knew about Whitney's disappearance or just read about it in the newspaper.

Again, the case was just another file—and for now the Portland police and the Oregon State Police didn't think to connect the cases. They seemed too different as one woman had disappeared in a city, the other about fifty miles away on a freeway.

On March 18, 1969, a high school teacher discovered the body of Stephanie Vilcko, age sixteen, along the banks of Gales Creek near Forest Grove about twenty-five miles west of Portland. She had been another missing girl who had disappeared after she had left her home to go swimming in July 1968. All that was left was a badly decomposed skeleton. There wasn't enough to tell forensic pathologists anything about how she died, but the discovery of her body added one more mysterious disappearance that would soon reach critical mass.

On March 27, 1969, Karen Sprinker of Salem disappeared, and Detective Jim Stovall of the Salem Police Department began working on the case. When Stovall first got the case, there were few clues. All he knew was that Karen, age nineteen, was on a short vacation between terms at Oregon State University in Corvallis and was staying at home with her parents. Her father was a prominent Salem veterinarian, and she hoped to follow his footsteps into a career in medicine and was a dedicated pre-med student. Her parents also described her as a highly principled girl who was still a virgin, at a time when many other students were rebelling against old-fashioned traditions. When she didn't show up to meet her mother at the restaurant in the Meier and Frank department store, her mother grew increasingly concerned. It wasn't like Karen not to be prompt, and after her mother returned home that afternoon and her parents called all of Karen's friends and the hospital, they reluctantly called the police, who took a preliminary report and asked the Sprinkers to go home and wait in case Karen called or returned. "We normally wait twenty-four hours before we take a formal complaint and investigate," the police explained.

The next day, after the Sprinkers heard nothing from Karen, the police detectives, led by Stovall, began their search at the Meier and Frank parking garage, just in case Karen had arrived there but never kept her date at the restaurant with her mother. At first, as they went floor to floor, and nothing looked unusual. On the roof was Karen's car. It was parked diagonally in a parking space and locked, just like any other customer's car. Everything about the car looked quite ordinary as well. A few of Karen's books had been left on the front seat; there was no sign of any kind of struggle or injury—no blood or semen on the seats or door panels, and all the latent prints found on the car turned out to belong to Karen or other family members. The best the detectives could surmise was that perhaps someone had confronted her when she was alone and vulnerable and then had taken her away. But they couldn't tell much more.

The strange disappearance powerfully moved Stovall, who became a leading force in trying to solve the missing woman cases. A tall, graying, longtime police veteran with a Jack Webb "just the facts" look, Stovall felt touched by the way Karen disappeared because his own daughter was twenty-one, so he could closely identify with the pain the Sprinkers were feeling. Even if he might not be able to bring Karen back, he wanted to do all he could to solve the case.

But it was slow going. The local Salem papers—the *Capital Journal* and the *Salem Statesman*—printed Karen's picture and asked the question, "Have you seen this girl?"[70] Besides the usual crank letters and informants eager to supply tips, even if they knew nothing, the police found nothing. Meanwhile, after one motorcyclist described how he had given a hitchhiker with long black hair (like Karen's) a ride to a hippie commune in Portland, Karen's boyfriend tried posing as a hippie to see if he could learn anything. He dressed up by wearing jeans and a batik shirt, and he let his beard grow so he looked the part. But nothing came of it—and it was unlikely that Karen would run off and become a hippie anyway.

The search seemed fruitless. Yet there was one odd story that led Stovall to wonder if perhaps it might mean something. Two high school girls said that a few weeks before Karen vanished they had been shopping at Meier and Frank when they saw a person who looked odd in the parking garage. At first, they thought it was a woman wearing a dress and high heels, but the figure was tall and heavy, very mannish in appearance, and he or she seemed to be waiting for someone and was "tugging at her girdle and fixing her nylons."[71] Could it be anything? Stovall wondered this after another investigator theorized that maybe a man dressed up like a woman had pretended to be ill or called Karen over to ask a question. Maybe she might have gone over, wanting to help, and then maybe the man might have grabbed her and taken her away. Then again, maybe the story meant nothing. The girls might have been mistaken, or even if they saw a transsexual or transvestite, he might have been perfectly harmless, just some man who liked to wander around a store looking like a woman in a dress and high heels. So Stovall felt the case was at a dead end, though from time to time he glanced up at the picture of Karen he had tacked up on the wall over his desk—like a sign to her that he would keep trying to find out what happened to her; he wouldn't forget.

Although Karen's disappearance was never headlined, the papers were starting to hint that there might be a maniac on the loose; what happened to Karen might happen to other women if he wasn't caught. On Wednesday, April 23, about four weeks after Karen disappeared, the fear in the valley became even worse when Linda Dawn Salee, a very short, attractive twenty-two-year-old who had won a Miss Smile contest a few years back, was kidnapped in what seemed like a replay of the Sprinker case. After Linda left her job at the Consolidated Freightways in Portland around 4:30 p.m., she stopped at the big Lloyd Center shopping mall to get a gift for her boyfriend's upcoming birthday. She parked her red VW on the sixth floor of the parking lot, and one of the clerk's remembered her because Linda had bought a leather watchband for her boyfriend, and then changed her mind, and went back to return it. "It's not what I wanted after all,"[72] Linda said. These were the last known words she reportedly said to anyone before she disappeared. Her boyfriend, who expected to meet her at the YMCA, was surprised when Linda never showed up, because she was usually prompt—and she had been eager to celebrate his birthday that night. When Linda didn't show up at her job the next morning, her friends and family became concerned that something terrible had happened to her, and one of them called the Portland Police, who advised other nearby agencies as well, including the Oregon State Police, who were already on the alert since the Whitney case. As a result, Oregon State Police investigators were soon on the scene at the parking lot helping the Portland detectives search the garage and nearby grounds. Again they found nothing—though the signs of the kidnapper's approach were eerily the same—a locked car, and no signs of a struggle in or around the vehicle.

Now there was enough to finally link the cases of the four missing women who had disappeared within a fifty-mile area. All were young and attractive; none seemed a likely runaway; they all were settled into jobs or school; had close family and friends, even attentive boyfriends in two cases; none had reported any fears of any jealous or rejected boyfriends; there were no apparent stalkers or callers. There were also no witnesses and no evidence at any of the scenes. It was as if the kidnapper had appeared at a time when they were alone, unable to get any help, and then the girls had gone willingly. This must be some kind of crafty, elusive person who found random suspects—the hardest kind of person to catch. The police felt totally frustrated, unable to do much beyond sending a warning teletype about the missing girls to police agencies in the thirteen Western states. When he got the teletype, Stovall felt frustrated, too. He felt sure that whoever had done this had also kidnapped Karen. But he felt no closer to solving that case either—just more determined to do so.

Finally, on May 10 came the first major break. A fly fisherman on the Bundy Bridge across the Long Tom River, about twelve miles from Corvallis, noticed a large, bulky shape floating just under the surface of the water. It looked curious—too soft to be a log, but too firm to be just a bundle of clothing someone might have dropped into the river. When he walked down to the bank from the bridge, he stepped back in horror, realizing it was a human being with light hair spreading out as the river flowed by. In moments, he raced back to his truck and called the Benton County Sheriff's Department. A few minutes later, sheriff's deputies were on the scene, and they pulled in a young woman's body that showed the decomposition signs of being in the river for some time. It was clear it wasn't just an ordinary accidental drowning. "The body's weighted down with a car transmission," a deputy reported. The engine part weighed about as much as the person did.

When he got the news about the body, Stovall, like other detectives in northern Oregon, was instantly on the alert to learn who the woman was and how she died, though initially, because the body was found in Benton County, local sheriff Charles E. Reams and District Attorney Frank Knight were in charge of the investigation. Soon, officials from the Oregon State Medical Examiner's office were on the scene, including Chief Medical Examiner Dr. William Brady, who arrived from Portland. As they carefully examined the body, Reams sent deputies through the area to see if any nearby resident saw anyone dumping a body. No one had, but the body held the first tantalizing clues of what happened to not only this victim but perhaps to the other missing women.

From the description of the victim and subsequently from prints and dental records, they soon realized that this was Linda Salee. Strangely, her kidnapper had taken her over seventy miles from the shopping center where he grabbed her. Presumably, while he had hoped to weight her body down enough to forever sink her in the river, he had misjudged the water's depth, or didn't care, or perhaps had dumped her body so as to be found. In any event, the weight and method of tying her body might be an important clue—the killer had bound her to the transmission with a nylon cord and copper wire, such as might be used by a mechanic or electrician. There was a bit of reddish fabric intertwined with these cords and wires that looked like the industrial cloth used by a mechanic. Certainly, any killer might have gotten such material at a hardware store. Then again, maybe it could be someone who worked with these materials. At least it was a lead.

Meanwhile, Dr. Brady's examination results came back to report that Linda had been strangled, since she showed the usual signs of a sudden asphyxiation, such as the small hemorrhages of the muscles of the neck, lungs, and heart that occur when the lungs are suddenly deprived of air. He couldn't tell if she had been raped, because the signs of any semen would have been eliminated by the several weeks in the water. He did find some unusual needle marks on either side of her rib cage, and there were signs of slight burning after death. It was the first time Dr. Brady had ever seen anything like that, and the police kept the information from the press, as a way to tell if a suspect had this critical knowledge and wasn't just another crank confessor lured by media attention. Brady also noticed a number of bruises showing that Salee had struggled in the last moments of her life before she finally lost.

Two days later came the next big break. Over the weekend, sheriff's detectives and scuba divers continued to comb the river for other clues, perhaps some of her clothing or a purse left where she was dumped, or something the killer left behind. On the morning of Monday, May 12, one of the police divers located another body, about fifty feet from where Linda had been found. As they pulled it up, they discovered it had also been weighted down by a car part—this time a cylinder head. The pathologist estimated that the body had been in the water about two months, and this suggested it might be the body of Karen Sprinker, who had disappeared in late March.

On hearing the news about the second body on teletype, Jim Stovall raced to the scene, accompanied by another Salem police investigator, Detective Jerry Frazier. Meanwhile, the evidence at the scene made it clear that Karen had been killed by whoever killed Linda. Not only was her body weighted down by an auto part, but it had been tied to the engine with nylon cord and copper wiring, and a red mechanic's cloth was tied to the engine head.[73] Dr. Brady's preliminary examination showed Karen had died from traumatic asphyxiation, too.

At this point, Stovall felt more determined to find Karen and Linda's killer than ever, and he was present at the postmortem, as was Lt. Gene Daugherty of the Oregon State Police, with whom he worked closely in the following months as the lead investigators on the missing women cases, while Frazier continued to help. Some of the revelations at this postmortem were especially disturbing. Though Karen had been fully clothed when discovered in the river, in the same green skirt and sweater she had been wearing the day she disappeared according to her mother, she didn't have on the usual simple cotton bra she usually wore. Instead, it had been replaced by a "waist-length black bra that was too big for her."[74] When Brady took off the bra, he found that both of her breasts had been removed, and the killer had inserted scrunched-up lumps of wadded brown paper towels. Possibly the paper towels were used to absorb blood and fluid, but it also looked like the killer had tried to manufacture makeshift breasts to replace those he had cut off. It was a shocking find, and it was also withheld from the public at the time. But at least it helped give Stovall a sense of the likely killer he was looking for—probably an electrician and a car mechanic—because both bodies had been tied with electrical wire and then tied to a car part.

The big question was, where to go next? Even if all the cases of missing women were all connected, the two killings and the disappearances of at least two other women had occurred over an area of about 100 miles from Portland in the north to Eugene in the south.

Over the next few weeks in May, Stovall, Daugherty, and Frazier tried visiting dozens of junkyards in Portland and Salem, thinking this might be a way to find the source of the transmission and cylinder used to weight down the bodies. They knew the parts came from a Chevrolet made between 1953 and 1962, so at least that was a lead, though there were hundreds of thousands of such cars produced, and they had no serial numbers. But it still offered a better chance of being traced than the cord, copper wire, or mechanic's cloth. Stovall and the other detectives deduced the killer must be strong or working with an accomplice to be able to carry the weighted bodies to the river.

Stovall tried to do a kind of preliminary profiling approach (later used more widely and systemically beginning in the 1970s), reviewing what he knew to date and imagining what the killer might be like. He soon had a list of possible characteristics. Probably the killer was between about twenty and thirty, since the victims were young. He was of at least average intelligence, since he had to be skilled to tie the specific knots he did in tying the bodies to the weights. He was likely to come from a broken home, missing a parent, or from a home with a strong mother and weak father, because he showed a strong dislike for his mother by the way he "desecrated" the bodies of his two victims. Perhaps the killer had a long record of antisocial behavior and he wasn't a steady worker, since the girls had disappeared in widely scattered locations at different hours of the day.[75]

Then Stovall noticed this odd fact—all of the girls had disappeared toward the end of the month: Slawson in January, Whitney in November, Sprinker in March, and Salee in April. Perhaps there was some kind of pseudo-menstrual or monthly cycle going on, Stovall theorized.

Looking at the map showing where the women had disappeared and where the bodies were found, Stovall felt sure that the killer had to be familiar with the area, especially around the river, because he probably dumped the bodies at night. He had to know the area, Stovall reasoned, because otherwise he would risk falling in the river. Stovall felt certain it was just one strong man able to dump the bodies in the river, because the bizarre desecrations suggested someone propelled by a psychological compulsion to act as he did. Plus, he probably looked fairly normal—someone who could entice the women to go with him willingly and then slide back into a seemingly normal life without attracting attention.

Looking at the map again between Portland and Eugene, Stovall noticed that Corvallis, about twelve miles from the Bundy Bridge, was somewhere in the middle, and Karen had been a student at the Corvallis campus. Stovall decided to start there. He and Daugherty took over a room and began talking to every girl on campus, asking what they knew about Karen and if they had seen any unusual strangers around. The Corvallis police department provided two detectives to help them, and over the next weeks, they interviewed hundreds of girls, spending about fifteen minutes with each one. They asked them what they knew about Karen's dates as well as about their own. Had they gotten any unusual phone calls? Gone to any strange places? Had they seen anything that might have been the least bit out of the ordinary?[76]

After a couple of weeks, this process seemed to be no more fruitful than checking the junkyards. And then Stovall's and Daugherty's ears perked up when three or four women mentioned receiving phone calls from a man they didn't know who had asked for them by their first name. None had ever met him before. They recalled some snippets of conversation. He had mentioned being a Vietnam veteran, and he had talked about having special psychic powers. At the end of a conversation, he had asked for a date, though most of the girls turned him down. But one, taking some psychology courses, had actually met him at her dorm lounge, mostly because she felt sorry for him after he described how he felt lonesome after the war and had spent some time as a patient at Walter Reed Hospital, where he learned some new methods of study in psychology she might find of interest. They talked for a while, but she hadn't been interested in seeing him again because he seemed odd and not particularly attractive. As she described him, he was "overweight, freckled, and looked as if he was in his thirties."[77] He also was not a very good dresser, and his car looked like an old junker.

She described how he did something very odd. He suddenly placed a hand on her shoulder and commented, "Be sad." When she wondered why, he said, "Think of those two girls whose bodies were found in the river." When she declined going for a drive with him, he made the strange comment, "How do you know I wouldn't take you to the river and strangle you?"[78] Then he left, saying he might call again in a couple of days, although he hadn't. She wasn't interested in seeing him again anyway.

For Daugherty, who interviewed her, the remark set off warning bells, and he asked the girl to arrange to see him again if he called. "Then, let us know and give him some excuse why you can't meet him right away." He gave her the Corvallis police department to call so the officers could be there before the man even arrived. Just in case, Daugherty warned her: "Be sure not to go anywhere with him." The girl agreed.

Over the next few days, Stovall and Daugherty waited anxiously for the man to call, if he would. Finally, on Sunday, May 25, the Corvallis police received the call. The "Vietnam veteran" had phoned a few minutes earlier, asking to come over, and the girl had arranged to see him in about an hour.

Two detectives met him instead. He turned out to be an overweight man with freckles, just like she said, and he calmly told detectives that his name was Jerry Brudos and he lived in Salem. He was only a little embarrassed when he admitted he had a wife and two children. Why was he in Corvallis? He explained he was working nearby. "I'm an electrician," he told detectives.

At this point, Brudos had committed no offense for which the officers could arrest him or even take him in for questioning. So they simply escorted him out to his car, parked outside the dorm—a green Comet station wagon—and noted his license number.

With that information, Stovall began the process of checking him out, and soon was sure that Brudos was the man he was looking for. Everything seemed to fall into place. He discovered that Brudos, now thirty, had been in the state mental hospital and had a record of violence. Moreover, at the time Linda Slawson disappeared in Portland, Brudos had lived there. He now worked as an electrician in Corvallis.

When Stovall and Frazier went to interview Brudos at his home and spoke to him in his garage, even more information seemed to fit their profile. As they walked around, Frazier observed a hook in the ceiling and then noticed lengths of rope lying around the room. One of them was knotted with the same kind of knot used to bind the bodies in the river. Brudos also described how he had worked at times as a car repairman, including working for a time near where Jan Whitney's car was found on the freeway.

In the files of the Portland police, Stovall discovered one more case that provided more evidence plus a living potential witness. On April 21, two days before Linda Salee had disappeared, a twenty-four-year old woman named Sharon Wood had just left her job as a secretary at the Portland state history department and entered the basement of the parking garage to get her car to go home. As the heavy stair door closed behind her, she realized she was on the wrong floor, and as she headed toward the daylight entrance across the garage, she felt the presence of someone behind her. She hurried faster, to the safety of daylight, and she felt a tap on her shoulder. When she turned, she saw a tall, heavy man with freckles holding a pistol. "If you don't scream, I won't shoot you," he said. Though she didn't know then it was a toy, Sharon knew she wasn't going anywhere with this man with the gun, and unlike the other women who had gone off with him, she fought back, which is why she lived, though she was severely battered. Though he tried to grab her around the neck, she kicked and took a deep bite out of his hand, and then, just as she saw a VW bus drive toward them and she lapsed into unconsciousness, he ran away. The next morning, on April 22, a fifteen-year old girl told police that an overweight, freckled man tried to grab her on the railroad tracks near Salem as she headed for school, though she had screamed and run away toward a woman working nearby in her yard, and he had run away and taken off quickly in his car, too. Soon after the calls from the mysterious stranger to the girls at the Oregon State University dorm had started, perhaps because that now seemed like a safer way of getting women after two failures in two days.

Though the police in Portland and then in Salem made no connection at the time to the missing women or the two bodies pulled from the river, Stovall did. He showed the fifteen-year-old girl a collection of photos, including one of Jerry Brudos, and she immediately picked it out.

Finally, there were grounds to arrest Brudos for an attempted abduction, and Stovall set out to do so. On the way, he heard on the radio that Brudos and his family had left Corvallis and were on their way to Portland. A police patrol car stopped Brudos's station wagon, which was being driven by his wife, Darcie, (though her name is recorded differently in other sources as Ralphene and Susan). For a moment, it looked like Brudos might not be in the car, but then the officer noticed a bulging form under a blanket in the back seat, which turned out to be Brudos. Back at the police station, when Brudos was asked to change into prison overalls, his jailers noticed this strange fact—he was wearing ladies' underwear.

For the moment, Brudos wasn't talking when Stovall questioned him over the next few days. Finally, at their fifth interview, Brudos suddenly started talking about his interest in women's shoes and underwear. Soon the whole story of what happened to the missing women and why began pouring out—a bizarre, puzzling saga that both shocked and fascinated Stovall and soon the public, as Brudos's admissions quickly sealed his fate, leaving the only question as to whether he was insane.

Brudos began by describing how he had followed a girl wearing attractive shoes and later had quietly broken into her home through a window and left with the shoes. Then he had found a large black bra hanging on a clothesline—the one later found on Karen's body. Stovall now knew Brudos had virtually admitted he had killed Karen,[79] and he continued to listen quietly, supportively, while concealing his own feelings of disgust, as Brudos went on, describing a world of fetishism and inadequacies with women that eventually led to murder.

For Brudos, the fascination began when he was five and found a pair of women's patent leather shoes in a trash dump. When he got home, he put them on. When his mother saw him, she yelled at him, telling him to return them at once. But Brudos didn't. Instead, he hid the shoes and wore them in secret, until his mother discovered what he was doing. She beat him and burned his shoes. But her angry reaction contributed to setting a pattern common for many men who later grow up to harbor secret fantasies—eroticizing the taboo by driving the fantasy underground.

Brudos went on with his story. His fascination with shoes continued, and in school he was so attracted to the high-heeled shoes his teacher kept as spares by her desk that one day he stole them and hid them in the schoolyard. Another student found them and gave them back to the teacher. When she sought to find out who did it, Brudos eventually confessed. When she wanted to know who did it, he raced out of the room, not wanting to tell her his guilty secret.

In 1955, when he was sixteen, he stole the underwear of an eighteen-year-old girl who lived next door and told her a fantastic story that he could help her get her underwear back because he was working for the police as an undercover agent. One evening when his family was away, Brudos invited her to come into his house, and as she entered the door, he called to her from upstairs, inviting her to come up. When she did, a tall figure with a mask suddenly jumped out at her and told her to take off all her clothes. Frightened at what the boy might do, she did, and he took some photographs of her with a flash camera. After the masked man left, Brudos came running in a few minutes later, claiming the man had locked him in the barn. Though the girl knew it was Jerry, she was too frightened to say anything about it at the time. Meanwhile, Brudos enjoyed looking at her photos as well as handling her stolen panties and bra.

When he was seventeen, in April 1956, Brudos's fantasies escalated a little more. He invited a seventeen-year-old girl into his car and then began talking as if they were on a date together as he left the main road and drove onto a deserted highway. By a deserted farmhouse, he dragged her from the car and began to beat her on her face and breasts, ordering her to take off her clothes so he could see her naked. She began screaming, and fortunately, a passing couple from a nearby farm came along, and after they stopped, they insisted that Brudos accompany them and the girl back to their house, where they called the police. Meekly, Brudos went along, and when the Oregon State Police arrived, he explained that he had just wanted to frighten the girl enough so she would take off her clothes so he could take pictures of her. The police arrested him, and when they investigated a little further, they found the women's clothing and shoes Brudos had hidden in his room at home, as well as the pictures of the girl next door, who told how he had appeared as the masked man the year before. She hadn't said anything at the time, fearing that Brudos might beat her up.

As a result of these two incidents, Brudos was referred to the Oregon State Hospital for evaluation and treatment, where he spent the following nine months. During the day, he attended high school at North Salem High School, though he was very much an outsider—very bright, especially in mathematics and science, but tall, pudgy, a kind of loser and loner, whom none of the girls wanted to date and who never went to the games or dances. They didn't know he went back to the hospital at night—and they didn't know much about him either.

After high school, he briefly joined the U.S. Army but was soon discharged because of his bizarre fantasies—one was that a Korean girl snuck into his barracks one night and tried to seduce him. When he left at age twenty, he moved back home with his parents in Corvallis, and after briefly staying in the second bedroom, he moved into a shed in the rear of the property, after his older brother Larry returned from college. It was the perfect place to give vent to his continuing fantasies and continue to be the loner he always was.

There were a few more odd incidents. One evening in Salem on an errand, Brudos spotted a young woman in a bright red outfit. Excited by her clothing, he followed her, jumped her in the doorway of an apartment house, and as she lay on the ground, he ran off with her shoes. Soon after, in Portland, he saw a woman with attractive shoes and tried to choke her. When she fought back, he ran off with just one shoe. Still, he enjoyed possessing it, like the other shoes, and slept with them in his shack.

Perhaps at this point he might have slipped over the edge to becoming a rapist in his early twenties, but at twenty-three, a young boy who came into the station where Brudos worked as a communications engineer introduced him to a woman named Darcie, who was then seventeen and wanted to get out of her house. She was the perfect submissive match, and, impressed with his job, she agreed to marry him. She was the one woman who didn't threaten him, though occasionally he had some odd requests, like asking her to dress up in silk underwear and high-heeled shoes and pose for photos. Though she was sometimes a little embarrassed and walking around the house in high heels when she did the housework hurt her back, she ultimately went along with what Brudos wanted. She usually did—until the very end, which helped preserve some of the evidence the police needed to document what Brudos did.

Despite the outward veneer of normality—a wife, and after a year of marriage, a baby girl—Brudos's fantasies continued. When Darcie was in the hospital having their second child, he felt the compulsion strongly, and soon after she was back home with their newborn son, he stalked a woman in Portland because he was attracted by her shoes. This time, after he followed her into her apartment to take them, she woke up. After he choked her unconscious to keep her quiet, he was overcome at seeing her totally helpless, and he raped her and then took her shoes and left.[80]

It was the beginning of a new, more violent phase in Brudos's long-simmering obsession with women's clothes and shoes. It finally exploded when Linda Slawson appeared at his home in Portland selling encyclopedias that January night. After he killed her, he spent the next hour or so dressing and undressing her body with the panties and bras he had stolen. She was like a large doll to play with, and he felt no desire to rape her. Late that night, when his family was asleep, he loaded her body in his station wagon and dropped it in the river off the Bundy Bridge, attached to the heavy car transmission to weight it down. Afterward, he kept just one part of her body—her foot—in his garage freezer so he could take it out from time to time to put some of his shoes on it.[81]

In November, when he found his second victim, Jan Whitney, whose car had broken down on the side of the freeway, his obsession became even stronger. This time after he helpfully invited her into his car, saying he was a mechanic and had to go home to get his tools, he brought her back to his home. After he checked that his wife was away visiting friends, he strangled her in his car, placed her body in the rear seat, and sodomized her. After dressing and undressing her as he had Linda, he suspended her by the wrists from a hook in the ceiling, and removed one of her breasts to make a paperweight, though the hardener didn't set properly. After raping her again, he briefly left her body in the pump house before he threw it in the river, this time weighted down with scrap iron. Ironically, the police nearly caught him, because while Linda was still hanging in the garage, a driver had lost control and hit the garage, knocking a hole in the wall. When police investigated, looking through the hole, they didn't see the body, and Brudos was able to take it away to the river before the police returned to inspect the garage again.

This close brush with the police led Brudos to hold off committing any more abductions for several months. In March he saw Karen Sprinker walk by in her high-heeled shoes and mini-skirt and he confronted her in the Meier and Frank parking lot. After he made her lie on the floor of his garage, he raped her and took photos, and dressed her in some of his collection of panties and bras. He tied her hands behind her, strangled her with a rope, raped her again, and cut off both breasts and succeeded in making them into paperweights. It's as if each killing was becoming more violent and bizarre.

Finally, with Linda Salee, whom he captured in April, Brudos both strangled and raped her as she died. As she hung from his hook on the ceiling, he tried an experiment by sticking two hypodermic syringes into her ribs and attached electric wires. He switched on the current, hoping he might see her dance for him in the air, but instead, the electricity only burned her. These were some of the bits of evidence that the police held back from the press in the hopes that they would hear this from the killer. Brudos freely told Jim Stovall this, as well as the other gruesome details.

Though Stovall was sickened by Brudos's story, he just listened quietly, trying not to react in disgust to stop Brudos from talking. Oddly, Brudos kept going, even though his own lawyer had advised him not to talk, as if he was just describing how he worked with a car engine.

The usually submissive Darcie provided the last bit of necessary corroborating evidence. Though Brudos called her from his jail cell and asked her to locate and destroy a box he kept in his tool box, she did not. After she called Brudos's lawyer, who told her she would be destroying evidence and could become complicit in the crimes as a result, she didn't get rid of the box. Instead, she told the police about it, and when they looked through the box, it contained all the incriminating evidence they needed to completely prove Brudos's guilt. One of the photos show the large black bra found on Karen Sprinker, and another photo showed a reflection of her hanging from the hook on the ceiling. Besides her reflection, there was a reflection of Brudos in the picture, too.

After that, Brudos's lawyer urged him to simply plead guilty before a judge to four counts of murder, and in return, the judge sentenced him without a trial to life imprisonment in the Oregon State Penitentiary. Under the circumstances, it was the best the lawyer felt he could hope for because the psychiatrists who examined Brudos felt he was quite sane. He knew exactly what he was doing; he planned it very carefully; and then he went on with a seemingly normal life.

As for Brudos's life in prison, he was segregated and ignored by the other prisoners, and his wife quickly divorced him in 1970, left with the children, and changed her name. Over the years, he began applying his ability for electronics to operate the prison computer system. Prison authorities let him obtain mail-order catalogs with pictures of women's shoes and undergarments to enjoy in the quiet of his cell. Over the years, Brudos began filing writ after writ for getting his property returned and getting out of prison. His appeals were all denied. Although he was eligible for parole, he was denied it at every hearing. He died in prison in March 2006.

Chapter 2

The 1970s

AFTER THE UPHEAVALS of the 1960s, the 1970s were a time of renewed calm, and the focus turned from changing society to changing oneself. There was an expanded interest in personal development and growth, spurring a whole new industry of self-help and personal growth books. This new attention to recovery and therapy in the media helped make personal problems, family dysfunctions, and conflicts with others more acceptable, setting the stage for those whose psychological problems and sexual drives might lead to murder to feel better about acting on such impulses. Perhaps that's a reason for the surge in the number of serial killers and mass murderers who appeared in this decade, not only baffling investigators in finding the elusive serial killers but police, psychologists, and others who tried to understand what was happening. In fact, the homicide rate climbed steeply in this decade generally, after a period of steady decline since the 1930s, with a slight rise starting in 1967 at the height of the Vietnam War protests (based on the FBI's Uniform Crime Reports). In 1971 the rise to the presently high levels began—much higher levels than any other similarly developed country.

Why? For one thing, the inner cities and the problems of drugs and poverty expanded, making the cities more violent than they had ever been. After the riots of the 1960s and the destruction of the Black Panthers, who had some positive community help programs when not confronting the police, people felt more discouraged than ever. The unemployment rate for blacks in the inner cities was at an all-time high. Also, in the vacuum left by the Panthers and other organized groups, local youth gangs became more important and powerful, beginning the saga of turf wars and violent attacks on strangers still occurring today.[1] At the same time, the inner cities increasingly became the center of drug dealing, as drugs offered a way to escape the despair of poverty—either by taking them or selling them—and criminal crackdowns only increased the profits of selling drugs and the violence, as in Prohibition.

As murder historian Roger Lane observes in *Murder in America*, the increase in both the number and types of homicides resulted in murder becoming more difficult to solve, even with new scientific technologies. As he points out, using the FBI Uniform Crime Report data and a study of homicide from 1972–74 conducted by criminologist Marvin Wolfgang, homicide was mushrooming and less solvable because "in comparison with the mid-twentieth century bottom, there were proportionately more killings of strangers, and in the streets, fewer at home; more deadly brawls involving many contestants, fewer one-on-on domestic fatalities; more robbery murders; proportionately fewer women arrested; more interracial murders, fewer involving family, friends or acquaintances."[2] From a 1955 murder rate low of 4.5 per 100,000 people, by 1974 the rate was 10.2; at the same time, the percentage of homicides that couldn't be cleared by arresting a suspect doubled from less than 10 percent in 1955 to about 20 percent in 1974.[3] In other words, while about 90 percent of the homicides were cleared by an arrest in 1955, by 1974 only about 80% of the homicides were cleared by an arrest—so while there were approximately twice as many murders per capita in two decades, the number that were unsolved had doubled, too. Clearly, something had changed—and the rise in the serial killers and mass murderers who suddenly snapped and went on killing sprees were part of this general upward trend.

As Lane points out, it is difficult to accurately compare rates before the 1930s because 1933 was the first year in which mortality statistics covered the whole United States. But generally, until the gang wars over liquor territories broke out in the 1920s and 1930s, the cities had been generally safer, more subject to law and civilizing influences than the rural areas—especially in the rural South and parts of the West, which had high levels of "murderous violence."[4] In particular, Lane credits an "increasingly nonviolent middle class" in the cities for helping to hold down rates there.[5] In the 1970s, as cities were increasingly taken over by lower-income groups and the middle classes fled to the suburbs and protected enclaves, city violence increased. At the same time, it became clear that problems in the United States were even greater than in similarly developed countries. The U.S. rate since the 1970s has been about 9 to 10 homicides per 100,000, it is well above the rate of 1 per 100,000 a year in Japan, whereas rates in Germany, France, and Britain have also been close to 1 per 100,000. The rates have been about 2 per 100,000 in Canada and 2.5 per 100,000 in Italy.[6] Not only have U.S. murder rates been higher generally, so has the number of serial killers and mass murders—as well as the growing popular interest in murder and true crime, as well as sex and scandal.

An increase in interest in crime was fueled by the events of the day, like the 1972 arrest of the Watergate burglars at Democratic National Headquarters, which led to hearings from 1973 to 1974 and eventually President Richard Nixon's resignation. People seemed to develop a new fascination and admiration for classy criminals, such as Clifford Irving, who concocted a fake "authorized" biography of Howard Hughes in 1972. The Patty Hearst story became front-page news as people followed the saga of the heiress after her 1974 kidnapping. The public wondered whether she had really joined her captors as Tania, especially after she helped them rob the Hibernia National Bank in San Francisco. She was captured in 1975, convicted in 1976, and eventually released from prison after her sentence was commuted in 1979. For many people, the events became like guerrilla or popular theater instead of a crime, despite the tragic deaths from various terrorist actions along the way. Similarly, Jim Jones led the members of Peoples Temple to Guyana, where eventually about 900 died in a group suicide in 1978. There was a sense of unreality about the chain of events—more like the invention of a dark novelist than something real. Yet such events served as a kind of bizarre counterpoint to the increasing outrageousness of some murders during this period—as if the killers were inspired by the times to be equally grandiose to get attention.

Meanwhile, in a period when films had become very much the bellwether of the state of current culture, some of the biggest films celebrated crime, like Francis Ford Coppola's *The Godfather*, first released in 1972, and followed by a sequel in 1974. Some of these crime films presented a scary new world of danger with mentally disturbed killers, like *A Clockwork Orange* (Stanley Kubrick, 1971) and *Taxi Driver* (Martin Scorsese, 1976). Some films focused on the difficulty of investigating international or diabolical schemes, like the Oscar-winning *The French Connection* directed by William Friedkin (1971), or celebrated criminal trickery, like *The Sting* (George Roy Hill, 1973). At the same time, the movies of the 1970s showed a much greater sensuality and eroticism than before, like in Marlon Brando's *Last Tango in Paris* (1972). Even adult film stars achieved a certain acceptance and celebrity as highlighted by some recent retro films about the 1970s like *Boogie Nights*. In films of the period, even the mentally ill and disturbed might become heroes, such as in *One Flew Over the Cuckoo's Nest* (1975), featuring Jack Nicholson as the crazed hero who intrigues a mental ward. It was a time in which entertainment, excess, and abandon were widely celebrated, where disco and bell bottoms were big, as John Travolta showed in the 1977 smash hit *Saturday Night Fever*. Flakiness was cool, as in Diane Keaton's popular portrayal of *Annie Hall*, the Oscar-winning Best Picture of 1977. John Belushi was an up-and-coming star known for his brash outrageousness in *Animal House*.

This social environment of the 1970s proved to be a fertile soil for many different types of killers to develop.

Many of these killings have been inspired by ideology or a generalized anger against society. One who got his start in the 1970s was the Unabomber (Ted Kaczynski). In 1978, he began sending bombs—and for seventeen years led the FBI on a frustrating chase until his ego and manifestos led to his 1995 capture. (In fact, one of the people he wrote to was murder historian Roger

Lane's publisher, worrying that he might be violating copyright law in quoting some of Lane's earlier work.[7]) The ideological turmoil of the late 1960s splintered into a variety of true believer groups, including "vaguely Marxist or African nationalist groups, supporters of Puerto Rican or of Native American independence, pro-life activists, racist hate groups, and religious cultists," according to Lane.[8] As Lane points out, there has been a spread of terrorism in the United States as well as world wide since the early 1970s,[9] and also a number of violent confrontations between federal agents and armed militants, starting with 1973 between FBI agents and Native Americans at Wounded Knee, South Dakota. Meanwhile, in the late 1960s and early 1970s, the left-wing Weatherman group began its own bombing campaign, mostly against property to protest the accumulation of wealth, with a few casualties along the way.[10]

The 1970 homicide records also show a growing trend to more mass killings and serial killings since the early 1970s. Yet these crimes' power to attract headlines like the ideological killings has contributed to making them especially scary, as has their unpredictable and random nature,[11] and they have become both an inspiration for and inspired by the popular media. They have fueled a growing industry of psychologists, criminologists, profilers, and others who have sought to better understand the motivations of these killers—to either help capture them or prevent them from killing.

Some key characteristics and differences between different types of killers have been discovered. Both mass murderers and serial killers are typically white, middle-class males inspired by personal rather than political motives. But they are otherwise quite different. Mass murderers are generally motivated by anger to lash out in a big burst of killing, which is often inspired by a suicide wish. They generally don't expect to escape or even try to do so. The spree typically ends with the killer committing suicide, being shot down by the police, or surrendering quietly after his anger is spent.[12]

By contrast, serial killers—generally defined as those who kill three or more people over thirty days or more—are not only becoming more common but also driven by a wide variety of motives, from anger and revenge to robbery and to satisfying sadistic and sexual impulses. Since the 1970s, Lane points out, hundreds of such killers have been interviewed—they have literally become a whole new field of modern study, there are so many of them. What makes them especially difficult to discover or understand is they tend to be clever, secretive, and sometimes "charmingly seductive," which helps them lure their victims and later get away. Some have no conscience and might be characterized as sociopaths or psychopaths; others live in their own delusional fantasy world that contributes to their actions and helps them justify and continue to do what they do. They enjoy it because it satisfies their own perverse idea of pleasure—or they feel a compulsion to continue. For a long time they might continue to get away with it because they are so clever. A classic example of this type of killer is Ted Bundy, who reportedly killed dozens of women in several states from the West Coast to Florida between 1974 and 1979, and his dashing charm helped him repeatedly find victims and get away.[13] In other cases, women have even fallen in love with killers and have contributed to their own subsequent victimization or helped the killers victimize others.

Although it is difficult to determine just how many of these killers were on the loose in the past (they are so elusive and earlier crime statistics are spotty), historians are generally agreed that since the 1970s they are much more common. New technologies and inventions help them do what they do as well, such as the easy availability of cars or trucks they can use to kidnap their victims or take them from the homicide scene to a hiding place or burial ground afterward.[14] Then, too, the anonymity of the city, coupled with the greater openness and sensuality of the 1970s, contributed to their ability to attract victims and escape later. Thus, although the local police and the FBI may have developed arsenals of new techniques to track them down, such as the use of Social Security numbers and a national fingerprint database, it would seem the conditions favorable to serial killers have contributed to their growth.

In turn, the press helped focus the attention of the public on the growing problem of serial killers with news about several major cases—the killing of boys and young men by Dean Corll and his accomplices in Houston and by John Wayne Gacy in Chicago, the murders of young women in Los Angeles by "The Hillside Strangler" (actually two men), Bundy's attacks on coeds in the Northwest and then in Colorado and Florida, and by David Berkowitz's (Son of Sam) shootings in New York. Perhaps more than any other place, California became, as crime writers Colin and Damon Wilson put it, "Virtually the serial-killer center of the world." Besides the Hillside Strangler case, which had the police and the public sticking pins in the map of L.A. to create a circle of dumped bodies around the house where the women were being killed, there were the killings by John Linley Frazier, who attacked the Ohta family in Santa Cruz in 1970, on the grounds they were too materialistic and deserved to die. There were also murders by Herb Mullin, who killed different types of victims randomly around Santa Cruz on the grounds they helped avert natural disasters. There were killings in the Sacramento area by Richard Chase, who got the name the Dracula Killer because he drank his victims' blood. Ed Kemper killed mostly coeds and hitchhikers around the state, mainly to get back at his mother. Juan Corona killed farm workers because of homosexual desires.[15]

One response to the rise of this new type of killer was the beginning of serious study by psychiatrists, psychologists, sociologists, and other academics to try to understand what was going on—ideas that in turn proved useful to investigators trying to track these killers and anticipate what they might do next. For example, in 1976, two researchers, Samuel Yochelson and Stanton E. Samenow, came out with their classic study, *The Criminal Personality*, in which they pointed out that criminality is closely connected with "inadequacy, laziness, and self-pity; it is another name for defeat-proneness."[16] That same year, Hervey M. Cleckley characterized the psychopath killer as one who reflected these primary characteristics: "unreliability, insincerity, pathological lying, and egocentricity; poor judgment and impulsivity; lack of remorse, guilt, or shame; an inability to experience empathy or concern for others, or to maintain affectionate attachments; impersonal and poorly integrated sex life; and an unstable life style with no long-term plans."[17] Other researchers talked about the serial killer's need for control due to a lack of self-esteem and self-doubts. Though he might appear quite normal and balanced to others, with family members and significant others he might seem like a "paranoid dictator" who always had to be in charge,[18] a quality noted by the Wilsons in looking at some of the classic cases of serial killers of the 1970s, like Bundy. A serial killer might be a loner with deep feelings of inadequacy, like Berkowitz. In any case, there began to be psychological explanations for why serial killers did what they did.

Another response was for police homicide departments to make changes to better monitor unsolved cases, looking for patterns that might suggest a serial killer at work. For example, in 1974, the New York Police Department acknowledged that it had failed to recognize the overall pattern in eight different murders and two assaults of women that occurred in the same hotel over a period of one and a half years. The killer confessed while being charged with another murder that occurred near the hotel.[19] They would now be more careful in looking for patterns—an approach the Houston Police Department realized it needed to adopt as well after it discovered that Corll, with the help of two accomplices had killed at least twenty-seven boys in the Houston area from 1971 to 1973. The police had absolutely no idea until one accomplice, Elmer Henley, called in August 1973 confessing everything. The police had dismissed many missing persons accounts as simply runaway boys and had failed to investigate or look for similarities in these reports.[20]

Unfortunately, at a time when there was a growing youth culture and a breakdown in the traditional family, there really were more runaways and less family supervision. So it was much easier for people to be missing without anyone suspecting anything seriously wrong—and therefore easier for serial killers to operate without being detected. For example, consider what happened in the early phases of Ted Bundy's murder career. Many of his victims were reported missing by friends and relatives, but most of the time the police treated these disappearances as routine missing persons reports. Only when the fourth victim was reported missing in May 1974 did the police begin to notice some similarities among the disappearances reported in Seattle, Olympia, Corvallis, and Ellensburg in Washington. They didn't start discovering the skeletal remains until early fall 1974. It was another six months—March 1975—before the police in Seattle formed a task force to look into the disappearances. In hindsight, after Bundy was finally caught and convicted, critics felt the police should have initiated joint investigation action much sooner, especially after the bodies started turning up.[21]

This was the same kind of problem that occurred in the notorious Gacy case in Chicago. There were reports of four missing boys, and four complaints were made against Gacy between 1971 to 1978 for homosexual assault behavior, but the Chicago police never connected the criminal information on Gacy to the boys' disappearances. In fact, Gacy was discovered when the police were checking on a fifteen-year-old boy who had disappeared after going for a summer job interview at Gacy's house in Des Plaines, Iowa, in December 1978. The police noticed an odd smell in his house and after initially unearthing two bodies on the first day of digging, they eventually found twenty-seven to thirty bodies in the crawl space underneath it according to various accounts. Until then, they had no idea they had a serial killer on the loose.[22]

Unfortunately, the more devious and mobile serial killers need more of a coordinated task force approach that cuts across county, state, and even international lines. In the 1970s, the police were only starting to recognize and respond to this problem, though it was clear there was a new type of killer committing "stranger to stranger" murders. In the 1960s, such killings only accounted for about 6 percent of such murders; by the mid-1970s, they represented 18 percent of all homicides—over 4,000 cases a year.[23] Clearly, something had to be done.

However, there were the beginnings of a more comprehensive and national approach as the FBI developed and expanded its Behavioral Sciences Unit (BSU) in the early 1970s. As former special agent John Douglas describes it, before J. Edgar Hoover died in 1972, psychology and behavioral sciences very much took a back seat to the tactical and firearms divisions, which were the real stars of the FBI. There was just a small group of about seven to nine BSU special agents, who were involved in instructing at the FBI Academy and helping with hostage negotiations. Beginning in 1969, Howard Teten began teaching a class on applied criminal psychology, and in 1972, he learned about profiling techniques from Dr. James Brussel, the psychiatrist who had helped crack the Mad Bomber case with these methods. Teten brought these methods of understanding criminal behavior and motives from evidence at the crime scene back to the bureau.[24] With Pat Mullany, who joined the bureau in 1972, Teten expanded this approach, in part with the help of a grant from the National Institute of Justice.[25] They started with a team of nine men, officially known as the BSU, designed to apply Brussel's techniques, which eventually led to launching a serial killer study in the late 1970s. Members of the unit began going to prisons across the nation to talk to well-known serial killers, such as Charles Manson, Richard Speck, Ed Kemper, Juan Corona, and David Berkowitz, and besides compiling a library of taped interviews, they began analyzing these accounts to learn just what motivated these men to do what they did.[26] They became in effect "mind hunters," putting themselves in the mind of the killers, so that they and other investigators might do this in future cases. This approach was used more and more in the 1980s and 1990s, particularly as more research about serial killers was collected from a growing number of them.

At the same time, other more sophisticated scientific and data-gathering techniques were developed to help investigators. For example, in 1974, the American Law Enforcement Assistance Administration began a pilot program to collect samples of paint from American car manufacturers and send them to

171 crime laboratories around the nation to help in identifying hit-and-run drivers and rapists,[27] and it was used in identifying killers, too. The program was so successful that it was continued and expanded in following years.

The 1970s marked the beginnings of using hair and blood samples for DNA testing.[28] The testing of a wide variety of trace evidence using precision microscopes—from shoe prints to hair and fiber samples—had become routine. Lab technicians could even measure bite marks on a victim's tongue, such as when nineteen-year-old Sharon Zellers disappeared on her way home from work at Walt Disney World in Florida on December 30, 1978. After the police found her car a few days later in an orange grove, they carefully examined blood stains, shoe prints, and a few strands of hair found in the car. When they found her body about fifty feet from the car, they used dental records to identify her. They were able to identify the suspect because a nurse who treated a man whose tongue was bitten discovered that the curve was the reverse of his own bite. Later investigators were able to show how Sharon had bitten it off, besides showing that the hair samples found in the victim's car matched those on the killer's head.[29]

While the number of stranger-to-stranger mass murderers and serial killers were growing, investigators were changing their strategies to use more psychological and sophisticated techniques to find the criminals.

At the same time, the media and public fascination with serial killers was starting to explode as well, which in turn helped inspire even more killers, attracted by the prospects of fame and recognition—preferably for their acts, and not themselves, so they could keep on with their activity without being caught. It was another aphrodisiac encouraging more killings for a killer often motivated by low-self-esteem and a sense of rejection by others, as well as a lack of self-control, a lack of caring for other people, and compulsive sexual drives.

Besides the burst of media attention for these cases, many of these killers became the focus for a growing library of books and then films. There were at least twenty books on killers in the 1970s—many more in the 1980s and 1990s. Among the early ones were books about Albert Fish (*The Cannibal* by Mel Heimer, 1971); Charles Manson (*The Family* by Ed Sanders, 1971; and *Helter Skelter* by Vincent Bugliosi and Curt Gentry, 1974); Carl Panzram (*Killer* by Thomas Gaddis and James O. Long, 1970); Dean Corll (*The Man with the Candy* by Jack Olsen, 1974; *Mass Murder in Houston* by John Gurwell, 1974); Charlie Starkweather and Caril Fugate (*Caril* by Ninette Beaver, 1976; *Starkweather* by William Allen, 1976); Juan Corona (*The Road to Yuba City* by Tracy Kidder, 1974); Herbert Mullin (*Sacrifice Unto Me* by Don West, 1974); Ed Kemper (*The Co-ed Killer* by Margaret Cheney, 1976); and John Norman Collins (*The Michigan Murders* by Edward Keyes, 1976, and *The Mysterious Deaths at Ann Arbor* by Robert Wilcox, 1977); just to name some of the more notorious killers. It was also the beginnings of compilations of these cases like *Murder and Madness* by Donald T. Lunde (1975) and *Murder USA* by John

Goodwin (1978). Some of these 1970s killers, like Ted Bundy, the Hillside Strangler, and David Berkowitz became the subject of a series of books in the early 1980s.

In short, serial killing was becoming something of a hot entertainment industry, and some of the killers began to be known by popular nicknames befitting pop stars, such as the Co-ed Killer for Ed Kemper, the Hillside Strangler for Angelo Buono and Kenneth Bianchi, the Freeway Killer for William Bonin, the Trash Bag Killer for Patrick Wayne Kearney, and so on. It was a way to help make sense of it all and perhaps make the phenomena seem less frightening, more a part of the growing media culture of the day. Each year brought a new burst of multiple killers inspired by different motives—some of them quite mad and delusional, others looking very much like the ordinary neighbor or business associate next door. Most were male killers who victimized women (like Kemper, Berkowitz, and Bundy) and killed for sex or out of their anger against women, there were a growing number of homosexual killers who targeted young boys or men (like Gacy, Corll, Kearney, Bonin, and Corona). A small number killed for money, such as Calvin Jackson who initially killed for money to buy narcotics, though his crimes later escalated into rape and murder, or Glennon Engleman, a dentist who conspired with his patients and killed seven people for their insurance payments. There were some who killed for ideological reasons, such as Vaughan Orrin Greenwood, the New York Skid Row Slasher who targeted alcoholics; Joseph Paul Franklin, an American Nazi supporter who killed mixed-race couples or blacks and whites involved in black causes; and John Linley Frazier, who targeted the family of wealthy eye surgeon Victor Ohta because he felt he was too materialistic and wanted to preserve the natural order. Some targeted the most vulnerable or available, such as Dayton Leroy Rogers, a devout Seventh Day Adventist who hated women and tortured about four dozen prostitutes, and Robert Diaz, a nurse who killed about twenty patients at a hospital, his way of playing doctor.

In short, as the number of serial killers multiplied, so did the wide variety of killers, victims, motives, psychological dynamics, and methods, contributing to the difficulty of discovering the killers. While the public and media were fascinated and social scientists and psychologists began their in-depth studies of the phenomena, the police, FBI, and other investigators were increasingly baffled. Even after the killers were discovered, the puzzlement and fascination continued, because now more than ever psychiatrists and psychologists played a role in trying to understand the killers and explain why they did what they did. In a decade when psychological analysis, self-help groups, and recovery movements were becoming popular, psychiatrists came to play a key role in the investigative process and were increasingly called on to argue for or against insanity defenses in court.

Psychologists were involved in some of the most puzzling and fascinating cases of the decade, too—which included the murder cases involving Kemper, who hated his mother and mostly targeted co-eds; Berkowitz, who mystified

Queens and Brooklyn as the "Son of Sam" and hated women generally; and Corona, a farm contractor in Yuba City, California, accused of killing and burying over twenty-five farmhands.

Following are their stories, reflecting the trends for the decade and the investigative techniques used to solve these cases.

THE CASE OF ED KEMPER

San Francisco Bay Area, Santa Cruz, California, 1972–73

On May 7, 1972, two eighteen-year-old roommates from Fresno State College disappeared while hitchhiking to visit friends at Stanford. The police thought Mary Ann Pesce and Anita Luchessa were runaways. Wearing jeans and backpacks, they had last gone to the end of Ashby Avenue in Berkeley holding up a hand-lettered sign saying "San Francisco" to help them get across the bridge so they could then make their way to Stanford. They were never seen again.

The supposition seemed reasonable, since the early 1970s was a time when students in the San Francisco Bay area and women generally felt freer than ever. The United States, especially the Bay area, was in an explosion of personal growth and self-discovery, when taking off on trips for exploring oneself or the world were common. It was a time when communal living and casual sex had become accepted in certain free-thinking areas, and often students simply dropped out of school to join utopian or religious groups like the Moonies and Hare Krishnas.

The police didn't seem very concerned, even though the friends and family of Mary Ann and Anita felt sure something terrible had happened. As family members described her, Mary Ann was a good student from an affluent family who loved to ski, aspired to try out for the Olympics, was a good debater in school, and was very interested in photography, which is why she carried an expensive German camera in her backpack the day she disappeared. Anita, an A student at Fresno, was the oldest daughter of a third-generation farming family, and she usually went home most weekends, though sometimes she joined Mary Ann skiing. All her parents knew was that around 4 p.m., two friends had taken them to the Ashby Avenue off-ramp, and they turned down an offer of a ride to Stanford because they were eager to hitchhike to meet new people. But again and again, when they tried to file a missing persons report with various police departments—in San Francisco, Berkeley, Fresno, Santa Barbara—the police either turned them down or dismissed their concerns, though one Berkeley officer, after much urging, took and filed a report. The problem, as several officers observed, is that "Girls ran away. Usually with boys," though some parents could never accept this. Besides, with the new law, "an eighteen-year-old was now legally an adult, and . . . an adult could not be a missing person."[30]

Anita's family even tried hiring a private investigator, who searched for three months. After several hundred hours, which including flyers, posters, and newspaper ads, he came up with nothing either.[31]

The story stood there for several months—just two missing co-eds. What the police didn't know was that they had been strangled, tossed in the backseat and trunk of a car, and then dissected. They didn't know this until much later, after more girls went missing and some parts of bodies began to turn up around the Bay area.

Even the disappearance of fifteen-year-old Aiko Koo four months later, on September 14, 1972, didn't seem to impress the police very much. She was waiting for a bus at University Avenue in Berkeley on her way to a dance class in San Francisco when she was offered a ride by a helpful stranger; tired of waiting, she eagerly took it. A few neighbors going to a movie saw her talking to another girl as she waited for a bus, and the girl who talked to her and later saw her picture on a telephone pole with the query: "Have you seen this girl?" reported to police she had seen her get in a late 1960s cream- or tan-colored sedan with a tall male Caucasian with light or medium brown hair.[32] That was the best description she could give.

The police put Koo down as another runaway, although Aiko's frantic mother did what she could on her own. She and family friends made posters and plastered them all over Berkeley. They contacted all the newspapers. They stood by buses for many nights, showing passengers Aiko's photo and asking if they had seen her. They wrote to all of the small police departments in California, Oregon, and Washington, as well as to communes around California and the United States asking for help. They even wrote to the FBI. But nothing turned up.

The police didn't realize there was a serial killer on the loose. Contributing to the problem was the fact that the mental health professionals who were in touch with this killer, Edmund Kemper, didn't have a clue either. In fact, the day after Aiko was killed, her body dissected, and her head left in the trunk of his car, Ed went for interviews with two psychiatrists in Fresno to show them he was normal so the court would seal his juvenile record and he could live a normal adult life. He wanted his record sealed because at age fourteen, he had killed his grandmother, whom he hated, because he "just wondered how it would feel to shoot grandma." He killed his grandfather when he arrived home soon after that. He passed the psychiatrists' interviews with glowing recommendations. One doctor's report to the court stated, "I see no psychiatric reason to consider him a danger to himself or any other member of society. His motorcycle and driving habits would appear to be more of a threat to his own life and health than any threat he is presently to anyone else." The second agreed his mental health was "excellent," and he found him to be "normal" and "safe."[33] This hurdle overcome, Kemper drove north, fantasizing about how he had to teach Aiko a lesson for being so pretty and hitchhiking in a dangerous place where girls just felt they could do whatever they wanted.[34] After stopping at home, he drove on into the mountains to bury Koo's head and hands near a religious camp.

The police suspected nothing at first, and neither did the mental health professionals. What made the investigation even more difficult was that there was at least one other serial killer operating in the Santa Cruz and Southern Peninsula area, Herb Mullin. For a time it was hard to sort out who was doing what. The whole Bay area went into a state of panic as the disappearances continued.

One factor contributing to the sudden rise of serial murderers and other mentally disturbed killers in the Santa Cruz/Southern Peninsula area, as well as in other parts of California, was a recent change in mental health laws and practices. Under Ronald Reagan as governor, new legislation was closing down the state's mental hospitals, using the argument that "warehousing" patients was inhumane and they could be better cared for in the community. The only problem was that most local governments were unable or unwilling to assume the costs for the care of these newly released patients, and the Nixon administration had cut down federal support for institutions providing patient care as well. Thus, as an increasing number of mental patients left the hospitals, there was a lack of local psychiatric wards and outpatient clinics to properly treat them.[35] Some of them turned out to be spree or serial killers who were able to operate in relative freedom given the open climate of the early 1970s, especially in California.

In the late 1960s, the Manson Family killings had provided a kind of model that inspired the first of these 1970s California killers—John Linley Frazier, who was truly mad, and soon got nicknamed the Ding-Dong, Avon-Calling killer in the Santa Cruz area. Frazier admitted that God told him to call at every house, speak to the man of the family, and with him decide if the rest of the family should live or die. Then these two chosen men would proceed to the next house, make a similar decision, and go on to the next. To his deranged way of thinking, this was a holy mission. At the first house he entered, he managed to tie up the wife, two children, and secretary of Dr. Victor Ohta, a wealthy eye surgeon. When Ohta resisted this mission, Frazier attacked him, threw him in his swimming pool, drowned him, shot the tied-up victims, and torched the house. Later, investigators found the ravings of a lunatic at the scene which described Frazier's crazed vision of killing to protect the natural environment and strike out against materialism. As his note attached to Ohta's car read in part:

> Halloween 1970 . . . From this day forward, anyone and/or company of persons who misuses the natural environment or destroys same will suffer the penalty of death by People of the Free Universe. I and my comrades from this day forth will fight until death or freedom against anyone who does not support natural life on this planet. Materialism must die or mankind must stop.

He then signed the note on behalf of various knights of the tarot card deck: the "Knight of Wands—Knight of Pentacles—Knight of Cups—Knight of Swords."[36]

In this case, the police were led to Frazier, a twenty-four-year-old garage mechanic and cultist in nearby Felton who was known as a fanatical ecologist and tarot practitioner. He was fairly easy to find, because witnesses soon told the police they had seen Frazier driving Ohta's station wagon a day after the murders and the police found Frazier's fingerprints on the wheel of the Rolls Royce where he left the note.[37]

Though the case was quickly solved and Frazier sentenced to death in 1971 (this was changed to life imprisonment due to changes in the California law), it left people in the Santa Cruz area already feeling jumpy when Herb Mullin began his own murder spree between October 1972 and February 1973. Mullin had been in and out of five different mental hospitals. Even though he was diagnosed as a violent paranoid schizophrenic who should never be released, he was let go. He went on his spree because he heard voices telling him he could prevent the massive earthquakes predicted for southern California with human sacrifices. He started with a transient he encountered in the mountains near Santa Cruz, and then went on randomly picking twelve other victims, including a young girl, four campers, a priest in a confessional, a couple who turned him onto LSD, a woman and her two children, and an old man who happened to be working in his backyard when Mullin passed him.[38] In one case, he was inspired by reading Irving Stone's biography of Michelangelo—*The Agony and the Ecstasy*—especially learning about how the great sculptor carefully explored human anatomy. He decided to do the same, and after picking up a Cabrillo Community College student named Mary in his blue station wagon in the fall of 1972, he stabbed her in the chest and back, and then proceeded to dissect her torso and examine her organs.[39] He was eventually captured after a few months and thirteen victims when a witness saw him shoot a retired fish dealer in February 1973 on a residential street in Santa Cruz and reported the car's description to the police, who soon captured him. He confessed to the killings, explaining his desire to protect humanity with his sacrifices. Before he was caught, his killings helped confuse investigators about who was actually abducting and killing the co-eds while contributing to the growing climate of fear.

In fact, before Mary's disappearance, no one had thought to connect the early disappearances of Mary Ann Pesce, Anita Luchessa, or Aiko Koo with what was going on in the Santa Cruz area; in fact, they had been pretty much file-and-forget kinds of cases. Mary's disappearance in early fall 1972 helped ignite a rising concern that one or more kidnappers or killers was at work in the Santa Cruz area, especially when her decomposed body was discovered in January 1973 by some men practicing sharp-shooting in the Santa Cruz mountains. This was shortly after the severed body parts of another girl were found by the side of a cliff south of Carmel; a neatly severed human rib cage washed ashore near the Santa Cruz coast a week later.[40]

The Santa Cruz area erupted in concern, a fear that soon echoed around the state and drew renewed attention to what happened to the three girls from Berkeley. College women especially were concerned as a growing number of bodies were washed up in the surf or discovered in the hills, since the killings seemed to be completely random; there were also a growing number of rape cases in the area. Women became increasingly scared that one of them could be next. Thus, they helped spread the warning that women should not hitch rides and should keep their doors locked to avoid being the next victim.

As author Margaret Cheney describes it, a newly formed woman's group picketed the county jail to protest that rape cases weren't receiving enough attention from law enforcement officers, whereon the Santa Cruz area Sheriff's Office issued its own advisory warning describing twenty-four cases in 1972 in unincorporated Santa Cruz County involving hitchhiking: ten rapes, eight assaults with an intent to commit rape, three incidents of indecent exposure, two kidnappings, and one incident of sex perversion.[41]

Meanwhile, a special rape line telephone number was installed in public telephone booths downtown, and two women organized a local group to fight rape. The university itself cautioned students through bulletin board announcements which urged girls: "When possible . . . stay in dorms after midnight with doors locked. If you must be out at night—walk in pairs. DON'T HITCH A RIDE, PLEASE. If you feel you must hitch a ride—do it with a friend, but NOT ALONE. Try to choose cars with University Parking decals (A, B, C or R)."[42] The college even helped organize a carpool, providing stickers and ID cards to the drivers and riders.

Unfortunately, it was difficult to discourage students from hitching rides, and there was a lack of sufficient regular bus service to the campus. As it later turned out, the killer himself had a university sticker, provided by his mother, who worked at the Cabrillo campus. No one suspected a thing, and the disappearances and killings continued. In fact, the killer hung out with some of the Santa Cruz deputies from time to time in a bar called the Jury Room, where off-duty officers liked to go. No one suspected a thing. He seemed like another conservative, straight-looking, very tall guy, who looked more like John Wayne, his hero, than some kind of crazy killer.

Herb Mullin was arrested on February 13, shortly before two more headless bodies of girls were found in the Eden Canyon area of Alameda County (later their heads were found on the Coast Highway just south of Pacifica, near San Francisco). Many people attributed all the killings to him. There were all sorts of theories bandied about—that Mullin was part of a devil cult, a homosexual, a transvestite, a medical student. The judge imposed a gag order on Mullin's case, which only confused the public about which killings he was responsible for and which he was not.[43]

Oddly, this confusion bothered the killer of the three Berkeley girls, plus three other girls whose headless bodies had recently been found. Kemper felt like the time was growing short before he might be caught because of the increased police attention. At the same time, he felt more driven to do what he felt he had to do—like a "walking time bomb," as he later explained.[44] He began to prepare for his final act or mission, which he would reveal to the world—killing his mother, with whom he had had a love/hate relationship since childhood. He was symbolically killing his mother each time he had killed a girl.

To Kemper's mind, the act was almost like completing the package, placing the final bookend. Nearly ten years before, he had killed his grandmother and his grandfather, because he hated his mother. His father, who had divorced Kemper's mother, wouldn't let Ed live with him, so he had to stay with his stuffy, old-fashioned grandparents instead. After he left the mental hospital, he killed six women as representatives for his mother. Now it was time to take the process to its conclusion by killing his mother—then he could reveal all. The cops had been too dumb to catch him so far; the mental health practitioners certainly didn't understand what he was doing either. He had been too smart for all of them. For the world to know what he did, he had to help. He felt a little like a superior being laughing at the lack of knowledge of the professionals and the police—a superiority he needed because he felt so rejected otherwise.

Like a villain revealing himself in the final act, Edmund Kemper got ready to do what he felt he must do—and then he would confess to the world. What he did on the morning of the day before Easter Sunday 1973 was kill his mother—whom he had always hated, yet loved, feared, and depended on—in a kind of strange fit of renewal and resurrection. He had always identified with Job and was a careful reader of the Bible, so for him this was like the final trial.

As the police soon discovered, as Kemper confessed it, at 5:15 a.m., he went into the kitchen and got a claw hammer and picked up the same pocketknife he had used to kill Mary Ann Pesce, his first victim. In his mother's bedroom, after he hit her on the head with the hammer, he slashed her throat, deciding "what's good for my victim was good for my mother." He cut off her head, dragged her body into the closet, and cleaned up the house. After briefly stopping downtown for a hacksaw blade and running into an old acquaintance who owed him $10 and paid him back when they got some liquor (otherwise, he would have become another victim, Kemper later said), he returned home. Realizing that the absence of his mother on Easter Sunday might upset the family, while her absence from work on Monday morning might puzzle others, he decided someone else had to die, too, as a cover-up or excuse, and he settled on a close friend of his mother's, Sally Hallett. He invited her to join him and his mother for dinner and a movie, and when she arrived, Kemper was his usual friendly, courteous self as he invited her in. As they walked into the living room toward the couch, it was as if the victim herself gave the signal when she said, "Let's sit down. I'm dead."[45] A few minutes later she was, after he attacked her with the hammer and knife. He removed her clothes and put her body on the bed, then he went to the Jury Room for a few beers and listened quietly to hear how the investigation, if any, had gone. Back at the house, he decapitated Hallett like his other victims, spent the night sleeping on the bed of his dead mother, put Hallett's body in a closet, loaded up a small gun arsenal he had collected, and began his long drive to confess.[46] It was Easter Sunday morning as he drove away. In Reno, thinking quite rightly that the car might soon be the object of an interstate search, he rented another car, transferred his guns to it, and dropped Hallett's car at a nearby Texaco station, telling the operator it had electrical problems, which he figured would take days to check. He drove for another eighteen hours until he arrived in eastern Colorado.

From a Pueblo, Colorado, phone booth, Kemper made a call to Lt. Charles Scherer at the Santa Cruz Police Department. Though he didn't know Scherer personally, he had seen him around Santa Cruz and knew he was investigating the disappearances and murders of the women students. As Kemper later told Scherer, he reminded him of his own father—the "John Wayne figure in my life."[47] At first the police, some of whom were his drinking companions, didn't take his phoned confession seriously. He had to wait at the phone booth and call several times. Around 5 a.m., the Santa Cruz police finally asked the Colorado police to go pick Kemper up. As he waited at the phone booth for them, Officer Conner in Santa Cruz got the details about the killings at Kemper's mother's house in Aptos. A few minutes later, Kemper quite docilely went into police custody in Colorado, and Santa Cruz officers began checking the scene in Aptos, which was just as he described. Within a few hours a team of Santa Cruz detectives, including Scherer and Santa Cruz district attorney Peter Chang, were in Colorado, ready to talk to Kemper and get what they could on tape.

At this point, they got everything, because Kemper was eager to confess. He waived everything—his right to an extradition hearing in Colorado, his right to remain silent, his right to talk to an attorney. He just wanted to talk. Over the next few days, he did—describing in graphic detail what he did. It was as if the compulsion to confess and find catharsis was as overpowering as the original compulsion to commit the crimes he now needed to confess.[48]

In careful detail, Kemper described how he had committed each homicide and why. In time, the story of his childhood and relationship with his mother came out, too. The only question left for his trial was whether he was sane. As the story came out, it rocked not only the law enforcement but the mental health and political community over how to deal with the mentally ill and protect the community from their crimes. What made Kemper's story even more difficult to fathom was that outwardly he seemed like an ordinary, friendly kind of guy, although he was very tall and ungainly at six feet, nine inches and a little on the shy and retiring side. He even wore a Junior Chamber of Commerce pin and had friends in the law enforcement community. He was very articulate and bright, with an IQ of 136, though he had never taken advantage of the opportunity to go on with his education and get a college degree. Instead, he had meekly resigned himself to a low-level job at the Department of Highways and Transportation. Part of his reason for turning to killing was so he could become known—as well as perhaps reflect his anger at those with a higher social status by taking their valuable daughters. At least, that's one explanation he gave to the many investigators and psychologists that came to talk to him. Others, like Dr. Joel Fort, who testified for the prosecution at his trial, felt it was mostly sexual pressure that drove him to do what he did, since he felt uncomfortable having a relation with a live woman; he could only feel the sense of connection and possession with one after she was dead.

In any event, one by one, Kemper described his year of killing, and subsequently the investigators confirmed it all. He also helpfully led them to the heads and bodies.

Kemper spent about two years practicing, by driving around, becoming familiar with the roads and picking up women hitchhiking to see how to best do it, like a man going to bars refining his pick-up lines. He thought through plans about weapons, disposal sites, and driving times. He worked out the details like a military commander, and later he felt some pride that he had been able to escape for so long. No one even suspected him until he called to confess; although by then the fear of losing control was building.

On May 7, while he was living in a small apartment in Alameda, the killings began when he picked up Mary Ann Pesce and Anita Luchessa. As he did with his other victims, he spent some time talking to them, briefly getting to know them, and he even felt a sense of special rapport with Mary Ann as she tried to talk to him and invited him to share any problems he had. As a teenager he had spent five years in a hospital for the mentally ill after killing his grandparents, so he was already wise to such techniques and didn't let the girls dissuade him from his plans. However, he did feel a special kinship to her, which led him to remember her later with a kind of reverence. Also, the experience led him to want to go on with his killings. As Kemper explained in his confession to Scherer:

> I was really quite struck by her personality and her looks and there was just almost a reverence there . . . (She had) very good efforts of communicating and discussing the thing. . . . I don't know how many times I stabbed her . . . I didn't even touch her, really too much, after that. That is, other than to get rid of physical evidence, such as clothing, and later the body.[49]

As he did with the other girls he killed later, Kemper took the bodies back to his apartment, took off their clothes, cut them up, and cut off their heads, which he kept for a while before he discarded them, too—the bodies in one site, the heads in another. It was like a plan he worked out to make it harder to discover what he had done as well as satisfying some unconscious need for possession and control. From time to time he returned to these and other murder sites, drawn by the desire to relive and remember the experience, as well as check to see if his handiwork had been discovered. Cheney, who studied his case at length, writes:

> For almost a year Kemper retoured the scenes of murders and the places where he had disposed of body fragments, in the manner of some fastidious and overly con-

> cerned cemetery caretaker. There were several reasons for this: an effort to recapture the excitement and horror of the deed, and perhaps, subconsciously, the wish to be caught and punished; but also his concern for the success of his game plan, his desire for perfection, and the needs of his insatiable curiosity.[50]

As he listened, Scherer felt sickened as Kemper described each murder in gory detail, but he kept his feelings concealed, so that Kemper would keep going and describe them all.

By the third killing, Kemper had involved his mother, stopping at her house while Aiko Koo's body was still in his trunk. As he told Scherer, he had wanted to talk to his mother to see if he still appeared normal, despite what he done. He was, as he explained, "testing on her whether or not anything would show on my face or my mannerism or speech as to what I was doing and why, and it didn't. She absolutely took no alarm or asked any undue questions."[51] Two days later, after he had dissected Koo's body in his apartment and buried most of her remains and still had her head in his trunk, he drove to Fresno for his psychiatric examination with the two doctors who thought he was perfectly normal.[52] He was a little disappointed from his earlier discussions with Aiko to learn that she was "not of the moneyed class whose death would serve as a punishment of society for its treatment of him."[53] But he felt compelled to go on.

About every four months the pressure would build in him, so in January 1973, he went looking for his next victim, who turned out to be Cindy Schall, a student at Cabrillo College, part of the UCSC campus. Kemper explained that he originally hadn't intended to pick out any victims in Santa Cruz, since he was now staying with his mother. After he read about the abduction and disappearance of Mullin's victim (Mary) in Santa Cruz, he felt that he could probably get away with doing likewise in the same area if he was careful. So he began looking for co-eds himself, and this time he brought the results of his killing even closer to home. While his mother, Clarnell Stranberg, was away from her duplex in Aptos, he noticed that the neighbors weren't even home, so he carried Schall's body to a closet. The next morning when his mother left for work, he took the body into his bedroom, where he raped her corpse. Placing the body in the bathtub, he used his buck knife and ax from the California Department of Highways to dissect her, and carefully cleaned up, dropping most of the body parts in a plastic bag off a cliff south of Carmel. But he left Schall's head in a box in his closet, and a few days later, when he read that the police had discovered some of her body parts, he buried her head in his mother's back yard.[54] It was as if Kemper was even more craftily making it clear he was doing all of this because of his mother—though she still didn't suspect a thing.

A month later, on February 5, Kemper killed two more hitchhikers he picked up at the UCSC campus—Rosalind Thorpe and Alice Lui. He brought them back to his mother's house as well. In fact, he used the sticker his mother had given him for the university parking lot to help reassure the women to get in his car, although the campus was already hysterical with fear about the Co-ed Killer who was picking up and killing women hitchhikers. After he took both girls to a quiet road with a beautiful view of the ocean and shot them both, he brought them back to his mother's house. In the morning after his mother had left for work, he cleaned the blood off both bodies in the bathroom, had sex with one of them, and put the bodies back in the trunk. Ironically, as he was doing this, a party was going on upstairs, and a window directly overlooked his car. But no one saw him. It was as if he was even more directly challenging someone to see him, but no one did. He dumped these bodies, too, in the East Bay in Eden Canyon, and dumped the heads off the Devil's Slide cliffs.

As he explained, he felt the pressure building for his final act and confession, since the investigation had stepped up in four counties, because the bodies or body parts of several of the women had turned up. Public hysteria was rising, and Mullin had been arrested just the week before.[55]

It was finally time to do in Mom. But why? That was the big question the public and psychiatrists would start asking. Was he sane?

As it soon came out, Kemper had had a very troubled childhood, growing up with a tall, strapping mother who was very domineering—a six-foot "domineering bitch" as he sometimes put it.[56] Clarnell married a series of weak men. She fought frequently with his natural father, E. E. Kemper Jr., a six foot, eight inch tall electrician who had fought in the Special Forces and went on some suicide missions during World War II. She accused him of having menial work, and there were frequent fights about money. Finally, he left for good when Edmund was nine.

As a small boy, Ed took to fantasizing, and these fantasies soon turned morbid. Once, he went into a cathedral and prayed that everyone else in the world except for himself would be killed.[57] He made a childhood death list, which included certain women friends of his mother, and he continued to keep their names and addresses for years afterward. From time to time he cut off the heads and hands of his sister's favorite dolls, and one time he enjoyed killing a cat by burying it alive in the yard. When it was dead, he took it into the house, cut off its head, and stuck it on a spindle, which he kept in his room.[58] His mother contributed to his torments by forcing him to sell newspapers on the street when he was eight or nine and telling him not to return until he sold them all; she made him sleep in the basement for eight months. From an early age, "death, sex, religion, and thoughts of suicide became confused in his mind . . . swirling with the actual killing of animals and the mutilations of dolls,"[59] according to biographer Cheney. He grew up in a lonely world without playmates, where fantasy loomed large, including a growing curiosity about sex, which he felt too awkward to express, and an abiding anger toward his mother.

At one point there might have been some hope when he briefly went to live with his natural father, stepmother, and their son in Los Angeles. But problems in school developed because he didn't fit in—one complaint was that he would "sit and stare at people until they became upset."[60] His father sent him to live with his grandparents on an isolated farm in North Fork in the Sierra foothills.

He hated living there, and felt "mad at the world," as he told the deputies who arrested him.[61]

After his grandparents' murder, he was found insane and sent by the California Youth Authority to Atascadero State Hospital, where he spent the next five years with convicted child molesters, rapists, and other adult sexual deviates. He was a model prisoner who was praised for his careful work in helping the prison psychologists give and correct psychological tests. His life in this environment helped shape his psychotic, paranoid attitude toward the world, particularly women. It also helped make him very conversant with the psychological jargon of the day, which he used to explain and justify his behavior to himself at the same time that he felt driven to act out his fantasies.

In fact, perhaps the pop culture of the day helped him do so, because he was sent to Atascadero at a time when it was becoming socially acceptable (if not chic) to act out one's hatreds and frustrations. Along with other activist causes like civil rights, women's equality, and activism against the Vietnam War, concerns were being raised about other social injustices leading individuals to commit mass murder, assassinations, rape, and other types of violence. It was the beginning of the victim and dysfunctional individual as celebrity and hero—still very much with us today—and Kemper was influenced by this growing tide of public sentiment. Writing in 1976, Chaney makes this observation:

> Mass murder, assassinations, rape, and widespread violence of every sort became rapidly developing phenomena that exploited "respectable" social injustice and in a perverse way absorbed some of the social okay for acting out of frustrations. Everybody who mulled it over discovered that he or she was a minority and was discriminated against, and everybody knew that the squeaking wheel got greased while the killer got, for a brief time, equal TV exposure with Hollywood celebrities, political crooks, and Mafia members. The French *invented* megicide but Americans glorified it—the worship of sensational killings that enabled weak men at least for a moment to claim the limelight.[62]

In a way, the early 1970s became Ed Kemper's time. Fueled by a dysfunctional childhood with a mother he hated, Kemper let his aggressions out and claimed the national spotlight to share what he did and his reasons with the world. As he came to realize at Atascadero, "I really killed my grandmother because I wanted to kill my mother."[63] After symbolically striking out at her through the six women he killed later, he finally killed his mother, too. Ironically, the doctors at Atascadero had recommended to the Youth Authority that he should never be returned to live with his mother. But that's exactly what happened.

At his trial, the question finally came down to whether Kemper was sane. If he had been mentally ill when he first killed his grandparents, shouldn't he be considered mentally ill now? Or had he really been ill then? At his trial, one prosecution psychiatrist, Dr. Joel Fort, a Bay area psychiatrist who lectured on sexual deviation and crime at the University of California, sought to argue that

Kemper knew exactly what he was doing but he had an overwhelming sexual curiosity, obsession with sex, and tremendous hatred, rage, or aggressiveness that included getting back at a society and a mother and father that he felt wronged him.[64] As Fort explained at the trial, he selected these women hitchhikers because he felt sexually inadequate and wanted to have a sense of power, control, or domination over them that he couldn't experience otherwise. He could only experience this in their deaths and in a few cases by eating parts of his victim's bodies. He would feel driven by cyclical buildups of tension to kill. As his trophies of death left him through decay, he felt driven to kill again. He felt no guilt holding him back. Without a sense of conscience, Kemper was able to do whatever he felt like doing at the moment, whatever he felt most expedient, or would give him the most gratification or pleasure.[65] Moreover, Fort found him quite in touch with reality. Kemper wasn't paranoid because his grandparents and mother actually *had* been rejecting him. Nor did he have schizophrenic delusions of grandeur. Rather, Fort concluded, Kemper sought out his status as a mass killer as a source of a "considerable amount of pleasure and satisfaction," a way of getting the recognition he desperately sought but hadn't achieved as a child.[66] Finally, Kemper had struck out at his mother, and even the way he treated her body after death showed the depth of his hate. As Fort testified, under a truth serum used in his interviews, Kemper revealed a detail not previously known—after his mother was dead, he had cut out her larynx and put it down the garbage disposal. It was, Fort said, Kemper's way of "getting back at her for all of the bitter things she had said to him over the years."[67] Through it all, Kemper always knew what he was doing; so he was sane.

Several other psychiatrists testified, trying to show how Kemper's acts were so bizarre and so abnormal, they couldn't possibly be sane, and his defense attorney tried to convince the jurors that "there are two people locked up in the body of this young giant, one good and one evil. . . . One is fighting to be here with us and the other is slipping off to his own little world of fantasy where he is happy."[68]

In the end, the jurors found him both sane and guilty on all eight counts of first-degree murder. Much as other jurors had found in the case of Frazier and Mullins, whether they were insane or not, the jurors didn't want any chance of Kemper being sentenced to a mental institution and being released again. The judge sentenced Kemper to life in prison, recommending that he never be released for the rest of his natural life. He was eventually sent to Folsom, and as of this writing, he remains there, serving out his sentence.

THE CASE OF JUAN CORONA

Marysville and Yuba City, California, 1971–73

The Juan Corona case, which turned into a legal cliffhanger, began on the morning of Wednesday, May 19, 1971, when farmer Goro Kagehiro noticed a large hole in his peach orchard in Sutter County, California—a land that had once been full of miners during the Gold Rush. The hole was about three and a half feet deep, two and a half feet wide, and six or seven feet long—much larger than an ordinary soil sample the state agricultural service or county agent might take because Kagehiro told them that some of his peach trees were sick. But he had a busy day, because he had workers for a farm contractor he hired, Juan Corona, thinning his peach trees, so he didn't get back to check on the hole until about 6 p.m. He was puzzled because then the hole had been filled in. Maybe it was someone burying garbage, which often happened. When the field workers or contractors did this, they usually asked permission. Besides, the hole seemed awfully big for that.

That night Kagehiro tried to call the Live Oak Police Department. He wasn't able to get through, so he drove over early next morning. But his ranch was outside of city limits, and the officer on duty called the Sutter County Sheriff's Department. Shortly thereafter, Kagehiro met Deputy Sheriff Steve Sizelove at his ranch and led him to the hole. At once, Sizelove offered to help Kagehiro find out what was in it, and the two began digging. Within a few minutes they had opened up what was to that point the largest mass murder case in U.S. history.

At first Sizelove's shovel struck something that "sounded kind of hollow." He uncovered a piece of fabric, which looked like part of a pant leg, and then he found a shoe, which came off, revealing a bare right foot. Within a few more minutes, Sizelove had sent out a radio call bringing half a dozen officers and detectives to the scene, including Sutter County Sheriff Roy Whiteaker, who headed up the ensuing investigation.

A half-hour later, they had dug up the body of a man Sizelove recognized, because three days earlier he had seen him walking along the Colusa Highway and the man had identified himself as Kenneth Whiteacre. Just another transient worker who helped with the spring planting, he had figured at the time. Now he was dead—stabbed in the left side of the chest, his left cheek slashed, and the back of his head smashed open, perhaps by a machete. Meanwhile, as one deputy detective poured a plaster cast of a tire track in the dirt a few feet from the road, Deputy Sheriff Roger Mason took photos of the scene. Later, these bits of evidence as well as the body itself became the basis of a huge courtroom battle over the collection of evidence. The processing was quite routine for now—just another dead fruit worker. After all the pictures were taken, two morticians from the Twin Cities Mortuary in Yuba City took the body, and after another detective took Whiteacre's fingerprints, a local physician and surgeon, Doctor Thomas P. Connolly Jr., performed the autopsy, confirming that Whiteacre had died from a stab wound in the chest, and then there had been five deep head wounds, plus other wounds—a surprisingly savage attack on someone who was already dead.

It was the beginning of what became a headline whodunit case after two dozen more graves were discovered. Perhaps a reason the murders attracted so much attention is that they occurred at a time of growing protest in the fields. César Chávez had been attracting attention with his protests on behalf of the farm workers, leading to marches and grape strikes since the mid-1960s. Though Whiteacre's murder was treated as a straight criminal case by the media, there was perhaps an undertone of concern that migrant farm workers were being killed, and a successful farm contractor was soon accused of their murder. There were possible homosexual overtones, too, when it came out that some of the next victims might have been involved in homosexual activities prior to their death. At this time, the gay rights movement was just beginning to organize and stage protests, starting with the riots at the Stonewall Club in New York in 1969. Plus, there was a growing public fascination with cult murders generally after the big stories about the Manson Family murders in L.A. and Frazier's tarot-inspired killing of the Ohta family in Santa Cruz hit the papers.

This was a big story! Much bigger than Sheriff Whiteaker, who at age thirty-one, had been elected as the youngest sheriff-coroner of California only five months before, realized at the time. Unfortunately, though he had campaigned as a progressive-minded professional who wanted to bring the skills of big-city detectives to Sutter County, he didn't personally have the experience to handle the investigation, although he certainly tried. At the time Whiteacre's body was discovered, Whiteaker had changed the sheriff's department to expand the patrols in rural areas, and he had started an on-the-job training program. He had also graduated from the Federal Bureau of Narcotics school and had more than 2,300 hours of police training. For all his efforts to professionalize and modernize a rural sheriff's department, this was the first investigation he was in charge of. The problems of the investigation became a major point of contention of the trial—the efforts of a small-town police force versus the wily doggedness and courtroom theatrics of a big-city lawyer. It made for compelling drama as questions about the mistakes in the investigation and the value of the evidence were hotly debated at the trial. It was like a precursor to the O. J. Simpson case, putting the police on trial.

Detective Sgt. John Purcell, who doubled as chief deputy coroner, was in the area of Kagehiro's farm with a team of detectives interviewing neighboring farmers and trying to trace what Whiteacre did the last two days of his life, as well as trying to find the site where he had actually been killed. Meanwhile, a small story in the Marysville *Appeal-Democrat* about the discovery of the body brought in a few leads from people who had seen a man in a long overcoat walking on the Colusa highway the night before the body was discovered.

One officer at the Marysville Police Department, Sergeant Olie Coleman, recalled an odd incident about a year before in which a man had been beaten and cut up very badly at the Guadalajara Restaurant in Marysville, and he called Detective Gregory at the Sutter County Sheriff's Office to report this. The restaurant was owned by Natividad Corona, and at the time one suspect besides Natividad had been his half-brother Juan. Back then, an informant had claimed that Juan Corona was known to have "fits of temper that were so bad the family had to take ropes and tie him down until he became quiet again," and on the night of the beating, Corona had been seen in a building with a short-handled hoe like that used for weeding beans. The informant also claimed that Natividad was a homosexual, but the mere mention of this made Juan very angry. At the time, the investigation never went anywhere and no charges were brought, because the victim "couldn't or wouldn't identify his assailant."[69] The injured man sued and won a judgment against Natividad, who sold the restaurant and returned to Mexico.

It was an odd bit of old information that helped turn Juan Corona into the Sheriff's number one suspect. But for the time being, there was absolutely nothing to connect Corona to the dead body in the ground. Or was there? Sgt. Gregory talked briefly to Coleman's informant, who wanted to remain anonymous, and then he headed toward the Sullivan ranch, a few miles from Kagehiro's spread, where Juan Corona had a small crew of Mexican workers providing foreman Ray Duron with some extra help. This time, Gregory had a copy of the picture of Whiteacre that Mason took at the mortuary, and after Duron said he didn't recognize the man, Gregory showed Corona the picture. "No," he said, shaking his head after staring at it for about thirty seconds. After handing the photo back, he asked to see it again, and commented to the foreman in Spanish, "This fellow looks like he is dead already."[70] It seemed a casual yet odd statement.

Four days after the discovery of Whiteacre's body, a detective working with Sergeant Purcell, Detective Wilcox, learned in interviewing Kagehiro again that Corona had been hired to thin his peaches and the body was discovered on his last day on the job. Plus his 1971 Chevy reportedly had wide tires with tracks like those at the scene. Purcell and Gregory were now especially suspicious of Corona, though Corona was also a religious, hard-working family man. Purcell made a note to check further on the plaster cast lifted from the dirt track to see if it matched the tread on Corona's car.

But before he could do so, all hell broke loose. Ernesto Garcia, working with a tractor on the Sullivan ranch, came across a large indentation in the ground, which looked oddly like another grave. "Yeah, it does," thought foreman Ray Duron, when Garcia and another worker led him out to look the next morning. After Duron told J. L. Sullivan, the ranch owner, they called Purcell, and a few minutes later he was out there with Gregory. Soon they were digging, while police photographer Mason and the undersheriff were on their way.

As Mason took photos, they were digging up another body—though this one had been in the ground much longer. But the oddly mismatched clothing indicated that this badly decomposed body was also that of a drifter. Purcell and Gregory retrieved what items they could from the pockets of the man's clothing, which helped pinpoint his death from about two weeks before—there were two Safeway cash register receipts dated May 8. But otherwise, these were the remains of an unidentified man who lived on the edge—a package of matches, a half-bar of soap wrapped in paper, and a safety razor.

It wasn't much to go on. During the day, after the Marysville police department heard about the discovery of the second body on the police radio, they wanted to let Sheriff Whiteaker know they had a missing person report on a wino named Pete Beierman, and when they booked him a few months before they had gotten a good set of prints on him. Plus they had a report of the fight at the Guadalajara Restaurant, which involved a cutting with a machete. When Whiteaker called the Marysville Police Department, he learned that a friend of Beierman's, Roy DeLong, had last seen Beierman going off with a Mexican labor contractor in a yellow Chevy van like the one Corona owned.

Whiteaker, like Purcell and Gregory, now believed he had a suspect, too. Could there be any more victims? If so, Whiteaker reasoned that if Corona was the murderer, he might bury the victims where he worked, and he might have buried even more of them on the Sullivan ranch, since it was very large and Corona had worked his crew there for some time before Whiteacre's body had turned up. Whiteaker decided to send a team of men to do a foot-by-foot search of Sullivan's ranch, and he called on the men from his own department as well as from the nearby Yuba City and Live Oak Police departments, too.

On May 25 the search went on without finding anything, and by twilight, they were close to quitting. One deputy suddenly noticed a cleared-out area in the brush by the riverbank. Several deputies pushed their way through the thick growth and suddenly saw some loosened dirt in the same rectangular shape that had concealed the two graves found before. As they dug, other detectives arrived and soon had a few more clues—a possible footprint, which one detective captured by pouring a plaster cast, a small cigarette butt found in the grave beneath some decaying leaves, and a small dark feather. Then came the most seemingly damning clue of all—Sizelove and another detective spotted two folded pink papers. One was a receipt for $78.35 dated Friday, May 21, just four days earlier, from the Del Pero Bros. and Mondon meat market; the second was a sales slip for $25.63 for 25 pounds of tongue and 17.5 pounds of spare ribs. Right there on the receipt was the name of the person who bought the meat—Juan V. Corona.[71]

When Whiteaker heard the news, he was more certain than ever that he was building a solid case against Corona. It was still purely circumstantial evidence, but the mosaic of connections was building. Then Purcell had even more supportive news—according to Sullivan ranch foreman Ray Duron, around 1956 Corona had spent some time in a state hospital.

Still, as Whiteaker knew, the evidence was tentative. There was only an inference that Corona might be the killer. Just in case, Whiteaker assigned several detectives to tail Corona. If he had really killed three men, he might try to kill again. Then Whiteaker went to talk to the Sutter County district attorney Dave Teja to consider the options. For the time being, they decided it would be best not to try to arrest Corona, because they still had to verify the receipts with the owners of the two markets. Even if the receipts were verified, they still couldn't definitively link Corona directly to the two men. After all, there was no proof he had been at the site when the receipts fell in. Someone else could have had them.

Thus, Whiteaker and Teja decided to start with a search warrant to look at Corona's records showing who was on his work crews and where they worked. These would provide Social Security numbers and records of payments. If the names of Whiteacre or the other missing men were there, this could help to establish that link. Then, too, the search warrant could enable them to check Corona's place for possible weapons, bloody clothes, even something the dead men might have owned, like a wallet, ID, even some of their clothing.[72]

Even before they began this search, there was more gruesome news. Some of the men who were digging had discovered another grave about 100 yards from the third grave in the brush along the river bank. The men reported seeing what looked like three more graves about 250 yards further on.

After that, the search for more graves intensified. A new twist was entered into the case after the fourth body was dug up and it was discovered with his shirt and sweatshirt pulled up over his face. He wasn't wearing trousers, and his penis was exposed through his shorts.[73] Investigators began to wonder if there might be a homosexual component to the killings—a suspicion that grew stronger when the next body and several additional bodies were dug up and were similarly undressed and exposed.

Meanwhile, after the discovery of the receipts in the third grave and the continuing discovery of bodies, Whiteaker and Teja felt they certainly had enough for a search warrant. They asked for one so they could search Corona's home, cookhouse, and any vehicles for knives, axes, machetes, shovels or other weapons, blood-stained clothing, or other records that might provide links to the two victims that had already been identified (Whiteacre and Beierman) and the other John Does still unknown. By this time the butchers at the two markets had confirmed giving Corona the sales slips the previous Friday, and Teja now obtained the file showing that Natividad had asked the court to commit his brother to a state hospital for the mentally ill. Corona had spent three months there before being released. Later the defense tried to argue that this fifteen-year-old commitment was long in the past, a temporary lapse by a highly religious man who feared that the huge floods in the area that winter had caused everyone to drown and Corona had long since been cured by shock treatment.[74] But to Whiteaker and Teja it was even more compelling evidence they had the right man.

At 2:30 in the morning on May 26 the judge signed the warrant, and at 3:15 Whiteaker and two search teams of deputies were at Corona's house and at the barracks and cookhouse on the Sullivan ranch, along with a squad of newsmen and cameramen. Corona had been a respected businessman who had created a solid middle-class life after years of hard work. After returning to Mexico after his 1956 commitment, he had returned to the United States determined to make a success for himself. After taking odd jobs, he had gradually built up a labor contracting business under Natividad's contracting license, recruiting only Mexicans with green cards but never the older derelicts and transients from Marysville's skid row like Natividad did. With Corona taking on more of the contracting business, Natividad opened up his Guadalajara café in Marysville, and the brothers drifted apart, especially after Juan married his wife, Gloria Morena, who had been working as a cook at a nearby labor camp. By the mid-1960s, Corona was well respected as a serious-minded husband and businessman. He even belonged to La Associacion de los Charros, a prestigious Mexican American association devoted to horseback riding.[75]

Whiteaker arrived with his men and the media. Within a few hours Corona was under arrest and in jail, while the police and district attorney prepared the largest homicide case in the United States against him. It certainly looked like a slam-dunk case. Over the next days, the body count mounted. But that was before Corona's lawyer, Richard Hawk, stepped in, claiming Corona had been framed in a set-up. A seemingly solid case turned into a legal whodunit, as Hawk challenged every bit of evidence gathered against him.

For the time being, the case against Corona mushroomed, and he looked more like a monster with a secret life. Outwardly, at age thirty-eight, Juan Corona looked like a quiet, short, stocky, devoted family man with a wife and children. The reaction of everyone who knew him was total shock. In jail, Corona expressed his total shock as well. The evidence piling up seemed overwhelming, but a big question that kept hanging over the case was why?

As the media poured in and the newspaper headlines tracked the latest body count, with banners like "11 Machete Murders" and "Twenty Bodies—Death Map" in the *San Francisco Chronicle*, the investigation went on. On May 26, as a result of the first search warrant, which listed just nine bodies, investigators hauled off knives and tools from the kitchen and garage, including an ax, meat cleaver, and bolo machete, as well as two ledgers, check stubs, and a checkbook. They also found a knife with a blade stamped "Tennessee Toothpick" that had a small brown stain that looked like blood, and a pistol that seemed to have a blood stain under its barrel.[76] This evidence figured strongly in the prosecution's case against Corona. After forty-five minutes of searching, Captain John Littlejohn, heading up one of the search teams, along with Purcell, arrested Corona and took him to jail, where he stayed for the next eighteen months until his trial.

The digging and investigating went on. For help, Purcell called on the Department of Justice's Criminal Identification and Investigation division, who sent in a man from the Latent Prints Section and a criminalist from the lab to help examine the fingerprints and other evidence.[77]

Eventually, there were a total of twenty-five bodies, and as more were discovered, more reporters were on the scene. Soon Sheriff Whiteaker was something of a media star. He impressed reporters because he seemed well dressed and soft-spoken—not at all the image of the country bumpkin rural sheriff popularized by shows like *Hee Haw*, as he assured the reporters, "We're certain he committed the murders."

Bodies kept turning up in places where Corona had worked with his crews. Many of the leads that came in from people who read about the case in the newspaper led nowhere, but a few reported seeing Corona on the Sullivan ranch at time when no work was going on. One called to say he had seen Corona at the river bottom orchard where the detectives were now digging up more bodies.

Then the investigators found what seemed like the most damning evidence of all when the dug up the final body under a peach tree on the northernmost part of Sullivan's orchard and found that the victim was Joseph Maczak. They discovered it after Ray Duron, the ranch foreman, called again to report that one of his workers said the tractor driver had seen Corona in the orchard saying he was looking for his dog, though his dog had been seen playing around the mess hall throughout the night. With all the digging for bodies to remind them, the men recalled the incident, went to that area of the orchard, and found a depression that looked like a grave in the muddy earth. Like the others, Maczak was another wandering fruit worker, and he had been killed in a similar fashion with three stab wounds in the chest and seven hacking blows to his head. What was especially compelling was the discovery of a soggy shopping newspaper dated April 21, 1971, folded with a rubber band around it, and nearby two crumpled bank deposit slips with Juan Corona's name and home address printed right on them. It was, as authors Ed Cray and Richard Hawk put it, the last bit of evidence that "all but made the district attorney's case."[78]

The sheriff and district attorney felt their case was so solid they didn't need any more bodies for evidence—just more witnesses who could directly link Corona to the victims. But that was the shakiest part of the case. The witness who had seen one of the victims drive off with a man in a yellow-looking panel truck, a vehicle similar to Corona's van, couldn't clearly identify him. The various ranchers one investigator talked to described Corona as a "good worker—conscientious, honest." In fact, no one had seen him use Anglo workers except for Ray Duron, the Sullivan ranch supervisor, and that was only briefly during peach-picking season, August and September, when help was short.[79] The murders had apparently been committed between February and May, according to the various receipts and documents found in the graves. Another puzzling factor was reported by one Filipino casual laborer, Aguinalbo Baclaan, who had worked for Corona at Sullivan's ranch. One day in the middle of May, Corona had picked Baclaan up at his hotel and taken him to the ranch. At the end of the day Corona had driven him directly back from the camp to Wino Park in Marysville. Corona had taken no detours, made no unusual advances, and said nothing peculiar. He had just been very quiet on the ride back, then paid Baclaan $10 in cash for his work and said "Good-bye." Since he fit the profile of the many victims and they had been alone on the ride, why didn't Corona victimize him? It was one of the many puzzles Whiteaker, Teja, and other investigators confronted as they tried to figure out the motive, though the circumstantial evidence against Corona certainly looked solid.

Besides the damning receipts found in Maczak's grave, they had something else that seemed especially compelling. They had a ledger taken from Corona's house that had the names of eight of the identified victims on a list of thirty-four names. There were dates next to the men's names from March 30 to May 15, 1971. Perhaps these were the dates the men had been killed. Plus there was the name of a ninth man with the date of April 5, 1971, next to his name, and he had simply disappeared. Maybe he had been killed, too. What of the other twenty-six men on the list, Whiteaker wondered. Were they also buried somewhere?

Whiteaker arranged for two aerial reconnaissance jets to search for more bodies using sophisticated cameras and sensing devices to look for possible graves. But after they found nothing, for all practical purposes, the search for more bodies was over. Certainly, twenty-five was enough with all the powerful circumstantial evidence—especially the receipts and the ledgers.

But what if someone else had actually done the killings and framed Corona? What if someone else was still out there, committing more killings of homeless, forgotten men nobody missed? Corona's new defense lawyer, Richard Hawk, would try to make this case.

Hawk stepped in shortly after Corona went to his arraignment on June 2 represented by a public defender. As Corona stepped from the patrol car between two officers, he pulled his jacket up over his head—he looked like an East Coast gangster trying to hide from the flashing cameras. Inside he firmly pleaded not guilty, and it looked like the defender might be planning an insanity plea, especially since Corona had a previous mental commitment and the case looked so overwhelming. But then Corona's younger brother Pedro spoke to one of his workers who knew a good defense attorney who might be able to help. After Hawk flew to Yuba County from the San Francisco Bay area and met Corona, he was determined to show he was innocent, not insane. He believed this himself, feeling certain someone else had done it.

It was the beginning of what was a very long fight, which would put Whiteaker's investigation on the hot seat along with Corona. No one would know the outcome until the very end.

Hawk began finding all sorts of holes in the prosecution's case. He found a report by the state handwriting expert that stated it was not possible to identify all of the questioned writing in Corona's ledger as being made by one person. Furthermore, he couldn't identify the writing in the ledger when he compared it with samples of Corona's writing.[80] He also found that the bloody weapons hauled from Corona's house weren't all that the prosecution expected. As he commented in an interview to one reporter, Tracy Kidder, "There was chicken blood on the hatchet, redwood stain on the posthole digger, no blood on the machete, and just a little blood on the two knives."[81] He also discovered that the little blood in the back of Corona's van was there because Corona had transported an injured worker in it. Had he transported the victims with the huge injuries they had suffered, there would have been far more blood evidence everywhere.

Hawk learned that the state's own expert had discovered that Corona's machete didn't cut open the skull of the first victim, Whiteacre, the only victim whose wound could be so tested because the others were too decomposed.[82] He found that the tire tracks next to Whiteacre's grave didn't match the tires on any of Corona's vehicles, and the bullet found in one victim's skull could not be traced to Corona's gun. There had been mix-ups in the lab over some of the bodies, so it wasn't clear whether Corona's meat receipts were found with Whiteacre's recently buried body or with a body that had been in its grave for over a month.[83]

In Hawk's view, the press had simply been printing the prosecution spin on things, despite the judge's gag order on all parties not to talk to the press. On the surface the evidence looked compelling. Corona was a Mexican in a county where farmers hated Mexicans, and the new sheriff was too new to know better than to give out reports of their findings to the press. In fact, Hawk was already talking about filing a $350 million libel and slander suit with additional charges for the negligent infliction of emotional distress against many of the law enforcement officials of Sutter County.[84] Clearly this was going to be a long legal battle, and Hawk reveled in the media attention, thinking he might gain more fame than F. Lee Bailey. Hawk imagined this might be a case to excite political interest, if he could show it involved some kind of conspiracy against Corona as a high-rising Mexican who had flown too high—although ultimately this strategy never worked, because at the time, the Mexican community wasn't organized or radicalized. Besides, this was a horrendous crime, and all the evidence initially pointed to Corona.

Still, Hawk's attack on the investigation did bear fruit initially, because Whiteaker and the other investigators really had been overwhelmed and there had been lab mix-ups. Plus some of the evidence hadn't been sent out early on for additional testing, such as much of the blood, fingerprint, and handwriting samples, perhaps because Teja was so sure he had enough to convict and originally expected a plea bargain, perhaps based on insanity.

Then Hawk tried to develop the other prong of his attack—finding another likely candidate. His theory was that the killer or killers decided that the two meat receipts in the first grave weren't enough to frame Corona and so had dumped even more evidence, including the bank receipts in the last grave, as if to seal the case.[85] Since the search for more graves had essentially stopped after Corona's arrest, there was no way to tell if perhaps the killer was still out there. In fact, Hawk thought the police didn't want to keep looking and find anyone, because it would destroy their case against Corona.

But if it wasn't Corona, then who was it? At one point, Hawk considered the possibility of another worker or foreman at the Sullivan Ranch, maybe even Jack Sullivan himself, and suggested that possibly members of a hippie commune about thirty miles north of the Sullivan ranch might be involved.[86] Eventually he settled on his most seriously considered candidate—Natividad, Corona's older brother, because he was known as a homosexual and the sheriff himself had discovered a number of Natividad's registration entries on the guest ledgers of run-down hotels in lower Marysville. Certainly, Natividad must have gone there for sex, since he had a house just six miles away. If he was gay and sleeping with such men, perhaps he had developed a strong hatred for them as well because they were stripping him of his manhood in a culture that valued machismo. Hawk even found a leading expert on homosexuality, Dr. Evelyn Hooker, who would testify thus.[87]

A basic problem was showing that Natividad was even in the country at the time, since he had sold all his property and had gone back to Mexico after a $250,000 judgment was rendered against him in the Guadalajara restaurant case. Though Hawk claimed he had evidence that Natividad was in the Marysville area in May 1971, the week Juan was arrested, it was very shaky. A few people had said he was in town, but no one had talked to him.[88]

For a time, Teja's investigation of the case to fight off Hawk's challenges to the evidence went into a kind of limbo, after Hawk made repeated motions for bail and a change of venue. Though Teja won the bail motions and Corona remained in jail, after eight months, Hawk finally did get the case moved out of Sutter County. Only after that was settled did Teja take care of much of the testing, such as the blood on the weapons and in two of Corona's vehicles, or asked for new handwriting samples from Corona or for samples of Corona's hair. Reports on the saliva from a cigarette butt and the blood from a barrel of one of Corona's pistols that might match the blood type of the only victim that was shot didn't arrive until the trial was about to begin.[89] Some of those results weren't what the prosecution expected—the saliva and blood, for example, didn't match—although another test on the saliva showed it might match.

In short, this was a difficult, shaky time for investigators and the prosecution trying to organize so much information to support twenty-five homicides, instead of what often happens in multiple homicides—just trying to focus on proving the strongest few cases. When the trial finally began on September 2, 1972—fourteen months after Corona was originally arrested—Hawk made many of his own mistakes, most notably adopting an overly aggressive style of attack in court that subjected him to repeated citations for contempt and a sentence of seventy-four days in jail after the case.[90]

For a time though, it looked like the prosecution's case was falling apart, as Hawk picked apart the gathering of evidence. Hawk established, for example, that the police mixed up the numbers on four of the corpses, assigning them to the wrong graves at one time or another, although the prosecutor tried to show that after some confusion the mortician had finally gotten it right.[91] Hawk also pointed to many gaps in the fingerprint evidence, showing through cross-examination how no one had tried to get prints from Corona's ledger, which allegedly had the names of the victims, from his pistol, or from items the killer must have handled, such as a wallet that was found lying on one victim's chest.[92] He tried to suggest how certain people, especially Ray Duron, who had once been Natividad's partner in the Guadalajara restaurant, simply didn't like Juan and might easily want to put the blame on Juan. "Ray Duron, pretty helpful finding graves, wasn't he?" Hawk commented at one point,[93] though Duron pointed out their partnership lasted only for two months, and he thought Corona often acted oddly, "wandering around where he didn't belong" on the ranch.[94]

In turn, the assisting prosecutor Bart Williams fought back by detailing the sheer amount of evidence and the large number of homicides, describing in detail the wounds and showing glossy pictures of the corpses.[95] Then, too, Teja and Whiteaker sent a detective to Mexico to investigate Natividad a few months before the trial. When they found him, he was a frail man suffering from diabetes. It seemed unlikely that he could have the strength to have killed twenty-five men, even if he was in the country. Besides, the investigators had gotten a sworn statement by Natividad that he wasn't in the area,[96] though there was no clear proof one way or the other—no passenger records from the Mexican airlines, for example, to show he had been a passenger. There was no way to check with immigration, because the investigator didn't have and couldn't get Natividad's passport number.[97]

Even if Natividad couldn't be completely ruled out, more than any piece of evidence, Teja's strategy was to focus on building a mosaic of circumstantial evidence, so that even if a particular piece of evidence could be interpreted several ways, as long as it was "consistent" with Corona's guilt, it would fit the picture.[98] The goal was to present Corona as an outwardly soft and gentle man who had done these terrible crimes. Teja saved some of his best evidence for last. Initially, Hawk had argued that the small amount of blood in the back of Corona's van had come from an injured worker who would testify. The investigators had found an expert, Dr. Ruth Guy, who used a mixed-agglutination system of blood typing, and he testified that she had found types A, B, and O in the blood, meaning that it came from at least three people. Plus she had found all types of blood in the trunk of Corona's Impala sedan. In retesting Corona's blood and comparing it to the saliva from the cigarette butt, she found that they were both type O—whereas there had been something wrong with the original saliva sample from Corona she had tested that made her think he was type A.

Finally, the pièce de résistance: Teja showed Corona's two ledger books. One contained names, Social Security numbers, and amounts paid—a normal word record. But the other contained a three-page list of names, with only dates and sometimes places written beside them, including the names of six or seven victims that had been identified. This was a "death list" or an "appointment list" as Teja called it, arguing that it was a "kind of confession by Corona." Whatever it was, it helped establish a connection between Corona, who wrote the list, and some of the victims.[99]

Then perhaps Hawk made the biggest mistake of all. He had already alienated some of the jurors by his courtroom theatrics and his merciless attack on one witness who expressed some confusion in testifying about the location of various grave sites on a map—although jurors aren't supposed to let their attitude about the attorney affect their view of the client's innocence. Making it even more difficult for the jury, Hawk—believing that the prosecution case was riddled with confusion—decided not to present a case at all for the defense. Though he left tantalizing hints of how he would show there was another killer, a homosexual killer, he simply began and ended his case with the statement: "The defense rests."

Perhaps part of his reason for doing so was that Corona and his family didn't want to have Natividad portrayed as a homosexual. The family had asked him not to put Corona's wife on the stand, because her health was growing increasingly fragile and perhaps her relationship with Corona was already weakening—unfortunately, she was his only alibi for where he was on the afternoon of May 19, when the first body was discovered. In his closing arguments, Teja spoke firmly of Hawk's broken promises, the lack of any evidence that Corona did not kill twenty-five people and bury them on or near the Sullivan ranch, and about the mosaic of guilt that the defense didn't even try to explain.[100]

It was up to the jury, and for five days they struggled. They even came back at one point saying that they were hopelessly hung with an eight-to-four verdict. Thinking he was likely to get an acquittal, Hawk urged the judge to urge them on, and so he did. As it turned out, the jury was really giving them an average of their votes; they were stalled at ten to two for guilty. When they returned, they came back with their verdict. The last holdout had given in, and they agreed that Corona was guilty of all twenty-five murders, convinced finally by Teja's evidence pointing to guilt and Corona's lack of any defense. Most of all, it was the blood evidence—and the lack of any explanations to explain it.[101]

Afterward, Corona was sent to the Vacaville Medical Facility to serve twenty-five life terms. He worked on appealing his conviction, still arguing that he was framed, though he was retried in 1982 and was once again convicted on all counts. He is eligible for parole every four years, although as of this writing, he has not been released.

THE CASE OF DAVID BERKOWITZ

The Bronx, Queens, and Brooklyn, New York, 1976–77

When the first of six killings by the man who later called himself Son of Sam began, the police in Queens, New York, thought it was another hard-to-solve violent street shooting in a city that already had a high homicide rate. At the time, about 2,000 people were killed each year in New York, and about a third of the killers went uncaught and unpunished.[102] New Yorkers had become inured to this. It was the kind of city where you took a subway while warily looking around to see if you were going to be mugged. People regularly complained about all the terrible things that had happened or might happen; it was a way to feel better about the daily problems and dangers of living in New York City.

On July 29, 1976, eighteen-year-old Donna Lauria was shot to death around 1 a.m. while sitting in a parked car in the Bronx with her friend Jody Valenti, who was also shot but survived. The police quickly discarded the theory of a jilted lover. It seemed to be just another everyday homicide, and the newspaper showed a picture of the car's splintered window. It was a crime easily forgotten in the maw of New York's many other unsolved homicides.

In quick succession there were two similar shootings in the fall. One occurred in Flushing, Queens, on October 23. Rosemary Keenan, the eighteen-year-old daughter of a New York City detective was sitting in her VW at 1:45 a.m. with twenty-year-old Carl Denaro in the passenger seat, when several shots rang out, one of them striking Denaro in the back of the head. Though Keenan wasn't hurt, Denaro required two months of surgery, and the police found three .44-caliber shell casings at the scene. The local tabloids reported that a man had been shot.

A month later, there was an apparently random shooting in Bellrose, Queens, as Donna DeMasi, age sixteen, and Joanne Lomino, eighteen, were standing on the porch after returning from a night at the movies. A man approached, nervously asking the girls for directions, and he fired his gun. One shot shattered the front window of the Lomino home and one crashed through DeMasi's collarbone, though she recovered; the other hit Lomino and shattered her spine, turning her into a paraplegic.

The media began to pay attention with the first warnings about lawlessness and random crime. Parents began to warn their daughters about the dangers of staying out late.

Meanwhile, the killer himself regarded these first three shootings as a kind of apprenticeship. He had been nervous, uncertain, and not fully confident. But because he hadn't been caught and had the satisfaction of seeing his handiwork at least briefly reported in the media, he felt ready to approach the next killings more like a calm and controlled professional, without any fear.[103] Later he talked about how he felt driven by a compulsion, by demons, to kill. But for now, the police saw only the results.

In late January and early March 1977, two more killings intensified the manhunt. One was on the night of January 30, 1977. Around midnight, Christine Freund, twenty-six, and her thirty-year-old boyfriend, John Diel, were walking along a quiet street in Forest Hills, Queens. They got in their car and embraced, and shots rang out, shattering the car window. Two of them hit Freund in the head and neck, just as Diel kissed her, and she died in the hospital a few hours later. "Then the voices stopped. I satisfied the demons lust," the killer later explained.[104]

The next killing came on March 8 around 7:30 p.m., also in Forest Hills, a block away from where Freund was shot. Virginia Voskerichian, age twenty-one, a Russian language major at Barnard College, was walking home from school carrying her textbooks. A man on the sidewalk suddenly pulled out a revolver from a plastic bag and shot her right in the face. As he ran away, there was the first witness, who heard the man call out to him, "Hi, mister," as he ran toward his car. As he slowed to a walk, a passing patrol car pulled over briefly to question him, thinking he looked suspicious. Suddenly, the cops heard a call that a woman had been shot, and not making the connection, they quickly drove away while the killer got into his own car and drove off. He had come very close to getting caught.

The hunt for the mass murderer was on in earnest. To this point, the police had thought these were simply random, probably unsolvable, killings. But they had compared the ballistics and knew that at least three of the attacks in Queens were by the same man firing the same gun. They also had a vague description from witnesses and survivors, and they realized the murders had a pattern—the victims were young girls, and with one exception, the shootings occurred late at night.

This was the beginning of the mysterious .44 caliber killings going big-time. On March 10, the mayor of New York, Abraham Beame, and the Police Commissioner Michael J. Codd held a press conference in which they revealed that the same gun had been used for all of the killings,[105] and they appealed for any information the public might have. The media, in turn, dubbed the murderer the ".44 Caliber Killer," describing him as a "mindless" and "demented" beast, because there was no clear motive. The hunt was on.

With the next killing, the killer revealed a name—Son of Sam. The hunt turned into a kind of deadly cat-and-mouse game, which both intrigued and terrified by the public. It began with the letter the killer left at the scene, as if he wanted recognition for what he had done. At the same time, he was challenging and taunting the police because they had not caught him. It was a little like the Unabomber sending out missives with his bombs.

The next killing occurred on April 17, 1977, shortly after Valentina Suriani, eighteen, an acting student, and Alexander Esau, twenty, a helper on a tow truck, parked their car in the Bronx shortly after midnight and began to embrace. After four shots, both were dead. This time, the killer left a note addressed to Captain Joseph Borrelli in the street near the car for the police to find. "Come and get me," he said, in a rambling four-page letter that he signed "Son of Sam." It was his way of reaching out and starting a dialogue with the public and beginning his cat-and-mouse game with the police. He used the letter to fashion an identity that intrigued the public, much like Albert Fish had written his own crazed letters four decades before and the Unabomber did two decades later. The letter continued in part:

> I am deeply hurt by your calling me a wemon [*sic*] hater . . . I am not. But I am a monster. I am the "Son of Sam." I am a little brat. When father Sam gets drunk he gets mean. He beats his family. Sometimes he ties me up to the back of the house. Other times he locks me in the garage. Sam loves to drink blood. "Go out and kill," commands father Sam. Behind our house some rest. Mostly young—raped and slaughtered—their blood drained—just bones now . . . I feel like an outsider. I am on a different wave-length than everybody else—programmed too [*sic*] kill.[106]

He concluded with this taunting message to the police: "Attention all police: Shoot me first—shoot to kill or else keep out of my way or you will die! . . . Police: Let me haunt you with these words; I'll be back! I'll be back! . . . Yours in murder Mr. Monster."[107]

The letter was a bombshell, providing a kind of *nom de guerre* in Son of Sam, which, according to Dr. David Abrahamsen, who followed the case closely, made the killer "perversely seductive, titillating the fascination an fears of the public, challenging authority, and cleverly manipulating the news media."[108]

After leaving the letter and speeding away from the scene, in much the same way that Ed Kemper felt a kind of perverse reverence for his first victim, the killer drove past the apartment of Donna Lauria, the woman he had first killed in January, feeling "flushed with power." It was a feeling that inspired him to keep going—as did the attention from the media. There were also the voices, the demons. The chase became like a mystery thriller with overtones of the devil as it continued, both scaring and enthralling the people of New York.

The police geared up for a city-wide manhunt. On April 19, two days after Suriani and Esau were killed, the set up a special Homicide Task Force, headed by Inspector Timothy J. Dowd, and they assigned 225 uniformed policemen and 75 detectives recruited from precincts in the five boroughs to search for the killer. In turn, the newspapers called on the public for help, and calls flooded into the switchboard—hundreds a day. After several months, they turned up nothing, even after the killer struck again on June 26 in Bayside, Queens, as Judy Placido, a recent high school graduate, and Sal Lupo were talking near a disco. Amazingly Placido lived, though she was hit in the head, neck, and shoulders; Lupo was hit in the right forearm. Again, the killer successfully ran back to his car and drove away. Later, he reported that "the demons were protecting me. I had nothing to fear from the police."[109]

The police were certainly trying. Detectives in unmarked cars and on foot were steadily checking out the killer's apparent "hunting grounds" in the Bronx and Queens. They set up traps in popular trysting places by putting life-sized dummies in cars in the hopes these might lure the killer and the police waiting nearby could capture him. Even Mafia boss Carmine Galante, according to rumors, invited the police to use the services of his organization to help track down Son of Sam. Meanwhile, American pop culture had started to immortalize the killer, as vendors in Central Park and other locations began selling T-shirts that announced "Son of Sam—Get him before he gets you."

To help do just that, the police began checking all current and former mental patients in New York state. They traced down 400 holders of permits for .44-caliber revolvers.

As if to make sure the police and public remembered that it was almost the anniversary of his first killing, and to taunt the police even further at their failure to catch him, Son of Sam sent a letter to New York *Daily News* columnist Jimmy Breslin, who was sufficiently moved to take the letter to Donna Lauria's parents and discuss it with them. As the killer wrote (later, published in the paper):

> Hello from the gutters of N.Y.C. which are filled with dog manure, vomit, stale wine, urine, and blood. Hello from the sewers of N.Y.C. which swallow up these delicacies when they are washed away by the sweeper trucks. . . .
>
> I'm just dropping you a line to let you know that I appreciate your interest in those recent and horrendous .44 killings. I also want to tell you that I read your column daily and find it quite informative.
>
> Tell me, Jim, what will you have for July Twenty-Ninth? You can forget about me if you like because I don't care for publicity. However, you must not forget Donna Lauria and you cannot let the people forget her, either. She was a very sweet girl but Sam's a thirsty lad and he won't stop me killing until he gets his fill of blood.
>
> Mr. Breslin, sir, don't you think that because you haven't heard from (me) for a while that I went to sleep. No, rather I am still here. Like a spirit roaming the night. Thirsty, hungry, seldom stopping to rest, anxious to please Sam. I love my work. Now, the void has been filled. . . .
>
> Not knowing what the future holds I shall say farewell, and I will see you at the next job. Or, should I say you will see my handiwork at the next job? Remember Ms. Lauria. Thank you.[110]

The killer went on to taunt the police and sign his letter thus:

> In their blood
and
From the gutter
"Sam's Creation" .44
P.S. J.B., please inform all the detectives working on the slayings to remain.

After his signature, Son of Sam, he affixed a symbol that looked like an X-shaped mark with the biological symbols of a male and female, along with a cross and the letter *S*.

Needless to say, the police stepped up their patrols even more intensively as the first anniversary of Lauria's murder arrived on July 29, 1977. The public waited with a mix of fear and fascination. In fact, some admired Son of Sam's ability to elude detection by the largest manhunt ever mounted by the New York Police.

Perhaps because of the intensified manhunt, Son of Sam did not strike on July 29 or even on July 30. Rather, he waited until July 31 and then moved into a new area in Brooklyn, choosing a middle-income area known as Gravesend Bay. The killing occurred just after Bobby Violante, a twenty-year-old clothing salesman, pulled into a parking space with his date, Stacy Moskowitz, a twenty-year-old telex machine operator. As they kissed and embraced, Son of Sam fired several shots. Stacy was hit in the head and killed; two others shot Violante in the face. He lost one eye and most of his vision in the other. As before, the killer quickly ran away to his car and drove off, feeling a sense of peace as he parked about a block away, bought a newspaper, and sat on a park bench reading. This time, he later reported, he got an erection as he saw the couple kissing and embracing before he fired his gun. He seemed satisfied to read the news about his latest killing.[111]

What the killer didn't read about was the clue the police got. The break came around 2 a.m., when Cacilia Davis, a middle-aged woman who lived near where Violante parked his car, was walking her dog. She saw a car being ticketed for parking too close to a hydrant. Just after the police left, a man holding a dark object brushed against her as he passed by, walking quickly. For a moment, he looked at her carefully and walked on. The encounter had unnerved her, and she ran back to her house. Just as she got inside she heard the sound of gunshots. Four days later, after she read about the shooting in the neighborhood, she called the police.

It was the break the police needed. They began to check every car that had gotten a ticket in the area of the Moskowitz murder. A few days later they had a list of four possible cars and addresses—one of them a 1970 four-door yellow Ford Galaxy belonging to a man named David Berkowitz who lived in Yonkers.

The police might have soon zeroed in on Berkowitz anyway, due to a number of other occurrences that were starting to point to him. One such occurrence was that Sam Carr, a man who lived near Berkowitz, had been receiving some anonymous letters since April bitterly complaining that his black Labrador retriever had been tormenting the letter writer who said he was prepared to eliminate the dog's owner. When his dog was shot, Carr had called the police.

In June, the Cassara family in New Rochelle had received a get-well card purportedly from Sam Carr, although no one in the family was sick or had heard of Sam Carr. When Mr. Cassara called Carr about the mystery and discovered that the handwriting on the card matched that on the threatening letters Carr had received, they remembered that they briefly had a tenant named David Berkowitz who disliked dogs. They reported this to the Yonkers police. After they read about the death of Stacy Moskowitz, they called the Yonkers police again to suggest that Berkowitz might be the Son of Sam, although the officer didn't take the call very seriously. The patrolman who had originally taken Carr's complaint about his dog was beginning to wonder if Berkowitz was the Son of Sam and passed his suspicions on to the intelligence division of the New York City Police.[112] The police added that to their thousands of Son of Sam leads to check out.

There was a odd third incident as well. An investigator for the Westchester County Sheriff's Office, Craig Glassman, had moved into the same building with Berkowitz, and in June he began to receive strange, threatening notes that included references to Satan and demons. On the morning of August 6—a week after Stacy was shot—he woke up to discover that a fire had been set outside his door. After the Yonkers police arrived and put it out, he showed them the strange letters he had received. They thought the handwriting looked like that on the letters to Carr and the note to Cassaras. Berkowitz was the prime suspect, though no one had yet tried to contact him about the matter.

A call came through to Yonkers from New York City Detective James Justus, who was checking on the registrations of the Brooklyn parking ticket and had come up with Berkowitz's name. Ironically, the Yonkers dispatcher who took the call was Sam Carr's daughter, and after she told Justus of the suspicions about Berkowitz that were already building in Yonkers, he was sure they had their man. Perhaps the building suspicions in Yonkers would have led to Berkowitz anyway. The parking ticket proved the catalyst. The police organized a stakeout of Berkowitz's building starting at 6 p.m. on August 10 and got ready to arrest him when he left to go to his car. That same day, Berkowitz's upstairs neighbor, Glassman, had also decided to check out Berkowitz's car, because he had become certain that Berkowitz was the author of the odd letters he received. After he went to look in it and started back to the house, he was stopped by several detectives who questioned him. As soon as he identified himself as a member of the Westchester Sheriff's Department, the New York City and Yonkers police invited him to join them on their stakeout. Two officers were in position on the roof of his apartment; two others were in a car two lengths behind Berkowitz's car, along with Craig Glassman.[113]

Four hours later, the largest manhunt in New York history was over. Not suspecting anything, Berkowitz headed toward his car, carrying a paper bag. A duffel bag he had previously put in the back of his car contained the small arsenal he planned to use to carry out his plans for his next big splash—an attack on a nightclub in Riverdale. It would, he imagined, be a blaze of glory as he fired a semi-automatic rifle with four loaded magazines, a twelve-gauge shotgun, and two .22-caliber rifles. As he started the car, the two detectives and Glassman approached with their guns drawn, and Glassman, putting his gun through the open window, told him, "Freeze, you're under arrest."

Berkowitz calmly turned, offered no resistance, and simply smiled, like he was a kid playing a game who had just been caught. As they led him out of the car and asked him to spread his arms and legs so they could search him, Berkowitz quietly commented, "Well, you got me. How come it took you such a long time?"

It was an oddly calm and anticlimactic moment after such an intensive manhunt. Even more surprising, David Berkowitz looked nothing like the evil monster Son of Sam. He appeared to be a quiet, unassuming Jewish boy, who seemed more like a shy, awkward clerk, which is what he was—a clerk who worked in the post office.

Now that Berkowitz/Son of Sam was captured, an even bigger mystery was about to begin—an attempt to understand just who he was, what motivated him to kill, just who were his "demons," and whether they were real. It was a battle that was be conducted by psychiatrists, rather than by lawyers and the courts, in deciding whether Berkowitz was sane or insane, after he quickly confessed.

Much as in the case of Ed Kemper, once the manhunt was over, he wanted to share his story—as much as the psychiatrists and eager public wanted to hear it.

Initially, the psychiatrists and the public seemed ready to buy the story Berkowitz told the police that he had killed on command, after Sam, a 6,000-year old man, passed on instructions to kill through his dog.[114] Berkowitz's own appearance made people doubt that he could possibly be the mass murderer himself; he must be insane because, as Abrahamsen describes him, "the face was so soft, so round, almost feminine; the smile so sweet, nearly seductive, his manner so mild and gentle. He looked like the boy next door, a nice Jewish boy from the Bronx."[115]

Initially, Berkowitz's three lawyers—Mark Heller, Ira Jultak, and Leon Stern—took the tack of claiming Berkowitz was not criminally responsible because he had a mental disease or defect, then the test for insanity in New York. They filed a motion in the state Supreme Court explaining this was their intention, and they had two psychiatrists who agreed. Berkowitz was definitely a paranoid schizophrenic, delusional, out of touch with reality, and compelled to act by his demons.

However, David Abrahamsen, the psychiatrist called in by the prosecution to examine Berkowitz, simply didn't buy this theory. Instead, he found Berkowitz highly intelligent, alert, and perceptive; in fact, Berkowitz had even read Abrahamsen's own book, *The Murdering Mind*, which he found in the Yonkers Public Library along with other books on murders, which suggested to Abrahamsen that Berkowitz had a need to intellectually understand his own behavior.

As Berkowitz began to talk about his childhood and teenage years, Abrahamsen came to believe that the roots of his murders lay in his own loneliness, anger against his parents and women, his ability to manipulate, and his outwardly shy, conformist behavior that concealed a growing pool of resentment and hatred. It was like there was a good outer Berkowitz and the inner seething person identified as Son of Sam, the source of his demons. This was finally released after Berkowitz, who had been adopted, sought to track down his birth mother, Betty Falco, after he learned she hadn't died when he was born. He finally found her, whereupon he learned she was not only a fairly ordinary, now dumpy housewife, but that his "birth" father really wasn't, because Betty had only put his name on the birth certificate. She had had an illegitimate child with a long-term married lover, and her husband had long ago abandoned the family. According to Abrahamsen, this was the ultimate shock—that Berkowitz was illegitimate and unwanted, early on rejected by his own parents. The murders became a way of getting back at the mother who had conceived him as a teenager with a lover in a car and finding his identity through becoming this popular figure known as Son of Sam.[116]

Abrahamsen began to develop his ideas about the real Berkowitz when he first talked to him and noticed that he liked to show off or had a "propensity for histrionics." After Berkowitz told him his first memory from childhood was "playing army games, cowboys and Indians," Abrahamsen began to notice how "playing" was a deep part of his character, which contributed to his love of fantasy and game-playing as he grew older. Early on, he developed a fascination with accidents and death, perhaps inspired by the attention he received after he was hit by a car and another time when he ran into a wall. For whatever reason, he was especially aware of car accidents in which people were hurt or killed, set hundreds of fires as a child, and killed and tortured animals, including his mother's parakeet by giving him small doses of cleaning materials, so his mother never suspected he did it. He comforted his mother after the beloved bird's death, playing the role of the innocent, helpful hero. As Berkowitz told Abrahamsen in various interviews, "I always had a fetish for murder and death. I had homicidal fantasies as far back as I could remember. Sudden death and bloodshed appealed to me."[117]

Abrahamsen found that Berkowitz had a long history of enjoying getting away with things, from setting fires to tormenting animals. As he grew up afraid and awkward around girls, he began fantasizing about being close to the young girls to whom he was sexually attracted. In reality, he was too shy or not handsome or popular enough to attract them himself.[118] So his fantasy life became his way to help him compensate for his lack of real satisfaction,[119] a process that contributed to his ability to manufacture his demons to explain his murderous behavior, though he truly felt guilty for what he had done.

In fact, that feeling of guilt convinced Abrahamsen early on that Berkowitz was sane and was creating his demons to escape guilt, responsibility, and punishment for his crimes, as well as to satisfy a fascinated public. Abrahamsen noticed this when he asked Berkowitz how he felt about his killing of Stacy Moskowitz, and Berkowitz described feeling sorry for her, explaining that Sam had told him to kill. "I had a job as a hired gun. I ran away from them—the demons. They wouldn't let me stop. It got to a point where I hated killing. I got sick of it. I wanted to stop . . . I was glad in a way they caught me."[120]

To Abrahamsen, this contradiction of being asked to kill and being glad he was caught meant that Berkowitz felt guilty and in his own mind felt he should be caught to be punished. If he felt guilt, he wasn't insane. Plus, he didn't show the signs of confusion, memory loss, and an ability to understand characteristic of schizophrenia, as the other psychiatrists thought. Rather, he showed great cunning in the way he selected the times and places of his murders and great skill in being able to elude the manhunt.[121] Then, too, Berkowitz functioned well in the everyday world, such as when he worked as a security guard and then at the post office—shy, reserved, polite. Outwardly he seemed perfectly in control, perfectly in touch with everyday reality, able to adapt his behavior so that he appeared to fit in.

Meanwhile, the resentment was building, particularly against the women in his family and young girls generally because he felt a keen sense of personal rejection. He resented his adoptive mother; after she died, he resented his new stepmother and his adoptive father for marrying her. He resented his twenty-five-year-old stepsister, Carol, who lived with them and was held up to him as a model for good behavior because she was smart and had many friends.[122] He felt increasingly insecure, and then his search for his adoptive mother proved to be a final blow. In one interview, Berkowitz even suggested this himself, telling Abrahamsen,

> My adoption caused me mental and emotional problems. . . . Then the question came up as to why I was adopted. I had to find out. I had to find out someone from my real family. I needed family real bad—a mystical and perfect family—a blissful family—a perfect relationship. Of course this wasn't to be. I guess this was one pathway that eventually led to murder. My dream family didn't exist. It was my last hope.[123]

Worse, he learned how his mother had conceived him, perhaps by sitting in a parked car, with her lover who wouldn't marry her[124]—an image that perhaps contributed to his later killing of women in parked cars in most of his murders. Though he never told his mother his feelings of anger, just like he kept his anger toward others bottled up, according to Abrahamsen, the meeting with his natural mother was the key to what followed.

> In Berkowitz's life there were now five women, all of whom he feared and hated. . . . Of all the cruel blows this meeting dealt him, the cruelest was that he now realized he was an "accident, a mistake, never meant to be born—unwanted." . . . There was no forgiveness for such rejection. His hatred toward women was becoming all-consuming, a fireball, and absolute.[125]

In fact, a month after his first murder, he wrote a poem titled "Mother of Satan" that expressed his anger and hinted at his future use of demon imagery to express his feelings of hatred. It reads in part:

> Old Mother Hubbard
> Sitting near the cubbard
> with a hand grenade
> under the oatmeal.
>
> Who will you kill now
> Daughter of Satan? . . .
>
> How many have you decieved [*sic*]—
> lured to slaughter like a
> fat cow?[126]

Berkowitz also confessed to Abrahamsen that his rage had been building until his ultimate disappointment on meeting his birth mother because from the time of his adoption to his terrible job as a night watchman, his life had been a series of "defeats and disappointments." After he left the army, he couldn't find a girlfriend. The anger kept building until his first attack on a girl, which the police didn't know he did. On Christmas Eve 1975 in the Bronx he accosted and repeatedly stabbed a fifteen-year-old girl, and then ran away afraid and confused. He realized he had tried to kill her, but he didn't know how. He felt sick and had nightmares afterward, upset by the feeling of compulsion to do something he knew was wrong. He tried to somehow justify what he did. As he told Abrahamsen, "I wasn't going to rape her or take her money. I was only going to kill her. That's all."[127]

The emotional tension kept building. Finally, he was compelled to go out and kill, explaining,

> I was determined and in full agreement with myself that I must slay a woman for revenge purposes and to get my back on them for all the suffering (mental suffering) they caused me . . . I . . . realize that this was a poor excuse for all I've done. However, at the time I sincerely believed that I was justified. I believed that I had every moral right to slay a chosen victim. . . . I psyched myself up to believing this.[128]

At the same time, he carefully plotted how he was going to do it and became very aware of and adept about the game he was playing with the police. As he put it: "I familiarized myself with the streets and possible escape routes from those central areas. . . . Towards the end of my spree, I developed a keen perception of police tactics. I began to figure out just where and when a cop car would pass or where a 'stakeout' car would be parked. I really got good at this—expert."[129]

Even so, at the very end when he got a ticket and was aware that the tickets of cars in the vicinity of a murder scene might be traced, he still killed. He even paid the parking ticket. It was as if by the end he really felt so guilty that he wanted to be caught—much like Ed Kemper, who was similarly motivated by his hatred of women and finally gave himself up.

In any event, it was this rational planning and awareness that convinced Abrahamsen that Berkowitz wasn't insane. He was drawn to kill out of hatred. As he got the spotlight for his crimes, he was driven to keep killing and fashion the more colorful Son of Sam persona. As Abrahamsen observed:

> He used every means to avoid suspicion and one of his ways was to shoot women he didn't know. Berkowitz prided himself on his caution. . . . Yet, he also wanted it to be known. He sometimes had an overwhelming, desperate wish to proclaim to the world that he, David Berkowitz, was the "Son of Sam"—the most feared murderer of recent times.[130]

In fact, Berkowitz later wrote to Abrahamsen confessing that he sometimes stared at his telephone and thought of picking up the receiver to announce his secret to the party at the other end. Perhaps in the end, he unconsciously did this in the way he left his car at a hydrant to be found and also sent a series of letters to people in Yonkers, set a fire at a neighbor's door, and shot a neighbor's dog. It was like a cry to finally be caught.

At the same time, he felt the drive to continue, particularly in response to the growing hue and cry in the papers, with headlines like: SECOND KILLING STUNS FOREST HILLS. As Berkowitz told Abrahamsen,

> During the fourth shooting when I first used two hands . . . I was more determined than ever . . . I finally had convinced myself that it was good to do it, necessary to do it, and that the public wanted me to do it. . . . I believe that many were rooting for me. This was the point in which the papers began to pick up vibes and information that something big was happening out in the street. Real big![131]

In other words, David Berkowitz was just a lonely, rejected, underachieving washout. But now that the public and news media had become involved, they spurred him on. It was like a game with "Berkowitz pitted against an entire city. It was as if they would be disappointed if he did not now continue with his murderous deeds."[132]

With each successive attack, Berkowitz became bolder and less cautious. He felt more and more power and mastery, in both dooming his victims and being the only one who knew who the killer was. He had thus become, in Abrahamsen's view, "omnipotent. The 'demons' had transformed the unassuming and quite ordinary David Berkowitz into one of the most sought-after killers of modern times."[133] The process was much like turning the angry and alienated Ted Kaczynski into the much feared and fearless Unabomber—he ultimately was so magnified by the press that his own hubris gave him away.

In turn, all these dynamics convinced Abrahamsen that Berkowitz was quite sane, though he had an egocentric, manipulative, narcissistic personality—all the signs of a sociopath who cared nothing for others and was compelled by his unsatisfied sexual frustrations, hatred, and revenge fantasies to finally kill. The Son of Sam persona and the demons became a convenient, dramatic way to help escape responsibility and punishment, as well as continue the public interest. He was, Abrahamsen though, still "playing" the game, just as playing had been his very first memory as a child.

On October 20, 1977, when the competency hearing on Berkowitz began at the prison ward of Kings County Hospital, that's what Abrahamsen argued, as defense psychiatrists tried to argue that Berkowitz was delusional and insane. In the end, the judge agreed with the prosecution and set the trial date for November 2.

But the trial never took place. After Berkowitz's lawyers filed a motion for a change of venue due to all the publicity in New York and the motion was denied, they made a motion for a new competency hearing with a new psychiatrist. However, even Berkowitz had decided to give up his belief in his demons and he decided to plead guilty, telling his psychiatrists in March 1978 that he wanted to "face the charges and punishment like a man and then wherever they send me from there I'll work . . . for the Lord." In April he told Abrahamsen that he had been reading the Bible every day, had found Christ, and wanted to repent his sins. Finally, he felt his conscience had been cleansed. As for the demons, "They have gone," Berkowitz said.[134]

That was the end of the court proceedings. Berkowitz pled guilty and on June 12, 1978, Judge Corso at the Kings County Court building sentenced Berkowitz to 365 years of prison—based on twenty-five years to life on each count of murder.[135] After some processing at the Ossining Correctional Facility and the New York Psychiatric Center, he was sent to Attica Prison to serve his time.

Subsequently, there were some stories about whether David Berkowitz really acted alone, including claims that he had three or four accomplices who were part of a cult. Supposedly there was some new evidence, such as new proof that the Son of Sam letters had been written by different people. Maury Terry first suggested this story in March 1979 and subsequently wrote about it in his book *The Ultimate Evil* (1987).

For Abrahamsen, this was just one more fantasy story created by Berkowitz or others who didn't want the Son of Sam story to die and be what it always was—a creation of Berkowitz's own mind. Abrahamsen wrote about Sam's creation:

> This hatred of himself, the source of his hatred of others, was central to his double behavior. It started when he was a child. . . . Always a role player, he wanted everyone to see that he was on the side of the angels, and then secretly switch to the side of the devil. . . .
>
> With his expansive imagination, he once speculated that if the evil side of his nature could be isolated from the rest of him, he could find tranquility. . . .
>
> His intense desire—his craving—to expose and display himself . . . stimulated his tendency to exaggerate which, already present in childhood . . . gradually took an aggressive and violent form. It drove him from truancy, pilfering, lying, and fire-setting to game-playing with demons, the Son of Sam, and murder. He had to be noticed, attract attention, create a sensation, at any costs. . . . His life had become a performance, his very being a stage for his theatrical experiences. These hysterical, role-playing traits—law-abiding vs. criminal, compliant vs. sadistic—were the stamp of his personality. . . .
>
> Each side of his character had its own feelings, fantasies, and points of view. One was compliant, representing the more-or-less practical person who adhered to the rules of his community and was in steady contact with his environment. The other was his *doppelganger*, the personification of which was "Son of Sam" . . . A kind of co-consciousness existed.[136]

Son of Sam was born, nurtured, and grew to commit murder, until finally David Berkowitz's compulsion overcame his caution—and the clues he gave away in the very end provided the keys that led the police right to him. At this point, perhaps unconsciously, his guilt made him feel he had gone too far.

Chapter 3

The 1980s

IN THE 1980S, the homicide rate remained high, especially through 1982, when it topped the charts at slightly over 10 homicides per 100,000 people. It then dipped slightly from 1983 to 1990, down to about 9 per 100,000.[1] Also in the 1980s, the serial killer phenomena continued to grow and chill the nation.

There was a big shift in the social climate, resulting in a crackdown on crime of all types, including homicide. The 1980s were the Reagan years, and with them came a new conservatism and new crime bills providing for tougher law enforcement at all levels. Besides providing more money for state and local law enforcement, these new laws created new federal offenses, including new categories of killings deserving the death penalty.[2] The role of the FBI and federal courts in dealing with murder was expanded, including beefing up the federal crime lab and databases and the Behavioral Sciences Unit for profiling and applying psychological methods to understanding criminals.

These changes also resulted in an increased attention to the growing number of serial homicides—as well as a change in the way the serial killers were regarded once caught. In the 1970s, psychiatrists and psychologists played much more of a role in psychoanalyzing these criminals (even though the juries didn't necessarily buy it), trying to show how they were insane, suffered from terrible childhoods, and were unhappy, rejected loners experiencing uncontrollable sexual urges—as in the cases of Ed Kemper and David Berkowitz (see Chapter 2). With the new, more conservative thrust, these killers were seen as the embodiment of pure evil, as indicators of a society that had gone wrong due to the rebellions and excesses of the 1960s and 1970s that led to the breakdown in traditional institutions, including religion and the family. Something had to be done to fight back. Along with all the new crime control legislation, there was an even greater fascination with all sorts of murder in the press and popular culture, reflected in the growing number of true crime and fictional works about homicide, serial killer and slasher films, cop shows on TV, and increasingly sensational tabloid stories about the latest killing. Meanwhile, cops and crime fighters became the new heroes who would help society fight back against the evil in its midst. This was a way of dealing with the growing fear of killers by viewing them as not merely disturbed but evil, and turning fear into fascination and stepped up efforts to fight back.

In short, the 1980s were characterized by a kind of conservative war on crime, much like the 1960s and 1970s had been fueled by various liberal efforts to change society and the self. The conservatives blamed these very changes for unleashing the unruly forces that often led to murder.

This conservatism of the decade was reflected in numerous ways. The landslide victory of President Ronald Regan over Jimmy Carter in the 1980 election was just the beginning. For the first time since 1964, Republicans also took over the Senate. There was a growing obsession with money and material things. It was the decade of the yuppies—the young upwardly mobile professionals. On TV, *Dallas*, which celebrated the good life in Texas, had the highest rating ever for a regular TV series, particularly when over 88.6 million viewers agonized over "Who shot J.R.?" in 1980. Such interest in wealth was not surprising, because this was also the decade of the dead—it was a time of buy-outs, mergers, and acquisitions; mushrooming home prices; insider stock deals. and Ivan Boesky telling a graduating UC Berkeley class that "Greed is healthy. You can be greedy and still feel good about yourself," shortly before pleading guilty to insider trading. There were new multilevel marketing opportunities and opportunity seminars; it was a time when popular seminars featured new techniques for success in the workplace, from assertion for women to dressing for success for everyone.

Popular culture reflected a growing nostalgia for a close, warm family (like *Terms of Endearment* in 1983), for honoring the military and personal valor (like Tom Wolfe's book *The Right Stuff* in 1979, which was later be made into a film; and the Richard Gere film *An Officer and a Gentleman* in 1982), and for the cop as hero (as in *Hill Street Blues*, which received the Emmy Award for the outstanding drama series in 1983; and *Beverly Hills Cop* in 1984, which helped establish Eddie Murphy as the next big star). With fear of crime and criminals at a high point, Bernhard Goetz became a popular vigilante hero in 1985 after he shot four black suspected muggers on a New York subway. After being cleared of attempted murder, he was convicted in 1987 for illegally owning a gun. The lone hero who could single-handedly decimate the forces of destruction became a new staple of the movies with the big success of the Rambo films with Sylvester Stallone, who starred in *Rambo: First Blood Part II* in 1985, and by the *Die Hard* films with Bruce Willis, which began in 1988. Many other films reflected the growing fear of a changing culture that undermined the traditional family, such as in the controversial *Fatal Attraction* (1987) with Glenn Close as the spurned lover who terrorizes the married man who wants to end the affair. Pop music showed a similar fascination with crime and violence. Michael Jackson became the King of Pop with his hit album *Thriller,* which sold over thirty-seven million copies and won eight Grammy Awards—the most sales and awards for any album at that time.

In fact, until the stock crash of 1989, it was a decade characterized by a kind of grandiosity as stock prices soared ever higher. The world's three most expensive paintings sold for astronomical sums—Van Gogh's *Irises* sold for $49 million in 1987. Computers spread around the world and Bill Gates, founder of Microsoft, first became a billionaire in 1987. Films like Michael Douglas's *Wall Street* (1987), Paul Newman's *The Color of Money* (1986), and Kevin Costner's *Field of Dreams* (1989) expressed the hopefulness, concern with success, and money hunger of the age.

At the same time, there was the dark undercurrent in the increasing crime and the growing fear and crackdown it inspired. Of particular concern was the rising number of serial killers with a growing variety of victims. Classically, the victim was a woman, often a young, attractive one. Now there was a dizzying array of targets—prostitutes, alcoholics, the homeless, homosexual men, and children. Social scientists began to chart and categorize these new phenomena; concerned members of the public and policy makers began to use these statistics and case studies to fight the growing tide of killers, particularly the pedophiles who targeted children, with new laws.

For many, this reaction was a repudiation of the trends of the 1960s and 1970s that some believed triggered this new wave of crime. One social scientist, Philip Jenkins, explains that moral conservatives in the 1980s felt the events of the previous fifteen years had had "a catastrophic effect on the fiber of American society." They felt "the tolerance of divorce, abortion, homosexuality, drugs, and sexual promiscuity had contributed to a pervasive moral breakdown that urgently needed to be reversed."[3] For them, the rate of violent crime that reached its highest peak in the years 1980–81 illustrated the crisis, and many felt it was time to take immediate action to change the course of society and the high level of crime it produced.

This meant a change in assessing the cause of social problems. In the 1960s and 1970s, the approach of social scientists had been to view crime and other social problems as due to social and economic dysfunction. The solution was changing society, such as through efforts like Lyndon Johnson's War on Poverty that pumped money into the cities in the 1960s, or through federal funding to try out new more socially progressive law enforcement programs, such as with grants and evaluation programs offered by the Law Enforcement Assistance Administration in the 1970s. These initiatives funded programs to promote diversion and crime prevention to get at the social roots of crime and find more community-based solutions.

In the 1980s, the trend was to view crime and deviancy, including murder, as due to personal sin and evil. Or as Jenkins put it, "For conservatives of the

Reagan era, the central issue in morality (as in economics) was a renewed emphasis on the responsibility of the individual, and a denial of the effectiveness or validity of solution that emphasized the state or the social dimension."[4] In fact, Reagan himself, along with his wife, Nancy, took a firm moral stand and helped guide the way toward this new view.

This approach was accompanied by a harsher, more punitive response to crime, replacing the more social and therapeutic approach of the 1960s and 1970s.[5] The drug war, typified by Nancy Reagan's "Just Say No!" campaign was one highly publicized example of this. Another was the push to restore capital punishment and execute convicted killers awaiting the death penalty, which culminated in the 1989 execution of serial killer Ted Bundy. Despite the horror of his crimes, he had become something of a popular hero with his suave ways, courtroom bravado, and ability to escape from prison several times. But in the 1980s, the tide turned. At his execution there were death penalty supporters carrying posters and selling T-shirts like "Burn, Bundy, Burn," and a nearby bar served Bundy "fries" and Bundy "toast."[6]

The execution statistics also reveal this change in attitudes. Between 1967 and 1976, there were no executions; there were only four between 1977 and 1981. Between 1984 and 1987, there were eighty-two of them, and among the first to be executed were the serial killers, most of them white males, so critics couldn't claim the executions were racially motivated in a society where a much higher proportion of blacks and other minority group members were in prison for various crimes. Rather, the choice of serial killers was one on which most people could agree that if anyone deserved the death penalty, they did. There was no longer the kind of sympathy that had surrounded killers like Kemper and Berkowitz the decade before.

In fact, the decade was marked by a general crackdown on crime of all sorts. For example, in 1981, an armed robbery by leftist radicals in New York was followed by a expansion of internal security operations generally, and more harsh legislation against political conspiracy and sedition.[7] At the same time, the federal government gained more authority in the nonpolitical, domestic arena where ordinary citizens seemed to be especially menaced, so the feds (not just the local police) should be involved—most notably in the areas of child abuse and abduction, drug dealing, and serial murder.[8]

In the cases of serial killings, there weren't any reliable statistics before the 1980s, in part because there was a lack of local police forces coordinating records when killers operated in different jurisdictions. Even so, the Justice Department did its best to come up with some statistics showing how serious the problem had become, suggesting that there were possibly as many as 4,000 or 5,000 such killings a year, up to a quarter of all American homicides—more than ever in U.S. history (or world history for that matter). Making the threat even worse, such killers were very mobile, moving easily between different states and jurisdictions.[9] The actual number of serial killings was often vastly overstated, but there were certainly many more of them—probably more like about 350 cases from 1975 to 1992, according to U.S. Department of Justice Statistics. This was far more than in previous periods—an estimated thirteen cases from 1900 to 1924, twenty from 1925 to 1949, and sixty-six from 1950 to 1974.[10] So the problem was real—though perhaps not as prevalent as the media and politicians seeking a crime crackdown wanted to make it.

Although such figures have been actively disputed and are probably highly exaggerated, the statistics helped build this concern to a peak in the mid-1980s, resulting in new crime legislation and a growing interest in such killers in the news media and in the literature, films, and pop culture of the day. Such statistics also helped in popularizing the killers as the ultimate evil who were variously turned into monsters and supernatural figures of savagery in pop culture, including vampires, werewolves, cannibals, and mysterious stalkers.[11] For example, Thomas Harris's 1988 novel *The Silence of the Lambs*, later made into a movie starring Jodie Foster, featured Hannibal Lecter as the evil cannibal.

The 1980s was also the decade when the phrase "serial murder," recently coined by members of the FBI's Behavioral Sciences Unit, was popularized by the media. Law enforcement authorities began to distinguish between different types of multiple homicides, based on the times between attacks. Those committed in a brief period in one place came to be called "mass murders," and those carried over a few days or a week were referred to as "spree killings." The phrase "serial murder" was used to characterize killings over months or years. They began to develop classifications examining the characteristics of these different types of killers as a way of better understanding how to track them down. This was especially important for the much harder to solve serial killers, because they were typically intelligent and crafty. They used planning and organized strategy to hide their crimes and often tended to look like the neighbor next door, which helped them get away with it for so long. Ted Bundy, for instance, was a sharp-looking law student who at one time worked as a volunteer with the Seattle police. John Wayne Gacy, the "killer clown" who killed over three dozen young boys, was a civic leader involved in local Democratic politics.[12]

A reason for the greater awareness of this problem is that the big metropolitan papers like the *New York Times* and *LA Times* increased their coverage of regional news after 1950, and newspapers increasingly became part of chains, so sensational stories were more likely to go nationwide. In the 1980s, there was a growing trend toward sensationalism and a "tabloid approach to news gathering," resulting in more crime reporting.[13] In fact, this interest seemed to build on the curiosity about multiple acts of irrational murder, stimulated by the Manson Family murders of 1969, according to Jenkins, along with the rise in the number of ripper crimes and lust murders in the late 1960s and 1970s, such as Jerry Brudos, the mysterious Zodiac killer, and others.[14]

Yet another reason for this growing awareness of multiple and serial killers in the 1980s is that due to improved investigative techniques, more killings in disparate times and places were put together as due to one killer—and more of these killers were caught and convicted. Before then, as Jenkins observes, it was "quite possible for poisoners to claim dozens or hundreds of victims undetected."[15] Many of these poisoners were likely to be women, who were often less likely suspects than the young white male killers, who were more likely to be the sexually driven serial killers or angry mass murders who killed in an explosion of fury.

Whatever the actual prevalence, these homicide and other crime statistics were used by various politicians, bureaucrats, and groups to argue there was a serious social threat from "monstrous random killers," each of whom might be responsible for hundreds of deaths and kidnappings. A few notorious cases helped stir the pot—in particular, the Son of Sam killings in New York, Gacy's murders in Chicago, and the Hillside Strangler in Los Angeles during the 1970s. In the beginning of the 1980s, the Atlanta child murders helped rouse concern even more. They became especially notorious because of the youth of the child victims; the racial conflict because all of the victims were black, which was unusual in serial killings; and because it was so difficult for the police to solve the crimes.[16] Further stirring up interest in these cases—plus fear of the dangers of serial killers—was the growing number of true-crime books and television documentaries on these high-profile cases.[17] There were dozens of books that came out in 1980 and 1981 alone, such as four on Bundy—*Ted Bundy: The Killer Next Door* by Steven Winn and David Merrill (1980); *The Stranger Beside Me* by Ann Rule (1980); *Bundy: The Deliberate Stranger* by Richard Larsen (1980); and *The Phantom Prince* by Elizabeth Kendall (1981). Other books dealt with John Wayne Gacy (*The Man Who Killed Boys* by Clifford Linedecker, 1980), Herbert Mullin (*The Die Song* by Donald Lunde and Jefferson Morgan, 1980), the Zebra murders (*Zebra* by Clark Howard, 1980), Ed Gein (*Edward Gein* by Robert H. Gollmar, 1981), Kenneth Bianchi and Angelo Buono (*The Hillside Strangler* by Ted Schwarz, 1981), and David Berkowitz (*Son of Sam* by Lawrence Klausner, 1980).[18] Movies jumped on the bandwagon, too, coming out with more films on the theme of multiple murder in 1980 and 1981 than in the previous two decades.[19] It was as if a killer got a window of fame and fascination, while at the same time making people even more fearful of the evil monsters lurking in their midst.

Like cowboys riding to the rescue, the FBI's Behavioral Science Unit (BSU) at Quantico played an increasingly active role in investigating these cases and providing a more comprehensive understanding of this kind of killer. The unit was established in the early 1970s, but it shifted its attention to profiling serial killers in the late 1970s, and this included pioneering lengthy interviews with convicted and incarcerated criminals, including mass and serial killers. Eventually, the program was formalized as the Criminal Personality Research Project. In 1982, Robert Ressler and John Douglas headed up an investigation funded by the National Institute of Justice to interview in depth thirty-six incarcerated multiple killers. These results were then used to create the extensive classification schemes of serial offenders with a goal of helping investigators analyze crime schemes to reconstruct the likely characteristics of the person committing the crime.[20] In 1981–82, the group gained especial acclaim for its help in solving the baffling Atlanta child murders—one of the cases highlighted in this chapter.

The members of the BSU were also involved in pushing for increased interagency cooperation, so serial killers operating in different jurisdictions wouldn't fall through the cracks. As a result, beginning in 1981, U.S. Attorney General William French Smith sponsored a Task Force on Violent Crime to examine ways to improve such cooperation, which led to a proposal to create a National Center for the Analysis of Violent Crime (NCAVC) under the auspices of the BSU, which was eventually formed in 1984. Around the same time, a new national databank was proposed, the Violent Criminal Apprehension Program (VICAP), to enable law enforcement agencies to share information about unsolved crimes from different jurisdictions. Under this program, local police departments would submit their information on unsolved crimes in response to nearly 200 questions; the NCAVC would collect and analyze these data and provide leads to local investigators to help in arresting violent offenders who moved about from district to district.[21] Although there were some heated debates in Congress about these measures—primarily because opponents were afraid the FBI might abuse its powers as it did under J. Edgar Hoover, provoking such a strong anti-FBI reaction in the late 1960s and 1970s—eventually the fear of crime and homicidal killers won out. By the mid-1980s, there was broad support both for the new NCAVC and the expansion of computer facilities needed for the VICAP database.[22]

Another major reason for the crackdown on crime was the growing concern about the danger to children, especially because many serial killers were targeting them, such as Gacy and Dean Corll. The Atlanta child murders added to the furor. After his own child was kidnapped and later found murdered, Adam Walsh, later the host of the TV show *America's Most Wanted*, became a national spokesman for victims' and children's causes.[23] Eventually, all this concern led to hearings by the Juvenile Justice Subcommittee in the Senate between 1982 and 1984 dealing with child pornography, child molestation, and hearings on missing and exploited children. These hearings resulted in new legislation that further strengthened the FBI. One was the Missing Children's Act of 1982, which made the FBI's National Crime Information Center a clearinghouse for this information and created the National Center for Missing and Exploited Children in 1984. This gave the FBI even more information to go after serial killers targeting children.[24]

At the same time, all of the legislative scrutiny led to a kind of panic between 1983 and 1985, spurred on by a U.S. Justice Department news conference in October 1983 on the growing danger of serial murder.[25] Among other things, the Justice Department experts at the meeting, Roger Depue and Robert Heck, announced with vastly overstated data there might be 35 serial killers active in the United States at any given time, as well as up to 4,000 victims.

Around this time, in Texas, convicted killer Henry Lee Lucas announced at a news conference that he had killed around 360 people in 20 states with the help of a number of friends, including murderer Ottis Toole. Later it turned out that he claimed far more victims than he actually killed—more like the dozen or so for which he was convicted; perhaps he just liked the excited attention. For whatever reason, Lucas became a national celebrity with interviews in 1984 and 1985 on major news shows, plus a 1985 TV documentary.[26]

The result was a deluge of media stories that trumpeted the news that serial murder had become an epidemic—quoting the use of this word by Robert Heck at the Justice Department. There were stories in *Time* and *Newsweek* about these terrifying random killers on the loose, along with the suggestion that were responsible for up to two-thirds of the estimated 5,000 unsolved homicides each year.[27] Beginning in 1985, the VICAP data bank began functioning, collecting information on apparently random, motiveless, and sexually oriented crimes; several states launched their own data-gathering programs. The effort to fight back was on, though the media kept everyone both fascinated and afraid.

As the serial murder panic died down, in part because of the new legislation and additional crime fighting techniques between 1985 and 1990, there was a booming market for true crime and scholarly books on the subjects. The notion of FBI agents like Ressler, Douglas, and Roy Hazelwood being mind hunters for the FBI captured the public imagination, especially after they used profiling to help solve the notorious Atlantic child murders.[28] Though profiling didn't always work, the FBI and media publicized the times it did—and soon Ressler and Douglas were media stars in their own right.

Intriguingly, while much of the more scholarly literature sought to delve into the psychology of these killers and explore the social dynamics producing them, the films and TV shows of the 1980s (like the first of the *Halloween* films) often portrayed these killers in supernatural terms. They were like "superhuman monsters, representatives of total, incomprehensible evil."[29] At the same time, the role of the investigator and cop was exaggerated and dramatized, too, turning ordinary police officers and detectives from local agencies—who are usually the ones involved in discovering serial criminals when they make a stupid mistake—into mind hunters and supercops.[30]

For all the exaggeration of fear about killers and the abilities of the investigator, there was some real progress in the decade, especially in the scientific front, giving investigators even more tools to track down more hard to find killers. One new technique was the development of DNA testing. Building on the work that had gone before, in September 1984, Dr. Alec Jeffreys at the University of Leicester in England devised the new genetic fingerprint for typing an individual. He had been studying gene coding for a certain type of proteins that carry oxygen to the muscles, called myoglobin proteins, when he discovered a building block made up of repeated sequences of ten to fifteen sections within the DNA. He cloned and isolated two of these blocks and made them radioactive with an isotope so he could track them. Eventually, he introduced these blocks into human blood and followed their movement, noticing that similar blocks were drawn to others with the same pattern. The result of all of these efforts is that Jeffreys was able to isolate DNA from the protein surrounding the nucleus, chopping it up into tiny pieces, and then analyzed these DNA pieces on a radio-sensitive film so he could see the marks identifying each piece. In short, what he did is discover the DNA autograph that is unique for every individual on earth (except identical twins).[31]

This autograph took the form of long columns of light and dark patches of different lengths, thicknesses, and spaces between them imprinted on a piece of X-ray film—essentially a "human bar code." As a result, an investigator could put together the genetic fingerprint of two individuals and no two columns or bands would be the same, except for identical twins.[32] It was a tremendous breakthrough, and with the use of two independent samples using multi-locus probes—like points on a fingerprint analysis—Jeffreys estimated the chance of two unrelated people having the same pattern at less than 1 part in a billion billion—that's a 1 followed by thirty zeros.[33]

Jeffreys's technique was first used in paternity cases to prove beyond doubt that a particular man was the parent of a child. In November 1987, the police in England used his technique to determine the guilt of a suspect by checking whether a suspected burglar and rapist a woman picked from a lineup really was the perpetrator. The police tested semen stains from the woman's clothing using Jeffreys's test and after they proved a match, the man was jailed for rape and robbery. In another case, the police used this technique to prove a suspect's innocence, when they took blood samples from every man in an area, thinking the killer was a local man, and learned that one man had paid a co-worker to act as his stand-in and give a sample.[34]

Soon the technique spread to the United States, and in 1987, a DNA fingerprint was used to secure a conviction for the first time. It occurred after a Florida woman, Nancy Hodge, was raped in her apartment in May 1986—the first of a series of similar break-ins, rapes, and robberies. A man was arrested after leaving behind two fingerprints at the scene of another rape and robbery, but when Hodge identified him at his trial, he denied the charge and claimed that he was home all night. His girlfriend and his sister backed him up. The prosecution presented its DNA evidence, arguing that there was only one chance in ten billion that he *wasn't* the rapist. Though the first case ended in a mistrial because of some confusion over the evidence, at the retrial the prosecutor had expert witnesses to explain the use of DNA fingerprinting and show how truly accurate such statistics were. As a result, the man was convicted and sentenced to over 100 years.[35]

Thereafter, DNA evidence was used successfully in other trials, so that by the end of the 1980s it had been used in over sixty successful rape convictions and several murder convictions.[36] It was a powerful tool that came into even more common use in the 1990s—especially after it was explained to the world in O. J. Simpson's trial.

Meanwhile, there were advances in ballistics and in understanding gunshot wounds. Even without recovering a gun or the bullet or cartridge case, a great deal could be determined about what happened, including where the killer and victim were positioned when the shooting occurred. Such improvements were inspired by the high level of gun ownership and shootings in the United States, which has a more highly developed ballistics analysis system than other countries. One British writer, Brian Marriner, tracking the development of the forensic sciences in solving murders had this to say:

> In 1975, there were 21,000 murders in the USA, of which 16,000—over half—were by shooting, compared to 500 murders in Great Britain. Truly, with drug gangs in the USA using machine guns routinely, the figures are staggering and can only get worse. . . . America needs a good ballistics system; thankfully we do not.[37]

Among other things, Marriner notes how precise ballistics or wound analysis can be. After the first step of photographing the body and carefully measuring the position of the bullet holes at the scene to determine trajectory, the postmortem examination can then offer the most detailed analysis, which has provided the basis for likely reconstructions of the events of the crime. In fact, video reconstructionists have built on these techniques in the late 1980s and 1990s to create dramatic presentations where allowed, such as at the Jim Mitchell trial in Marin County in 1992, after Jim was alleged to have shot his brother, Artie, claiming it was an accident. The reconstruction was used to illustrate if the shooting was an accident or premeditated murder.

More specifically, this modern analysis involves such steps as carefully examining the clothing for bullet holes or powder traces and examining wounds to determine entry and exit points. Knowledge about the victim's position, such as if seated or standing, can be used to learn something about the killer—such as how tall he or she might be, based on his or her distance from the victim, which can be estimated from the size and angle of the entry wound. As Marriner describes,

> The entry wound will be small; a neat round hole. The skin, being elastic, closes up around the bullet as it enters the body and actually wipes it clean. . . . If the bullet strikes at an angle, the entry wound will be oval rather than round. If the bullet was fired at point-blank range then the wound will be gross, with . . . a bruise and scorching around the entry wound or clothing.[38]

Particles of lead or burned powder from the bullet found on the skin or clothing will tell their tales, too, and the velocity of the bullet provides its own calling card in the form of a wider than normal entry wound, because the wave of air pressure causes the flesh at the site of the entry to balloon out. Plus if a bullet hits bone, there can be even more damage, which might be mistaken for a bludgeoning wound, though a skilled examiner can tell the difference.[39] Conversely, an exit wound, unless the bullet hits a bone as it goes through the body, can be very small, helping the examiner trace the results of a shooting. Sometimes, an examination of a wound can even lead back to the manufacturer of the gun. As Marriner notes, a forensic scientist can examine powder grains under the microscope to determine the type of cartridge used in the shooting, as well as the manufacturer of a particular cartridge.[40]

Other developments also helped in the identification of bodies—even long dead and decomposed ones. The medical pathologist in the coroner's office may still be the primary person in charge of the postmortem, but many other specialists in different scientific disciplines have increasingly been used to provide input. For example, as described by Marriner, a veterinary surgeon can help in distinguishing between animal and human bones; an anatomist can examine a skeleton to determine the sex, age, height, and often the race of the victim. If there is blood or bone marrow evidence, a serologist can determine the victim's blood grouping. From teeth evidence, a forensic odontologist or teeth expert can determine the victim's age or race, such as by noticing if there are pits on the inner surfaces of the concave incisor teeth, which would indicate an Asian victim. Fillings can be used to identify the victim by looking at dental records. Of course, some of these identification techniques date far back in history—for example, the Romans used to identify their dead by examining their teeth, and a dentistry professor in Paris published a medical-legal textbook on identification by teeth in 1898.[41] But in the 1980s, there was a more extensive and systematic use of these various techniques, and this teeth evidence contributed to Bundy's conviction. The evidence against him had been circumstantial but not conclusive except for one thing. There were bite marks on the buttocks of one of his victims that were matched conclusively by an odontologist who examined Bundy's teeth impressions.[42] The evidence helped convince the jury that Bundy was lying, no matter how charming he was, and the evidence withstood his years of appeal as his own courtroom and prison lawyer.

By this time, the preservation of evidence along with the precision of examining it under the microscope had gotten so good that in one Florida case, prosecutors were able to use the bite on a tongue ten years after a murder to obtain a conviction. This occurred after Sharon Zellers, age nineteen, disappeared on her way home from work at Walt Disney World on December 30, 1978. At the time, the police found her abandoned car in a orange grove near a motel, and they obtained various bits of evidence, including some blood stains, a few hair strands, and shoe prints from military boots. A forensic odontologist positively identified the victim from her teeth and dental records. Meanwhile, some detectives discovered that on the night Zellers was killed, a guest at a nearby motel had called for an ambulance and was bleeding heavily from his mouth as they took him away. Though he claimed he had cut his tongue during a fight at the local skating rink, there was no fight at the rink according to guards, and a nurse said the man couldn't have bitten his own tongue, because the curve was in reverse to his own bite. Presumably someone bit it off. By the time detectives had put this assessment together, the suspect, Robert C. Cox, had returned to his military unit in Georgia and the police could not do anything. The best the detective in charge of the case could do after questioning Cox, who denied knowing Zellers, was take some hair and blood samples for possible DNA testing, which was just beginning to be used. For about eight years, the case was on ice. But in mid-1986, the detective on the case found that Cox was now in prison. He got some hair samples from the prisoner and sent them to a Chicago laboratory, which was able to make a positive match with the hairs found in the victim's car. In his concluding arguments, the prosecutor referred to the way Zellers had bitten off a piece of Cox's tongue, commenting, "She marked him, God bless her, she marked him." So a bite and a few hair samples from a decade before helped seal Cox's fate. After the jury found him guilty of murder, he was sentenced to death.[43]

Archaeologists and paleopathologists have gotten involved in homicide cases too, because they can determine how long ago a person died. Among other techniques, they use X-rays to help show how old the victim was by the degree to which his or her bones ossified over time, creating a kind of skeletal calendar for forensic experts. In addition, if a victim's skull was ever X-rayed before death, investigators can use a radiological outline to compare the frontal sinuses on each X-ray, like comparing two skull fingerprints to see if there is a forensic match. This establishes identity beyond all doubt.[44]

Additionally, investigators gained another video identification technique from work pioneered in Israel and first used in Britain by Dr. Peter Vanezis, a forensic pathologist at the London Hospital. After a skeleton of a man who had disappeared in March 1988 was found in the woods near Essex, Vanezis superimposed the skull of the skeleton onto a photograph of the missing man using a video camera and was able to show there was a perfect match. Because there was no identification on the body, no dental records, and a lack of genetic or fingerprint material for testing because the body was so decomposed, this was the only way to make an identification.[45]

In turn, such techniques have been making it increasingly difficult to commit a murder in the hopes that time will decompose and wash the evidence away. As Marriner observes, "Very soon it may well be impossible for there ever to be a 'body without a name.' However mutilated or decomposed, forensic science will supply the name of the body in question."

Even handwriting analysis has become more sophisticated, with the introduction of the metrical analysis method, which measures the height of individual letters and presents them in the form of a graph.[46] This way investigators can assess the likelihood that two samples are comparable, much like comparing the banding in different chemicals to determine what a substance is.

Then, too, the role of the psychologist and professional profiler has become more important, helping investigators gain more of an insight into the type of killer to look for and literally get into the mind of the murderer to try to predict his or her next move. For example, at Quantico, the FBI mind hunters, working under VICAP, start with pictures of the crime scene to give them psychological clues into the case. They create a profile of the likely killer, including his age, marital status, car he drives, area where he lives, and lifestyle. It involves a bit of common sense—such as figuring that if a body is left at a remote hilly spot, the killer probably is a strong type with a Jeep. But then the investigators also draw on some of the typologies developed from the interviews of FBI profilers with convicted killers. Among other things, they identified critical incidents in a person's past that might contribute to becoming a killer—such as knowing that virtually all of these killers were intelligent but abused and rejected as children, leading them to retreat into a world of fantasy. Plus, serial killers tend to learn and become more proficient and clever with each killing, so methods can develop and expand over time.[47] One psychologist, Joel Norris, who studied serial killers and wrote a book about them (*Serial Killers*, 1988) discovered that most were both physically and psychologically damaged people—most, for instance, had scars on their bodies, missing fingers, and evidence of previous batterings. Many had unusual physical abnormalities, like webbed fingers or elongated limbs or had suffered head injuries (such as Earle Nelson or Raymond Fernandez, featured in early decades).[48]

In turn, profiling can help an investigator make the connections when crimes are committed over years in many different places. In fact, such psychological sophistication in understanding modern killers has become necessary because in many cases, even technological developments in detection aren't enough. The detective, as Marriner puts it after tracing the development of forensic science, can no longer be "merely a sleuth—he must also be a psychologist."[49]

An investigator also needs to have a good bit of luck, because so many murders are not solved by forensic science or by clever investigative work. Rather, the killers are caught by accident, because after they kill and leave so few clues, a slip-up may be the critical factor that breaks the case. The killer makes a mistake and gets caught for doing something stupid, like making an illegal left turn with evidence of the crime in his car; a jealous boyfriend or girlfriend might come forward to report what he or she knows; or the killer gets too cocky and talks too much to the wrong person. Once there are these mistakes or insights that target a particular suspect, the new technologies can play a very important role in confirming the suspect as killer and proving it in court.

This wide variety of techniques proved necessary in tracking down and securing convictions against the wide range of killers in the 1980s who varied widely in their choice of targets, methodology, motivations, and strategies for evading detection. In fact, many killings were so widely publicized that these killers even had their own nicknames and perverse followers—sometimes women who sent in marriage proposals and in a few cases later married the killer in prison. For example, among the many killers of the 1980s, there was Richard Ramirez, the Night Stalker in Los Angeles, who mysteriously entered homes to rape and murder women between 1984 and 1985; Robin Gecht, a Satanic Killer in Chicago, who went after prostitutes like Jack the Ripper between 1981 and 1982, and subjected some of them to Satanic rituals in which the women had to cut off their own breasts; Jeffrey Dahmer, the Cannibal Killer in Milwaukee, who targeted and killed at least eleven young boys starting in 1988 to 1991, cut up their bodies, and cannibalized them. There were several killers who targeted gay men, such as the Freeway Killer, Randy Kraft, who mostly killed homosexuals and military men in southern California and other states between 1982 and 1983. Raymond Copeland, in Missouri, joined his wife, Faye, in killing local transients they hired to work on the farms they owned for several years until the sheriff began investigating in 1989. Many killers targeted women, typically after they sexually assaulted them, such as Douglas Clark, called the Sunset Killer, who killed young blondes in Los Angeles with the aid of a woman named Carol Bundy, who was excited by the prospect of luring women to satisfy his compulsion and even decapitated her lover and left her children with relatives to join him.

There were also many family killers who killed their lovers and children, such as Marybeth Tinning of Schenectady, New York, who killed all nine of her own kids before they were age five by smothering them. Nurse and hospital orderly killers murdered various types of patients, including babies (Genene Jones, a nurse in a Texas hospital); elderly women (Gwendolyn Graham and Catherine Wood, nurses in a Michigan nursing home); and patients of all kinds (Donald Harvey, a hospital orderly in Cincinnati). There were killers whose lifestyle or approach to killing was so unique that there was wide public attention, such as when Joe Hunt, founder of the Billionaire Boys Club in Los Angeles, organized boys into an investment cult and killed several times for money. The mysterious Green River Killer led the police on a still unsolved manhunt for a spree killing of prostitutes dumped along the Green River in Seattle.

Perhaps most baffling and hard to solve were the Atlanta child murders in 1979–81, the bodies of elderly pensioners that turned up in the yard of a kindly old landlady named Dorothea Puente in Sacramento in 1986, and the 1985 killing in the David Brown family that was surrounded by lies and deception and initially led to the conviction of the wrong person. Following are their stories, reflecting the homicide patterns and investigative developments of the 1980s.

THE CASE OF WAYNE B. WILLIAMS

Atlanta, Georgia, 1979–81

The beginnings of what became a national manhunt involving five law enforcement agencies and national accusations about racism and Satanic cult involvement in Atlanta began quietly enough on July 28, 1979. The bodies of two young black teenagers were found in a ravine. The police simply thought it was another drug killing and did little more than identify the bodies and file the cases.

The bodies were found after a woman searching for cans and bottles smelled a foul odor in the woods and noticed a body in a tangle of kudzu vines. After she called the police, the investigators discovered the boy, who was dressed entirely in black and had been shot. About 100 yards away, they discovered a body of another teenager, also dressed in black.

There was no identifying information on the bodies. The medical examiner was nevertheless quickly able to determine the identity of the boy who had been shot—Edward Hope Smith, who had disappeared from his home several days before—by matching his teeth with his dental records. The police soon learned he had lived close to the ravine, an easy walk away.[50] They also discovered he had been killed with a .22-caliber weapon.

The second body took a little longer to identify, since there was no missing persons report on file yet. After the boy's mother filed a report with the Atlanta police, the officers soon made that connection, too. The second victim was Alfred Evans, and he had probably been strangled.

Thinking the killings drug related and with no witnesses and no active leads, the police simply filed reports and put the cases away. At the time, there was no reason for them to do otherwise.

Regrettably, such killings in Atlanta, a city of about 450,000 people at the time, with about 2 million in its greater metropolitan area, had become all too common. In 1979, the FBI's national crime statistics showed that Atlanta had become, in effect, the "murder capital of the United States," because it had more killings per capita than any other city in the country.[51] Many of these killings occurred in low-income black neighborhoods that were part of the city's underside, although outwardly, Atlanta had become a trendy, modern city, which combined recent migrants from the East Coast with its traditional Southern gentry. In fact, on the surface, the city appeared to represent a model of the new racial integration in the South, because now it had its first black mayor, Maynard Jackson, and its Public Safety Commissioner, Lee Brown, was a longtime black lawman with a doctorate in criminology.[52] Atlanta also had a growing reputation for its attractive underground shopping centers, nightclubs, and showplace hotel. Yet it had a growing problem in its inner cities, where a growing number of men were unemployed and single mothers were raising their children on their own. In despair, more of the poor were turning to drugs. In this context, the police regarded these deaths as just two more unfortunate murders probably due to drugs.

About six weeks later, in early September, fourteen-year-old Milton Harvey disappeared, and his bike was found on its side on a dusty road. Apparently, the police determined, he had not gone to school that day because he was ashamed of his old shoes. Somewhere on that dusty road, he had been abducted or enticed away. But with no further leads, his case was written up and filed too, and Harvey was never seen alive again.

Another strange disappearance occurred on October 22, when nine-year-old Yusef Bell went to a nearby store to do a favor for a neighbor, who asked him to buy a can of snuff. He never returned. Again, it was a file-and-forget case with no leads. Yusef was also poor in an area with an especially high level of homicides and an increasingly overwhelmed police force.

Thus, even when Harvey's and Bell's bodies turned up in November, nothing much was done. The first body to be discovered on November 8 was that of Yusef Bell in a maintenance trap at an abandoned school. A man had pushed his way in to urinate, and there amid shattered glass, broken boards, and plaster, he had found Yusef's body. He had been strangled, medical examiners later determined.[53] About a week later, Milton Harvey's decomposed body was found in a dump near Redwine Road in the East Point section of Atlanta. It was sprawled in the midst of rotting food and broken appliances and household goods.

The police didn't make a particular connection among these cases. There wasn't enough similar evidence, apart from the children being black. In a city of Atlanta's size, children often would run off or disappear, and unfortunately, some ended up dead. It was still nothing out of the ordinary, or so the police believed.

Starting in March 1980, the city began to wake up to the fact that something terrible was happening. The build-up of concern began on March 5, when twelve-year-old Angel Lenair set off for school but never arrived. Her body was found five days later, tied to a tree in a lot full of weeds. Her hands were tied behind her back, and the electric cord that strangled her was around her neck. Though she was fully clothed, including with her own underwear, a pair of panties belonging to someone else had been stuffed down her throat. The police initially suspected rape, but the medical examiner found no evidence that she had been sexually assaulted.[54] (Other sources suggest that there was a sexual assault, claiming that her hymen was broken and there were abrasions in the genital area, so there is some controversy over the evidence in this case.)

On March 12, ten-year-old Jefferey Mathis headed off to the store to buy a pack of cigarettes for his mother, and he disappeared, too. At this point the police were still stymied by the individual cases and hadn't yet made the connection that some or all of these cases were related. There were many differences as well as similarities among them. Just poor black children and teenagers seemed to be the common theme.

The journalists who covered the police beat began to be concerned that something terrible was happening to young black children in Atlanta. Some of them had spoken to Camille Bell, Yusef's mother, who was becoming increasingly vocal, urging the police to do something to find and arrest the person who had killed her son. She also began speaking to other parents of missing or dead black children.[55]

Finally, in mid-April came the first breakthrough in the media. Camille and other parents of these missing or dead children announced that they had formed a Committee to Stop Children's Murders. They asked for official help and recognition of the problem. In turn, the media began reporting the story, which soon went national, announcing that Atlanta's black children were "being systematically murdered."[56]

The media also described the disturbing and baffling pattern that seemed to characterize these murders. With one exception—the twelve-year-old girl tied to a tree—the victims were young, black, poor boys; most had been smothered or strangled, though the first boy found had been shot. The media noted that several of the bodies had been found in laid-out positions, with their arms folded over the chest or spread out from the shoulders, which suggested maybe the killer deliberately laid them out after death.[57]

The result was a rising alarm about what was happening, which included fears that these attacks were racially motivated or that evil cultists were behind the murders. One of the wildest charges was expressed by Dick Gregory, a comedian turned social activist, who warned there might be some kind of conspiracy involving the U.S. Centers for Disease Control, based in Atlanta, to take the blood of black children to manufacture interferon, a substance that was believed to help in treating cancer and herpes. As Gregory suggested, the blood of the children might be desirable for this purpose, because sickle cells found in the blood of some blacks was the best source of this ingredient.[58]

Others began to spread the story that the children had been kidnapped by an insane person or religious cult member who washed and cleaned their bodies and killed them in a sacrificial ritual. Some began to think there were two or more killers on the loose, either inspired by the earlier killings or part of a group out to kill children. Meanwhile, a rising chorus of voices began to accuse the members of Atlanta's power structure of a lack of concern about poor black children, so they weren't properly pursuing their killer, whereas they would have if the victims were white.

Even with all this hysteria, the killings continued. The next victim, fourteen-year-old Eric Middlebrooks, was found bludgeoned to death by a blunt-force blow to his head on May 19. He had gotten a telephone call a few hours before his body was found. Presumably, whoever had killed him had lured him to his death.

About three weeks later, on June 9, twelve-year old Christopher Richardson disappeared as he headed to a neighborhood swimming pool. Though his body wasn't found for eight months, near the body of another victim, his disappearance raised immediate alarm in light of the previous morbid discoveries.

Only two weeks after that, on June 22, the second young girl linked to the chain of killings, seven-year-old LaTonya Wilson, was taken from her bed late at night. It was the night before her eighth birthday. When investigators arrived at the apartment where she lived with her family, they found a window pane had been removed, allowing the kidnapper to get in. Could she have possibly been transported across state lines? That possibility made the child disappearances and killings a federal offense, and so was the beginning of FBI involvement in the growing national uproar. Until the end of July, the FBI was just involved quietly monitoring the situation, making sure it had the jurisdiction to enter. In quick succession there were several more murders—and the bodies were found more quickly, suggesting that the killer was becoming bolder—perhaps even enjoying this tantalizing "you can't catch me" game with the police, as the media coverage steamed up.

The next to be discovered dead on June 24 was ten-year-old Aaron Wyche, whose body was found under a bridge in DeKalb County, only a few miles outside Atlanta. His death was listed as due to asphyxia and a broken neck. At first, his death was described as accidental, presumably because he had fallen off the bridge and landed in a position that prevented him from breathing. His family members insisted from the beginning that this was no accident, because Aaron wouldn't play on a bridge—he was very afraid of heights. Several months later his name was added to the growing victim list.

On July 6 came the next gruesome discovery—the body of nine-year-old Anthony "Tony" Carter was discovered lying face-down on the grass. He had been killed by multiple stab wounds, but a lack of blood at the scene indicated that his body had been moved from somewhere else. All the police knew was that he had been playing with a friend in the neighborhood before he mysteriously disappeared.

The pressure on the police to make the connection and do something to find the killer grew. At this point, some local activists claimed that the killings were done by a white man or group of white men who had decided to get rid of the city's black children in a kind of mini-Holocaust. Perhaps it was even a Ku Klux Klan squad. Some thought the reason might be to kill off these children before they could grow up and reproduce. Such thinking was further inflamed when a day care center in Atlanta blew up, killing a black teacher and four of her black charges. Though the blast turned out to be due to a faulty gas furnace, the hysteria turned up the heat even more on finding the killer(s) of the children. In response, the police tried investigating a well-known local Klansman and some of his associates, but they found nothing.

In fact, the police were quite sure the killings weren't being done by a white man or group of white men, because there had been so much publicity about the murders by this time. Thus, it seemed unlikely—virtually impossible—that any white man could be moving around an up-in-arms black community kidnapping and killings kids.[59] Yet beyond being sure that the killer wasn't a white man, the police didn't have a clue.

Meanwhile, Mayor Jackson and Brown decided it was time to take some action to stop these devastating attacks that were panicking the city. Among other things, Jackson announced a strict 7 p.m. to 6 a.m. curfew for all children under age sixteen and offered a reward of $100,000 leading to the arrest and conviction of whoever was responsible for the murders.

Various national celebrities stepped in to contribute money or star power to the investigation. Among them was heavyweight boxing champion Muhammad Ali, who, along with corporate and private donors, added to the reward fund, increasing it to $500,000. There was a gala benefit concert, headed up by top singers Sammy Davis Jr. and Frank Sinatra that raised $250,000. Schoolchildren, housewives, and even prison inmates contributed small sums, and one former Klan leader, David Duke, offered to donate a $1,400 speech fee because he was concerned that the investigation would lead to retaliatory violence against white people.[60] Meanwhile, the growing list of victims raised more controversy because critics felt the list did not include all the victims or included children who weren't victimized by the same killer.

The killings were convulsing the city. To help cool fears and divisions, Jackson and Brown finally created a special Task Force on Missing and Murdered Children, after meeting with some of the victims' mothers, to help assist in the investigation. Eventually, this new organization came to include nearly fifty investigators from eight police and government agencies, including members of the Centers for Disease Control and county health experts, to look for common characteristics of the victims, which might both provide clues to the killer as well as provide a warning for other potential victims at risk. Meanwhile, the victims' mothers and others joined with a local minister to do what they could to keep other children from being victimized. This was the Committee to Stop Children's Murders (STOP).[61]

For all this furor, the killings continued. The next incident occurred on July 31, when eleven-year-old Earl Terrell was reported missing near Redwine Road, where Milton Harvey's body was found. The night this happened, Earl had gone swimming at a public pool with several friends, but a lifeguard had thrown him out after he began teasing some girls by the side of the pool. He never returned home. The police weren't able to immediately find him, but his disappearance did lead to something of a break permitting the FBI to finally officially enter the case. This occurred because the night Earl vanished, his family received several telephone calls from a man who said he was holding Earl in Alabama and offering to return him if they paid $200. The caller said he would call back with more details. He never did call back, but the claim of holding Earl in Alabama meant that the state lines were actually crossed, not just hypothesized as when LaTonya was taken out of her bed through a window. Now the FBI could step in. Although it soon became apparent that the ransom calls had been a hoax, and thus the FBI should step back out, several weeks later the FBI was called back in—this time for good. The FBI profilers, including John Douglas and Robert Ressler, played a major role in breaking the case.

As the FBI wavered over whether to get involved, the media and public went crazy, turning the case into an international sensation. There was even speculation that the disappearance or death of children in Europe and Japan might be somehow connected.[62] In Atlanta, the public frenzy resulted in a flurry of local developments. One effort was a police-led "Kids Don't Go With Strangers" campaign to remind children to be wary. Continuing monetary contributions continued to arrive from individuals and business and community groups. Ministers and lay leaders led prayer vigils in Atlanta and other communities around the nation. In Atlanta over 3,000 citizen volunteers of all races and ages participated in sweeps to look through any off-the-beaten track areas where the missing children might be—whether held hostage or dead. They tracked through vacant lots strewn with garbage, dilapidated housing projects, and ravines full of weeds and vines. One such search turned up the skeletal remains of LaTonya Wilson in an abandoned lot, four months after she had been abducted.

Finally, in September, after another body—that of thirteen-year-old Clifford Jones—was found strangled in an alley, the police finally agreed there was a connection between all these deaths. As urged by the media and public, they planned an organized investigation based on the assumption that all the murders were related.[63] On September 16, after ten-year-old Darron Glass was reported missing (though he had previously run away from several foster homes), Mayor Jackson formally asked the White House to have the FBI investigate and help solve these murders, regardless of whether there was a jurisdictional question of authority.

In turn, the frenzy over whether there was a conspiracy to commit genocide in the black community, possibly by the Ku Klux Klan or Nazis, gave the FBI another basis on which to assert jurisdiction, even if there was no interstate kidnapping involved. There could be a violation of federal civil rights, although the FBI, like the police, didn't think the killings were racist at all, because serial murders are normally personal crimes, not political ones. Also, though the overwhelming majority of serial killers have been white, almost always these killers choose victims of their own race. Both the police and FBI investigators felt it was likely the killer or killers were black.

In the meantime, before the FBI was in full swing, there were a few other intriguing developments. After nationally known psychic Dorothy Allison appeared on the *Phil Donahue* TV show on December 9, talking about how she could help solve the killings, there was public pressure on the police to bring her to Atlanta. They did so in October, causing another media circus. At a press conference after she arrived, she announced, "I can guarantee he won't murder while I'm here. I will control him. I have seen who he is. I see where he is. I follow him."[64] She described the killer as a black male, and though she vowed to stay in Atlanta until he was caught, she left three days later. The police still had no suspects, but she had correctly determined the killer was black, as the police and FBI believed. She also claimed to have given the police detailed descriptions of two suspects. At least there were no new reports of missing or murdered children in the few days she was in Atlanta.

Soon after Allison's departure was noted in the media, there were several more killings, including twelve-year-old Charles Stephens and nine-year-old Aaron Jackson. In November, sixteen-year-old Patrick Rogers, who sold newspapers for extra spending money, was found dead.[65] The FBI finally and quietly entered the case.

To start its investigation, which the FBI dubbed ATKID or Major Case 30, John Douglas and Roy Hazelwood flew down to Atlanta. They were selected as the most active profilers of the Behavioral Science Unit. Hazelwood was teaching a course on interpersonal violence and handling many of the rape cases of the unit—he was ideal for handling a case where there might be sexual overtones involved.[66]

Initially, the FBI wanted to keep its own role low-key to avoid stealing the show from the Atlanta police or creating too high expectations that they might not be able to meet, as profiling was still relatively new.[67] As Douglas describes it, he and Hazelwood began by reviewing the material in the huge case files the police had already gathered. These files included crime-scene photos, descriptions of what each child was wearing when found, statements from witnesses in the area, and autopsy protocols.[68] In addition, they interviewed the children's family members to look for common patterns that might have led the children to become victims. They also were taken to visit the neighborhoods where the children had disappeared and to each site where the bodies had been dumped.

Assuming the mind hunter point of view, Douglas and Hazelwood separately took psychometric tests given by a forensic psychologist in which they put themselves in the mind of the killer and then took the test. They answered questions about the killer's motivation, background, and family life—and significantly, both Douglas and Hazelwood answered much the same way.

Their basic conclusions were these were not racist-inspired hate crimes, and the killer was almost certainly black. They also felt that although many deaths and disappearances were related, not all of them were.[69] Their reason for taking this viewpoint is that most hate crimes tend to be very public, highly symbolic acts in which the perpetrators want to make a public statement or display and draw attention to their cause. But these were quiet, hidden types of crimes. They felt the killer was black because the body dump sites were in areas of the city that were largely or exclusively black. If a white killer was prowling around the neighborhood, enticing children to leave with him or dumping their bodies, surely he would have been seen. Even after the police conducted extensive interviews in these areas, no one reported seeing any whites near any of the children or dump sites. There was street activity in most of these areas around the clock, even at night—a white man would have probably been noticed. In short, all the signs pointed to what is usually true about serial or sexual killers—they tend to choose victims from their own race. Though Douglas and Hazelwood hadn't yet seen any clear evidence of sexual molestation, they thought these crimes fit a sexual pattern.[70]

They noticed certain characteristics of the victims that might make them vulnerable to a man in a car who picked them up and took them away. As they recognized, the victims were all "young and outgoing and streetwise, but inexperienced and rather naive about the world beyond their neighborhood."[71] Many lived in impoverished conditions, some in houses with no electricity or running water. As a result, a child might be susceptible to a come-on or con and be willing to leave with a convincing adult who had an aura of authority. In fact, when Douglas and Hazelwood did a test where Atlanta undercover officers went into the area posing as workmen and offered the children $5 to come with them to do a job, the kids went willingly. It seemed likely that the victims had been willing to go somewhere with a stranger—only they happened to pick a killer.

On the other hand, Douglas and Hazelwood felt that the two girls had been killed by the same man because the style of killing them was different—especially the unusual way that LaTonya Wilson had been abducted from her bedroom. Evidence in a couple of other cases suggested that the killer had been a member of the victim's family. But it wasn't very popular to try to distinguish the killings in this way, and when FBI director William Webster tried to do this by making a public announcement, he was attacked for doing so.[72] Perhaps it was easier to imagine pursuing a single killer—and the families of victims might be cut out of the funds coming in from around the country for the Atlanta child murder victims.

In any event, despite the possible existence of several killers, Douglas and Hazelwood came up with a profile of the primary suspect—a black male, single, between the ages of twenty-five and twenty-nine. They imagined that he would be "a police buff, drive a police-type vehicle, and somewhere along the way he would insinuate himself into the investigation."[73] They further believed he would not have a girlfriend and would be attracted to young boys. However, because they didn't see any definitive signs of rape or other overt sexual abuse, they felt he might be sexually inadequate. As for the ruse or con he used to lure the kids, they thought it might have something to do with music or performing, but then he couldn't produce results. Soon the kid would reject him or he would think they had, leading him to feel angry, rejected, and motivated to kill.[74]

Unfortunately, at this early stage of the investigation, this profile could fit thousands of men living in the Atlanta area. In fact, after the Atlanta PD checked their database of all known pedophiles or men with prior sexual offenses, they had a list of about 1,500 suspects.

Another tack was contacting children to see if any of them had been approached by a suspicious stranger. To this end, both police officers and FBI agents went to schools and asked children if any adult male stranger might have approached them and they didn't tell their parents or the police. They also rode around on buses, passing out flyers with photos of the missing children and asking if anyone had seen them. Some undercover officers even went to gay bars to listen in on conversations for leads.[75]

Then came what seemed like a break. Someone called the police department of Conyers, a small town about twenty miles east of Atlanta, saying he was the Atlanta child killer. Besides mentioning the name of the most recently discovered victim, he promised to kill more "nigger kids," and said that the police could find another body on a particular spot in the county. Though the police were excited, Douglas was dubious, thinking this was just another caller playing on the hysteria and trying to taunt the police. Just in case, Douglas told the police to go to the road but search the opposite side of where the caller directed them. His theory was the man would be watching and would call back to say how dumb the police were, which is exactly what happened. When he called back, the police were also ready to trace his call. They found a very embarrassed older white man. When they checked the correct area of the road just to make sure, there was, of course, no body.[76] It was one of many red herrings that plagued this case.

Then there came what seemed to be another break. On the theory that many serial killers return to the scenes of their crimes and dump sites, FBI detectives searched through the woods near where the earliest remains were found and discovered a girlie magazine. Was this left by the child killer? The detectives sent the magazine off to the FBI lab, which lifted latent fingerprints and got an ID, which led to a white male with a van who worked as an exterminator. He seemed like a good candidate to many, particularly because if he was an exterminator, perhaps he imagined taking his work one step further to kill black children. Perhaps, as some detectives imagined, he had pulled along the side of his car to look out over his conquest, and then masturbated while recalling what he previously did.[77] According to Douglas, excitement in the FBI grew as news of the man's arrest spread. The FBI director, along with the attorney general and the White House, were ready to announce that the Atlanta child killer had finally been caught. After they questioned the man, he first denied everything. When confronted with his semen and fingerprints on the magazine, he guiltily broke down and confessed how he had bought the magazine since his wife was almost nine months pregnant and he hadn't had sex for months. Rather than cheat on his wife, he had gone to the woods, hoping to achieve some relief in private.[78]

Among all the publicity given the investigation, including the red herrings, the investigators finally got their first real break. Though the original heavily reported search on Sigman Road turned up nothing, in January 1981, another body turned up in open view on Sigman Road—that of fifteen-year-old Terry Pue. It's as if the killer put it there to be found, if he had been following the investigation in the press and wanted to taunt the press and police with how superior he is, because "he *can* dump a body along Sigman Road if he wants to."[79] To Douglas, this response meant that the killer had broken his pattern to drive twenty to thirty miles from his usual dumping grounds to taunt the police and play a game. Unfortunately, it was too late to do what Douglas now realized they might have done—staked out the general area along Sigman Road, thinking that with all the publicity the killer might come back to claim the site as his own. Knowing the killer was following the case, perhaps there might be some way to use this information to track him down.

As Douglas thought about the ways profiling might be applied in this way, another major development occurred that would lead to the killer—as well as lead him to change his usual modus operandi. In early February, as reporters continued to hype the latest developments, and several psychics shared their observations with the police and the press, including Jeane Dixon, who told the

New York Post on February 16, that she was trying to "psych out the Atlanta killer,"[80] still another body turned up. It was the body of eleven-year-old Patrick Baltazar, found in DeKalb County on the Burford highway. Significantly, detectives found hair and fibers on his body, and after the medical examiner's office announced that these matched those found on five previous victims, the news received wide coverage.[81]

At once, Douglas sensed that this would lead the killer to change his strategy. As he reasoned, the killer would realize that if the bodies he left on the roads or in the woods still had hair and fiber evidence, he had to do something different to avoid leaving such evidence in the future. "He's going to start dumping bodies in the river," Douglas concluded. He urged the FBI to set up a surveillance of the rivers around the city of Atlanta, especially along the Chattahoochee, the major waterway on the northern boundary of the city between Atlanta and Cobb County, on the opposite side from DeKalb and Rockdale Counties.

Unfortunately, it took the FBI until April to organize and get approval for such a surveillance operation with the police jurisdictions for each surrounding county. In the meantime, just as Douglas predicted, the next body—of thirteen-year-old Curtis Walker—turned up later in February in one of the rivers, South River. And whereas the previous victims had been fully clothed when found, his body was stripped to his underwear, which could be a way of removing hair and fiber evidence.

As all Atlanta was left waiting to learn where and when the next body would turn up, the *Atlanta Constitution* and the *Atlanta Journal* received some taunting letters from someone claiming to be the child killer, and a minister near the site where one of the bodies was found reported receiving some anonymous phone calls from someone making the same claim. Was it the real killer or just another crazy? It was hard to tell if the letters and calls were even connected. But the letters were filled with bits of police jargon, leading many to believe that the killer was a policeman or someone posing as an officer to gain the children's trust. Or was he winning the trust in some other way?

The frustration of not knowing and waiting for the killer to strike again was maddening. Atlanta was in a near panic. As Clifford Linedecker describes it,

> The terror was building. Mothers sent their children outside with whistles around their necks in case they needed help. Atlanta youngsters were skipping school more often than ever before. They wet the bed, awoke shrieking with terrible nightmares. . . . Whites hesitated to venture into black neighborhoods, apprehensive that they would be accused of being the killer. Red-jacketed vigilantes from the Atlanta Youth Against Crime began helping police patrol the streets and shopping malls. . . . Fear was pervasive throughout the city.[82]

The killings went on. As if to confirm Douglas's prediction, two more bodies turned up in the river at the end of March, this time the Chattahoochee. Like Walker's body, they were stripped to their underwear.[83] They were the bodies of thirteen-year-old Timothy Hill and twenty-one-year-old Eddie Duncan. Though Duncan was much older than the others, investigators learned he had been mentally retarded, perhaps making him more vulnerable to the killer's enticements than others of that age, like one other twenty-one-year-old, Larry Rogers, who was also added to the list of victims.

At least by mid-April, the joint surveillance operation of FBI and Homicide Task Force Personnel from the police departments in various jurisdictions around the Atlanta area was approved. They began watching the bridges and potential dump sites along the river. After a month of long days and nights of nothing happening, by mid-May the authorities were beginning to feel the operation were fruitless and were close to shutting it down. The only things that had turned up were two more bodies in the Chattahoochee River. One was the nude body of twenty-three-year-old Michael McIntosh, who was also older than the earlier victims. He was only five feet, five inches tall and weighed only about 100 pounds—about the size of several of the teenage victims. He was described as "mentally slow"— perhaps his small size and low intelligence contributed to making him vulnerable. A week after that, the body of Jimmy Ray Payne, twenty-one, was pulled from the river, similarly undressed.

On another front, some members of the Task Force had been looking at various names that surfaced as possible suspects. One whose background seemed especially intriguing was a young black male in his early twenties named Wayne B. Williams, with a quiet, almost nerdy, pudgy bespectacled look. He had a background much like that profiled by the FBI. He was very intelligent, something of a "media whiz" and "police groupie" who lived with his parents, Homer and Faye Williams, who were retired schoolteachers, in a middle-class area of northwest Atlanta. In high school, he had won some local acclaim for constructing and operating his own low-powered radio station from the basement of his parents' home, and by age twenty-two he had become a kind of entrepreneur, using his skills as an electronic and media consultant, freelance news photographer, and music producer.[84] In fact, many Atlanta police officers and journalists already knew him as someone who drove around the city at night with a police scanner to pick up emergency calls about fires, accidents, and crimes. He would drove to the scene and take photos, which he sold to the media. In one case, he was arrested for impersonating a police officer after he used flashing red lights to go to a call. Eventually the charge was resolved in traffic court as the unauthorized use of emergency lights.

There was one other thing about Williams that intrigued the task force given the FBI profile that the killer might have an interest in music or performing. Williams had been trying to contact aspiring musicians, promoting himself as someone who managed and produced professional recording artists. The police had found copies of Williams's flyers about his efforts as a producer and promoter among the possessions of four of the murder victims. The task force members also learned that Williams had organized a black singing group called Gemini, so named because that was Williams's own astrological sign. Could that be the way Williams might be luring the children to follow him—promising them the chance to become famous and gain wealth as the next big hit group, like the Jackson Five?[85]

Before they could even pursue this lead, the task force was about to be shut down. All they had so far were more bodies and speculations about possible leads that looked interesting. Thus, the authorities decided to close it down, and the operation was scheduled to end with the 6 a.m. shift change on May 22, 1981.

At 2:30 that morning, on that last surveillance shift by the banks of the Chattahoochee River, a police academy recruit named Bob Campbell heard a loud splash. He heard it as he was walking under the Jackson Parkway bridge and noticed a car drive across and briefly stop in the middle of the span. Moments later he heard the splash. Quickly, he called it in on his walkie talkie and pointed his flashlight at the water, noticing a few ripples. Up on the roadway, a member of the stakeout team in a patrol car who got the call headed toward the bridge and saw the car, a green station wagon, pull off the bridge and drive into a liquor store parking lot. Apparently seeing the police car, the driver of the station wagon turned and headed across the bridge in the opposite direction, slowly at first, and then speeding up. An FBI agent in a second car joined the pursuit, and a few minutes later, they pulled the car over.

In the car was Wayne Williams. He acted friendly and cooperative, like nothing was wrong and he was surprised to be stopped. During questioning, he told the police he was a music promoter and lived with his parents. The policed looked through his car. Seeing nothing suspicious, they let him go.

However, the FBI and police decided to keep a close watch on Williams, beginning an around-the-clock surveillance on him. As they did, two days after Campbell heard the splash, the nude body of twenty-seven-year-old Nathaniel Cater came to the surface of the water downstream of the Jackson Parkway Bridge and near where Payne had bobbed to the surface about a month earlier. Though detectives thought the location and condition of the body could mean it was the same one dropped from the bridge, and the medical examiner reported that the man could have died before his body was dumped in the river, there still wasn't enough evidence to arrest Williams and get a search warrant. The nexus between the splash, the body, and finding Williams's car on the bridge just wasn't close enough to be the necessary probable cause.

Now came the waiting game. The police and the FBI stepped up surveillance, with several cars following Williams when he left his house. Small airplanes and helicopters were even part of the chase sometimes.

Not surprisingly, Williams was soon very aware that the police were following him, and like a fox in a hunt, he playfully led them on several wild goose chases around the city.[86] At one point, he led them to the street in front of Public Safety Commissioner Lee Brown's house and started honking his horn as he waited for them to catch up. It was as if he was basking in the public attention.

As the police and FBI gathered enough information to get a warrant, it looked like Williams might be taking some steps to get rid of incriminating evidence. One day in his backyard, detectives observed him burning photos. They also saw him wash out his car.

At this point, Douglas was strongly convinced that Williams was the right one because he fit the killer profile he and Hazelwood had developed "in every key respect." Williams even owned a German shepherd, as they imagined, and was an eager police buff. He had once been arrested for impersonating a law officer and after that had "driven a surplus police vehicle and used police scanners to get to crime scenes to take pictures."[87]

Still not quite ready to make a formal arrest, FBI agents asked Williams to come to the office for an interview. It was, according to Douglas, done in a too heavy-handed and direct manner, although Williams was cooperative and didn't ask for an attorney. He even agreed to a polygraph, which proved inconclusive. From the reports he read later, Douglas was convinced Williams would never confess.[88] His cooperation with the police and eagerness to stay on after the formal interview to talk about police and FBI matters was all part of his game and his interest in the investigation and the police.

Finally, on June 3, the police and FBI got their warrant to search Williams's home and car. They impounded his car, and although Williams had washed it out, they found hair and fibers linking him to about a dozen of the murders—the ones that Douglas had profiled as all being committed by the same killer.[89] In fact, not only did the hair and fibers create a link between Williams's room, house, car, and some of the bodies, but further testing by the Georgia State Crime Lab found even more damning evidence—some of the fibers found matched that from the clothing some of the victims had worn before they disappeared. Among other things, they found green, yellow, and purple fibers from carpet samples, sweepings, blankets, and clothing in Williams's home, as well as dog hairs, which had turned up on several of the victims' bodies.

Meanwhile, as the police and FBI checked the evidence they had gathered in their labs, Williams continued his game with the press. On the morning the warrant was executed, Williams stood in front of his house at 7 a.m. giving an informal press conference. He distributed copies of his résumé and gave his explanation for why he was on the bridge on 2:30 a.m. May 22—he was looking for a woman vocalist he expected to interview early that morning for a singing audition later that afternoon. He simply wanted to find her address before he returned home. "And I have nothing to do with the murders," he insisted, claiming the police, FBI, and press were slandering him.[90]

On June 21, Williams was arrested for the murder of Nathaniel Cater, the victim whose body had made such a splash in the Chattahoochee; a few days later, first-degree murder charges were filed against him for the death of Jimmy Ray Payne, whose body had also been found in the Chattahoochee.

This was the beginning of the end game for the Atlanta child murders. After Williams's arrest, the killings stopped, and the furor in Atlanta subsided. Douglas, Hazelwood, and other investigators were sure they had their man—for at least twelve of the killings and perhaps as many as two dozen, though Williams was only tried for two. Ironically, these were for two men in their twenties.

At the trial, which began in late January 1981, Douglas and Hazelwood weren't able to testify about the results of their profiling techniques as to modus operandi, signature, or case linkage, though they do routinely do so since profiling has become more accepted. At the time profiling wasn't yet recognized by the courts, so they could only advise the prosecutors on strategy or, if there was a conviction, give a professional opinion on the defendant's dangerousness on the future.[91] As an adviser Douglas was right there for most of the trial, sitting directly behind the prosecution table.

Williams did his best to claim his innocence, using a high-profile legal defense team, which included Jim Kitchens and Al Binder from Jackson, Mississippi, and Mary Welcome from Atlanta. In the end, the evidence against him was overwhelming. It included about 700 pieces of hair and fiber evidence that had been carefully analyzed to show linkages with the victims. In addition, although Williams was only being tried for two murders, the law in Georgia permitted the prosecutors to bring in linked cases. So they brought in testimony about the deaths of ten other victims on the task force's list to show that the killings were part of a pattern.[92]

Probably the biggest problem for the prosecution, headed up by Prosecutor Gordon Miller, was that Williams simply didn't look like a killer. He was, as Douglas describes him, "mild-mannered, controlled, well-spoken, and friendly. With his thick glasses, soft features, and delicate hands, he looked more like the Pillsbury Doughboy than a serial killer of children."[93] During the trial, Williams tried to tap public sympathy by claiming that he was completely innocent and his arrest was due to racial reasons. He even gave an interview to the press just before the trial began in which he compared the FBI to the Keystone Kops and the Atlanta police to *Car 54, Where Are You?*[94]

The prosecution tried to turn Williams's own racial accusations around by portraying him as an intelligent, ambitious young man who hated his own race so much that he was hostile to other blacks and that he was a homosexual or bisexual who paid boys to have sex with him. They brought in one witness to testify that Williams used derogatory names to describe other blacks; they found another who claimed he saw Williams holding hands with Cater only a few hours before Williams was found on the bridge from where the prosecutors claimed he dumped Cater's body.[95] The prosecutors painted Williams as someone who killed because he enjoyed the challenge and his ability to outwit the huge task force trying to find him. It helped that when Williams himself took the stand, portraying himself as the innocent victim of a racially biased system that needed a suspect, the prosecution was quickly able to wear him down. They broke through his soft-spoken, controlled veneer and got him to erupt in anger after the prosecutor kept drilling, asking him again and again: "Did you panic, Wayne, when you killed those kids? . . . What was it like when you wrapped your fingers around the victim's throat? Did you panic? Did you panic?"[96] For a few moments, Williams went into a rage, yelling about FBI goons, calling the prosecution team fools, and accusing Douglas of trying to "make me fit that FBI profile, and I'm not going to help you do it!"[97] He caught himself, but the image of innocence had been shattered.

Most of all, the hair and fiber evidence sealed the case against him. As Prosecutor Miller stressed in his closing argument after a nine-week trial, the combination of fiber match-ups created odds of 1 in 150 million, which was so significant it was like a signature, "just as if the defendant had signed his name on the death warrants" of his victims.[98]

Finally, on February 27, 1982, the jury returned its guilty verdict on both murders, and Williams was sentenced to two consecutive life terms. He was sent to the Valdosta Correctional Institution in the south of Georgia to serve them. He maintains his innocence, but he is there today, still trying to win a new trial.[99]

In fact, since 2005 there have been some new developments, according to postings in the Wikipedia. On May 6, 2005, DeKalb County, Georgia, Police Chief Louis Graham reopened the murder cases of four boys killed in DeKalb County between February and May, 1981 that were attributed to Williams, believing that Williams may be innocent of all of the murders. The remaining cases in Fulton County, Georgia, however, are still considered closed by authorities. On June 21, 2006, DeKalb County police dropped their reinvestigation of the Atlanta child murders shortly after Graham resigned and was replaced by acting chief Nick Marinelli, who felt that nothing panned out in the reinvestigation. The case is still being appealed by Williams's lawyer Jack Martin, who in January 2007 got lawyers for the state of Georgia to allow DNA testing of dog hair that was used to convict Wayne Williams in order to seek a new trial.

THE CASE OF DOROTHEA PUENTE

Sacramento, California, 1982–88

When the first boarders who lived at 1426 F Street in Sacramento disappeared in 1986—or maybe it was 1987, or maybe the year or two before—no one really seemed to notice. After all they were drifters, homeless persons, alcoholics, derelicts suffering from mental illness or drug addiction. Most had few or no ties with family members; they had lost touch with old friends. There was no one to pay attention to them, except the kindly, prim-looking lady with pulled-back white hair and spectacles who looked liked a sweet, gentle grandmother. Her name was Dorothea Puente, and she had gained a reputation in the Hispanic community for her good works as "la Doctera," ministering to the down and out, and for her contributions to many different charities. She had been photographed with powerful politicians, including Governor Jerry Brown, and had developed close ties with social workers and welfare workers, who saw her boarding house as a home of last resort for difficult-to-place clients who had little hope or future—just a small Social Security check, disability benefit, or veterans pension to see them through. These boarders had gone to 1426 F Street, where they were cleaned up, served home-cooked meals, and given medications to treat their various illnesses. Many of them disappeared—but no one knew or cared.

This was a time when it was easy for the poor and down-and-out to get lost in America, especially in California. The dispossessed were easy to overlook at this time because the mid-1980s was at the height of the Reagan years, when wealth and success were celebrated, and the war on drugs was at its height. Through the early 1980s, consumer spending had gone hog-wild, making the United States officially the world's largest debtor nation, with a deficit of $130 billion in 1985. Wall Street financiers and acquisitions and merger specialists had become popular heroes, although some, like Ivan Boesky, who pled guilty to insider trading in 1986, went a little too far, leading to a government crack-down. First Lady Nancy Reagan was known for her stylish dresses; the Reagans made a prime-time antidrug television special that was part of the "Just Say No" campaign. Pop singer Madonna gained fame more for her lavish, extravagant, and flashy lifestyle than for her singing; films like *Ruthless People* looked at doing anything to get to the top in a kind of envious way laced with humor. In 1987, the same push to gain admiration by doing well was reflected in such events as the sale of the world's three most expensive paintings, all by Van Gogh, at prices from $19 to $49 million.

There was a dark side to all this focus on acquiring money, reflected in the growing number of scandals involving big-time fraud—from insider trading and banking scandals to the fall of Rev. Jim Bakker after his adultery with a church secretary exposed how he used his church ministry at the PTL Club to defraud his members of millions of dollars. In fact, films like *Wall Street* showed the dangers of being caught up by the pull of greed; it destroyed personal relationships as well as a person given over to greed himself. This rush to achieve, spurred on by national and state legislation that promoted deregulation, meant that there was much less of a safety net for those at the bottom who didn't make it. There was simply less money for government-provided support services for the mentally ill, impoverished, and addicted. There was not much interest in the private sector in picking up the slack. The mid-1980s marked the spreading growth of a homeless problem in the cities of America, as the down and out fell further to the bottom.

It was a problem especially true of California, where the population had long been more rootless and spurred by personal dreams than the rest of the country, especially when legislation shut down mental health facilities and pushed a growing mentally ill population out into the community. They joined the poor, alcoholic, and addicted among the homeless in the underbelly of a wealth-seeking America of the 1980s.

There were always some kindly souls to reach out to the poorest of the poor, like Dorothea Puente of Sacramento. Unfortunately, Puente wasn't exactly the kindly grandmother helping the poor and homeless like she seemed to be. For many years, no one really knew what she was doing.

The first time anyone began to ask questions was in 1988, when Judy Moise, a street counselor working with the Volunteers of America's (VOA) Courtesy Outreach Program, began to worry about one of her charges, Bert Montoya, who lived at 1426 F Street. Moise was assigned to the detox unit, essentially the VOA's Central Reception Center, a long metal building in downtown Sacramento, where drunks could go to chill out after they were found drunk in public, instead of going to jail.[100] After a couple of nights, they could leave. It was a way to save the public money as well as divert the drunks out of the criminal justice system. Judy first met Bert, a shambling gray-haired man with missing teeth, one day after she started working for the VOA in spring 1986. He was standing on the sidewalk in front of the building, having a conversation with imaginary spirits in a graveyard. He was telling them, "Get out of here! Keep away from me!"[101] As Judy soon learned, Bert, about age fifty, had been confronting these demons for about thirty years. He wasn't an alcoholic; in fact, aside from an infrequent beer, he didn't even drink. However, he was delusional, perhaps even retarded, and there was something about his sweet, gentle manner that made Judy want to help him. He helped out doing chores at the detox center and became something of a mascot.[102]

Bert didn't really belong at detox, since he wasn't an alcoholic. He was there because he had no money, and had no money because he had no Social Security number. Judy was determined to help him, and making him her personal mission, she finally managed to track down his original birth certificate and get him a Social Security number in early 1988. When she looked for someplace to put him, another street counselor helping the elderly homeless had a suggestion—a "good clean boarding house" run by Dorothea Puente, who was willing to take difficult, down-at-the-heels types.[103]

Judy and another VOA worker Beth Valentine, thought everything looked fine. The house at 1426 F Street was a clean, well-tended, blue-and-white, two-story Victorian, and the grandmotherly Puente who greeted them at the door seemed caring and compassionate as they sat around drinking coffee. Puente talked about being a nurse and cooking both breakfast and dinner for her guests. As she explained, she lived upstairs and the guests downstairs, but they came up for meals. She emphasized that "I'm not in this business for the money . . . I don't need the money. It's just that life has been good to me, and this is my way of giving something back."[104] Judy and Beth were also impressed seeing the framed awards that Puente had received from contributing to Hispanic causes; when she took them on a tour of the house, they felt reassured by the sturdy and clean furnishings, the large number of televisions in many of the rooms, and the well-kept yard. It seemed very inviting with many flowering plants and shrubs and its vegetable garden. There were also attractive decorations like a ceramic cherub, a small windmill, and a religious figure in front that looked like a shrine.[105]

In moments, Judy and Beth decided it would be an ideal place for Bert, and when they brought him over that afternoon, he seemed to warm up to Mrs. Puente. On February 3, 1988, he moved in. It seemed like the beginning of a wonderful new life in a warm setting. When Judy and Beth came to visit over the next few weeks, Bert seemed to be thriving. Before, his hair looked shaggy and matted, and he had chronic psoriasis. But that cleared up. He also seemed to be talking less to his spirits and was more grounded, especially since Dorothea got him to start taking his antipsychotic medication again. She cooked for him and got him to church every Sunday.[106] She also seemed to be well organized generally, keeping track of her tenants' appointments with doctors, social workers, and dentists, and taking care of chores, laundry, and shopping herself.[107]

It seemed to be an ideal arrangement. Others who knew Dorothea Puente during this time were certainly impressed, such as Patty Casey, a cab driver Dorothea often used to go on errands. As Patty noticed, Bert sometimes called Dorothea "Mama," and he helped her out by carrying supplies or lifting heavy things for her. It was as if Puente had taken Bert under her wing and treated him like a son, and he thrived under her care.

Nothing seemed particularly unusual when Dorothea took Bert to the Social Security Office and had him make her the payee for his Social Security checks. As she explained, he was mentally retarded and had trouble managing his own money. On the form she wrote down that she was his cousin. No one bothered to check if she was; it seemed like another routine application, and in due process it was approved. Dorothea would now receive Bert's checks of $637 each month—just as she did for many of her other boarders.[108]

Starting in April, Judy began to become suspicious that something strange was going on. She started to dig up some disturbing information about Dorothea, which led to some gruesome discoveries at the placid-looking Victorian home. By then it was too late to save Bert.

The first inkling something was wrong came when two social workers—Mary Ellen Howard from the welfare department and Polly Spring from Adult Protective Services—asked Judy and Beth to meet with them to discuss an unusual problem that had just happened to a client they had temporarily placed at Dorothea Puente's boarding house. Apparently, Dorothea had kicked him out and he was living somewhere else. When Mary Ellen called Dorothea to try to work things out, Dorothea had cursed her angrily and hung up. The response had been so surprising that Mary Ellen began thinking about another landlady, also named Dorothea, who had had some problems years before. After she did some checking, a former social worker, Mildred Ballenger, provided the details. The landlady's full name was Dorothea Johansson, and she had spent time in prison in the early 1980s for victimizing elderly boarders. Mildred had alerted the authorities, and *Sacramento* magazine had done an article, "Unsung Heroes," describing how Mildred had alerted the authorities leading to her arrest.[109]

Judy was amazed. Could Dorothea Puente be the same person? It seemed incredible to think the sweet lady Judy thought was in her seventies was the 200-pound dark-haired woman in her forties Ellen and Polly described. The meeting got Judy thinking, so a few weeks later, she and Beth headed out to Dorothea's, ostensibly to see Bert. As they chatted with Dorothea in the parlor, Judy casually asked the question she had been wanting to ask: "You know, you're so fair skinned . . . you don't look Mexican. What was your name before it was, Puente?" "Montalvo," Dorothea responded quickly. Judy probed once again. What was her name before that?

At this point, Dorothea hesitated, eyeing Judy closely before she finally answered. "Johansson," she finally said. Judy tried to act calm and collected, like this was just another ordinary conversation. Afterward, she began probing further and found the *Sacramento* article. However, it used a pseudonym (Eleanor Anderson) to describe the dangerous but well-connected landlady who was sentenced to five years of prison on charges of "forgery, grand theft and administering stupefying drugs," and it hinted that she was never convicted of her worst crimes, as some believe.[110]

The article was unnerving, and it left Judy wondering if Dorothea Johansson and "Eleanor Anderson" were really one and the same. She wondered for a moment what to do about Bert, whom she had placed at Puente's. Should she leave him there? Finally, after reasoning that the press often sensationalizes anything having to do with social services and even if Dorothea broke the law some years ago she hadn't done anything now. She thought about how happy Bert seemed to be there. Her boarding house was among the best in town. There seemed no legitimate reason to suddenly uproot Bert.[111] She got busy with others things in mid-June, so she didn't have time to think about Bert for a while. When she called about seeing him in early October, he seemed to be gone. Judy became concerned, setting in motion a chain of events that led to the gruesome discoveries in November.

When Judy began to check up on Bert, she had one disquieting bit of news from another co-worker, Bill Johnson, at detox. As Johnson told her, at the end of July Bert had come to detox saying he didn't want to stay at Dorothea's any longer because he didn't want to take any more meds—the antipsychotic drugs he was taking to stop his auditory hallucinations. A few weeks earlier, Bert had mentioned that he wanted to get a place of his own once he started getting his Social Security checks again.[112] But when Bill had taken Bert back to Dorothea's, she had convinced him to stay. His meds weren't so bad, he agreed. He would take them. He didn't really want to leave, he finally said. Bert showed up back at detox in early August and slept on the floor, but Johnson had persuaded him to go back. After all, didn't Bert have his own room and TV? Why go back to a crowded detox and sleep on the floor?[113] The last Johnson heard, Puente was going to be taking him to Mexico along with some of her other tenants. When Johnson called Dorothea at Judy's suggestion to find out how Bert was, her chipper reply that "Bert's in Mexico!" made her even more unnerved.

The story that she had taken Bert to Mexico and left him there, when Bert had told her he preferred the city, didn't make sense. When Judy called Dorothea a few days later, what she heard was even more disturbing. Why should Dorothea's family enjoy Bert, who was mentally ill, so much that they would welcome him into their home? Dorothea claimed that Bert liked it so much that he was calling her three times a week to talk about what they were doing. The idea of Bert making international calls just didn't compute. What if he wandered off on his own and got lost? Dorothea simply laughed off her concerns. "Anyway, he'll be back next week."[114]

When Judy called a week later, Dorothea said Bert had stayed in Mexico another week for a fiesta; the following week there were more excuses. Frustrated, Judy decided to drive out to the house to talk to Dorothea personally. On November 1, when she arrived with Beth, Dorothea was still making the same promises. "I just need a little more time," she said. When Judy mentioned that she might have to place Bert somewhere else because he had been gone more than two weeks, a violation of Social Security rules, Dorothea appealed for understanding, adding affectionately, "Oh, dear, I'd really hate to lose him. I'd really miss having Bert here. . . . And I've already gone out and got Christmas presents for him. . . . I was looking forward to sharing the holidays with him."[115] Then she even offered to fly down to bring Bert back herself, so he would be back by November 7. Judy could see him then.

But on November 7, on her way into the office, Judy got a mysterious phone call from a man who said he was Michel Obregon, or Miguel, as he quickly corrected himself, and he was, he claimed, Bert Montoya's brother-in-law. "Bert doesn't have a brother-in-law," Judy told him, but Miguel was insistent. "Oh, yes he does." Supposedly, he had picked up Bert on Saturday in California to take him home, so now Judy could stop Bert's checks. When Judy asked to speak to Bert, he wasn't available, and he wouldn't give Judy the number so she could call back. He was calling from a pay phone, and he and his wife were moving so they didn't have a phone yet. Suddenly, he had to go and hung up.

The call was so unnerving that Judy immediately called Dorothea to find out what was going on. But after Dorothea simply repeated the story that Bert's brother-in-law had arrived on Sunday and taken him and all his things to Utah, Judy decided something was very wrong. "I'm going to have to call the police and report Bert to missing persons," she said. That call started the investigation that within five days became front-page news.

Had Judy not called, Bert's disappearance probably would have remained forgotten, and it's likely that the other vanished lodgers would have remained missing. Later that morning, on November 7, after stopping to talk to Judy and Beth, patrol officer Richard Ewing stopped by 1426 F Street to talk to Dorothea. "No, Bert left in a pickup truck for Utah," she assured the officer most cordially, as she led him around the house. Everything seemed perfectly ordinary, and Ewing encountered a tall, elderly tenant named John Sharp, whom Judy had urged him to talk to, in the downstairs lodger area. Sharp backed up Dorothea's story in every detail. Dorothea had gone to pick Bert up in Mexico and after they returned on Saturday, he left in a red pickup truck on Sunday. Briefly, Ewing accompanied Dorothea upstairs to her own quarters, thinking everything was fine. As he came back downstairs ready to leave, Sharp suddenly shoved a note scribbled on the back of an envelope into his hand that warned, "She wants me to lie to you." Quickly, Ewing slipped into Sharp's room, turned up the TV to cover up their conversation, and arranged to meet Sharp a few blocks away. When they met, Sharp had some disquieting news. There was "something strange going on," and he wasn't just talking about Bert. He knew about another tenant, Ben Fink, who had suddenly disappeared the previous spring. Dorothea had some ex-cons dig several holes in the yard that were empty one day and covered the next. Plus he had noticed a strange odor from a room upstairs—and since he had once worked in a mortuary in Kansas City, he recognized it as the "stink of death."[116]

Ewing was amazed. Could any of this strange story be true? Nervously, Sharp left to tell his story to Judy as well, while Ewing wrote up his report, which was passed on to Detective John Cabrera of the Missing Persons and Homicide/Assault division. He had written up Sharp's suspicions as best he could. It was up to the investigators to follow up and determine if anything was there.

On Wednesday, November 9, Judy received a strange letter postmarked from Reno. It was an awkwardly written letter signed Michel Miguel Obregon—to perhaps cover up the strange slip of the tongue her caller from Utah had made in identifying himself. The letter read in part:

> Mrs. Moise,
>
> As I told you on the phone Albaro, "Bert" as you know him Jose as we in the family call him. Until he was told he was going to have to move again after the holidays and he did not want. . . . What Jose did not tell you was he had called her at our home for the last 3 1/2 years. When we get settled we will send you photos and will let him call you about Thanksgiving if he wants to you.
>
> Yours truly,
>
> Michel Miguel Obregon
>
> P.S. As you know Jose does not write English . . . Also he has been wanting to go to Costa Rica for the Navidad period.[117]

The letter, coupled with Sharp's warnings, only made her more nervous that something terrible had happened to Bert. The suggestion that he would be gone for Christmas made her sure she would never see him again, and she left a message for Cabrera. She left repeated messages, nervous that nothing would be done. But finally, Cabrera called her back, scheduling a meeting for the following day, November 11.

By the time Judy and Beth crowded into his small office the following day, Cabrera was truly alarmed. He had read not only Ewing's report but earlier reports and criminal records about Dorothea Puente, and what he read was chilling. It was as if by presenting herself like a sweet old lady, she had repeatedly slipped through the law and the follow-up by various bureaucracies she had dealt with. Outwardly she might be the compassionate care-taking nurse who was well respected as a civic-minded contributor to the Hispanic community, but underneath this veneer she had a substantial criminal record. Among other things, it included charges of forgery, theft, and drugging and robbing elderly victims. Though four parole agents had visited her over a dozen times at 1426 F Street since she was released from prison in the fall of 1985, she had led them around as if she was just another boarder, and no one realized that she had tenants on the ground floor. A specific condition of her parole was that she wasn't supposed to be running a boarding house. She had fooled the agents checking up on her.

Cabrera had recently received a bit of disturbing news from a sometime prostitute and heroin addict Brenda Trujillo. Trujillo had spent some time in the county jail with Puente in 1982 when she had been charged with fleecing some elderly victims. Trujillo had lived for some time at 1426 F Street herself when she was out of prison. According to her, people were dying at the house and Puente was burying them on the property.[118] When he first heard her claims, Cabrera hadn't taken them seriously, since Trujillo was the suspect in another murder at the time (though the investigation was later dropped). With Judy's concerns about Bert, maybe there was something there after all.

On Friday, November 11, Veterans Day, Cabrera and his partner, Terry Brown, and Jim Wilson, a federal parole agent, met in his office with Judy and Beth. Cabrera was eager to hear what they had to say about Dorothy Puente and the missing boarder.[119] Wilson, who had recently become Puente's parole agent, shared the information in the parole files, noting that she had been on federal parole in 1978 for forging checks and was back on parole again after her release from prison on state criminal charges in 1985. But despite thirty-five contacts with parole agents since then, no one had reported that she was running a boarding house, had other tenants living with her, or was supplementing her assistance income in any way. "She's not allowed to," Wilson observed, noting that under her federal parole conditions, she was restricted in her travel, couldn't contact other parolees, and very specifically couldn't work with the elderly or emotionally handicapped.[120] Obviously, she had done all these things. She had literally slipped through the cracks of the system by knowing how to play it, and her sweet little grandmother role had helped her slip through.

After Judy and Beth shared their own story about Bert's disappearance, Dorothea's runaround to keep Judy from seeing him, and finally the strange letter from "Miguel," Cabrera decided it was time to check out Puente and the house, as well as confirm Trujillo's odd story about burials at the house by seeing if anything there resembled a grave. At least the search would satisfy the social workers who were insistent something be done and were threatening to take their concerns higher in the police department if something wasn't.

At about 10 a.m., Cabrera, Brown, and Wilson headed out to Puente's house, and Judy and Beth headed back to work, promising to stay in touch if needed. It was a quiet day because of the holiday.[121] Dorothea's two-story Victorian looked the model of proper middle-class decorum, with a well-groomed and trimmed front yard, neatly surrounded by a brick and wrought-iron fence.[122] It seemed so out of character what Judy, Beth, and Trujillo were suggesting.

When Dorothea appeared smiling at the doorway, Cabrera tried to be reassuring, as if this was a friendly check-up call. He introduced Wilson as Dorothea's new parole agent. She graciously invited them in for coffee and he declined, explaining they were there to follow-up on a missing person report. "Oh, he's in Utah with relatives," she reassured them calmly, explaining that the people in the house could verify that as well.[123] Just as casually and calmly, Cabrera asked if they might look around and talk to some tenants.

It was a masterful performance of tact and salesmanship, because the police had no warrant, and Dorothea could have easily asked them to leave. But Cabrera's easy-going manner helped make Dorothea feel comfortable. She invited them in. As they walked around for about an hour, talking to Dorothea and individually to some of the tenants, everything seemed quite in order; Dorothea had been the model of helpful cooperation. She volunteered that Ben Fink, the boarder Sharp had raised concerns about with Officer Ewing, had left during the summer and gone to Marysville, a small town about seventy-five miles north of Sacramento. She admitted the felonies on her record but said they were in the past. "I'm trying to straighten my life out now," she said.[124] She was very apologetic when Jim Wilson told her she was violating her parole by running a boarding house and failing to disclose this source of income. She didn't even protest when he said he would have to revoke her parole, which meant she would be likely going back to prison. She could have stopped the tour or interviews at any time and sent the police and Wilson on their way. But she did not.

After the tour of the house was over, the one place they hadn't seen was the yard. As diplomatically as he could as they stood on the back porch, Cabrera broached the topic. "Do you mind if we check outside and do a little digging?" he said. Quite easily Dorothea could have said no. That might have been the end of any further investigation, because Cabrera wasn't even sure he had enough evidence to support a search warrant.

Very quickly, Dorothea said, "Oh, go right ahead." After getting their coveralls and short-handled shovels from their car, the two detectives and Wilson began to dig, as the faint sound of drums, trombones, and cheers from the Veteran's Day Parade wafted by. Puente quietly watched. It seemed outlandish to think that they were going to find anything out of the ordinary in this attractive, well-tended garden, with its freshly planted fruit trees, tiny gazebo, tightly planted flowerbeds, and small statues of stone cats. They couldn't discount the possibility that if anything was buried there, these could be grave markers. But if Dorothea was hiding anything, why invite them to dig?

Still a little skeptical, the men dug. Soon, they had dug up three exploratory holes, and found nothing—just dark loamy soil. They began to think they were really on a fool's errand, based on unfounded suspicions about holes in her yard. It seemed rude to keep going, tearing up the yard of this lady, who despite her past record seemed so helpful and sweet.

Just as they were close to giving up, Wilson's shovel struck something about eighteen inches down in the far corner of the yard by the fence. It looked like a white powder, and when he reached down to touch it and sniffed his fingers, he found that it was lime. Digging a little further, he hit something that felt oddly hard and spongy. He called Cabrera and Brown over, so they could dig in case he had found something important. Soon, Cabrera had cleared the dirt away from what looked like dirty cloth wrapped around a tree root. After pulling out more bits and pieces of material, Cabrera pulled out a leg bone, still covered with bits of skin, and still with a tennis shoe attached.[125] Dorothea expressed a sudden gesture of shock, holding her hands to her face.

This was the beginning of a frenetic two days of digging that shocked Sacramento and the nation. In a few minutes, Brown had notified police headquarters; city workers with heavy equipment, crime scene investigators, forensic pathologists, and a coroner's deputy were on the way. The district attorney's office sent over two forensic anthropologists as well.

Cabrera escorted Dorothea to headquarters to interview her about what he had just found, as well as about the missing Bert Montoya. It was obvious this badly decomposed body had been in the ground far too long to be Bert's. Whose was it? "I need all the truth from you," Cabrera said softly, still finding it hard to believe that this woman who looked so old and small could be a vicious killer.[126] For about two hours, Cabrera asked Dorothea questions, while she continued to maintain Bert was really in Utah, that she had nothing to do with the bones in the backyard, that she had kicked Ben Fink out of the house and he had gone to Marysville, and that she had just put lime in the yard to "soften the dirt." She invited the police to bring in a contractor to dig up the yard so they could see "she had nothing to hide." Of course she was willing to take a polygraph, though she hoped they might wait until Monday, "to give my nerves a chance to settle," she said.[127]

So it went. In the end, Cabrera didn't feel he had enough evidence to arrest her yet—nothing to show the skeletonized body in her back yard was there due to a crime or that she committed it. Afterward, he drove her back to her home. At least, he had gotten the interview on videotape. It later proved very critical in court.

The investigation and digging at 1426 F Street was going on; by now the scene was becoming a media circus, with bright yellow police tape festooning the area. It became even bigger and crazier on Saturday. In the meantime, Dorothea returned home, free to come and go as she wished. Cabrera was playing by the rules in taking her home without making an arrest. He just didn't know how dangerous she truly was—or that Dorothea would use the rules to get away.

The investigators, excavators, coroner's deputies, and others were back in force early Saturday morning. A forensic anthropologist, Dr. Rodger Heglar, was there to help with the full recovery of the first body, as diggers carefully made a kind of pedestal of dirt around it and brushed away the last dirt to avoid damaging the body. Crime scene photographers carefully documented each stage of exhumation. It looked like a gray-haired, petite, elderly female, Heglar concluded after the diggers were finished. As a van took the first remains to the coroner's office to be examined, the police got ready to dig through the rest of the backyard for additional bodies.

Just after the first body was taken away, Dorothea approached Detective Cabrera and asked if she was under arrest. He said no, and she asked if she and John McCauley, one of her tenants, could go to the nearby Clarion Hotel for a cup of coffee. "I'll be back soon," she promised sweetly. Because she wasn't under arrest, after consulting with his superiors, Cabrera told her she was free to go. He escorted her outside through the yellow police tape and past the growing crowd of press and curious onlookers. He thought he was being chivalrous, and after a couple of blocks, he waved her on and watched her walk away.

In retrospect, Cabrera thought he should have arrested her. When he returned and began digging, a second body was found. By the time detectives went to find Dorothea at the Clarion Hotel, hours later, she was long gone. She had called a cab, headed to a bar in West Sacramento, and then taken another cab to Stockton, because she correctly figured that the police would already have all the major transportation centers in Sacramento staked out to find her. From there she boarded a bus to Los Angeles, quietly sinking back in her seat for a calm, anonymous ride to that most anonymous of cities. Once again, she had managed to escape.

Back at 1426 F Street, the investigators were digging up more bodies, and Cabrera had to face the embarrassment of having let the main suspect get away. It was an unfortunate slip, though technically she wasn't under arrest. The district attorney had said there was too little evidence pointing directly at her, and his next step was to seek a search warrant for the property, as the best way to preserve any evidence Cabrera or other cops found from future legal attack.[128] By the time district attorney Tim Frawley had changed his mind on Saturday—once two bodies had been found—Dorothea was already gone. About the best Cabrera could do at this point, on Frawley's instructions, was to arrest John McCauley, the boarder who had accompanied Dorothea and returned shortly after she took her taxi to Stockton. McCauley claimed she was still at the Clarion. He was arrested as an accessory to murder in the hopes he might say something about where Dorothea was, though Frawley wasn't too hopeful. McCauley had already lied to the police and had helped her get away. At least the police could show the press they were trying to do something.

The digging continued. Both bodies that were discovered and taken to the coroner's office so far were too old to be Bert's. While the identification process was going on, Frawley decided to charge Puente with Bert Montoya's murder, considering it unlikely, given what had happened in the last twenty-four hours, that he was still alive.

Eventually, the weekend of digging yielded a total of seven bodies by November 14, and one of them turned out to be that of Bert. As the more tedious process of cataloging and identifying the remains went on, the big question was, where was Dorothea? Was she on her way to Mexico? Would they be able to catch her before she eluded the authorities for good? Was there any way to link her definitively to the bodies found in her yard? Even though it was apparent that she had most likely killed at least these seven and perhaps more people, was there any proof she was involved in burying them in her yard? More than that, could the cause of death be determined to show there was a crime? The media circus in front of the house on F Street and the headlines that spoke of the search for the alleged murderer concealed how truly difficult this case turned out to be—especially when Puente still looked like a sweet grandmother accused of such an unspeakable number of crimes. It was like a replay of the case of Belle Gunness about eighty years before—except that Belle had stood out like an odd black sheep in her conservative Midwestern farm neighborhood. Dorothea was known as a pillar of her community—and she looked so gentle and sweet.

As the examiners worked on identifying the bodies at the morgue, the police set up a watch at the airports, bus stations, and train stations. The media helped by describing the search and featuring her picture on front pages across the nation and on the air. Although the search didn't immediately turn up Dorothea, it did attract a caller who reported one more suspicious death back in 1982—that of Ruth Monroe, a woman who had excitedly planned to go into the restaurant business with Dorothea, and had moved into her house on F Street. A few weeks later, she was dead of a drug overdose, presumed to be suicide.[129] Dorothea told the police Monroe was depressed because her husband was terminally ill. They believed her and judged the incident a suicide (Wikipedia, Dorothea Puente), though in hindsight, the death raises suspicions.

As a result of this call, the Sacramento police department got a search warrant, which permitted a complete search of the house. Some of the evidence that was taken was intriguing—such as a Folger's coffee can with "Lye" printed on the lid, various bottles of pills, and a book with the title *150 Commonly Prescribed Drugs*.[130] Could this book include anything Dorothea had used on her boarders?

The FBI finally entered the search and put out an all-points bulletin for Puente; McCauley was quietly released and went home. All he had admitted was that Dorothea had decided to flee because she knew the police would go after her "no matter what."[131] But as to where she might be, he wasn't saying.

As the hunt for Puente went on, much of the investigation shifted to the morgue, where a team of forensic pathologists working for the coroner's office performed the autopsies to learn not only who the bodies were but how they died. *When* they died might be helpful—but with such decomposed bodies, that was hard to determine. One member of the team was a forensic radiologist, Dr. Russel A. McFall, and he used X-rays to photograph each wrapped-up corpse. He then used the developed film to compare the bones with previously taken X-rays of former tenants of the house. This was extremely precise work that involved comparing not only the shape of the bones but the characteristics of the joints and even the amount of calcification that had built up. The work was so precise that McFall felt the bones could be used to make a positive ID, because every bone is unique, like a human fingerprint.[132] For identification purposes, another member of the team, a registered nurse, cut off the tips of the least decomposed fingers from three of the bodies to send to the Department of Justice labs to test for fingerprints. They were too decomposed to get prints on the spot. At the DOJ, experts might be able to get prints by examining the deeper layers of the skin.[133] Later the DOJ's latent print examiner was able to get some prints by injecting the fingertips with a fluid to rehydrate the tissue so he could dust with black powder and roll the prints on a card.[134]

It was intensive, grueling work, but gradually the bodies in the morgue began to give up their secrets, and all were identified. There were also some suggestions of what might have happened. One forensic anthropologist saw no obvious evidence of trauma—no knife or gunshot wounds on any of the bodies,[135] but the examiners did find the evidence of a sticky green substance in all of the stomachs, as well as small traces of a drug, later identified as flurazepam, sold under the trade name Dalmane.[136] It later provided crucial evidence for the trial, suggesting that each of the victims had been drugged and perhaps suffocated before being wrapped up and buried—typically in a blanket, with several layers of clear plastic secured by duct tape, and dusted with lime or lye.[137]

By Wednesday, November 16, Sacramento Police Chief John P. Kearns was still trying to explain away the embarrassment of losing their only suspect; the FBI still didn't have the slightest idea where she was either. Perhaps she fled to Mexico, went the popular thinking. Finally, the break came in Los Angeles. On Saturday, Dorothea had quietly checked into the Royal Viking Motel, a cheap, ordinary looking place, using "Johansson," a variation on a former husband's name. She spent the next few days quietly holed up there, only going out for meals at a nearby restaurant. Her idea was to quietly disappear, assume a new identity, and blend into the anonymity of the city once all of the media attention died down.

By Wednesday afternoon, she was feeling lonely and restless and decided to go out for a drink. She hailed a cab, which took her to a down-at-the-heels neighborhood bar called the Monte Carlo. She was well-dressed, wearing perfume and pumps, and she soon started talking to one the bar's regular customers, Charles Willgues, a thin, balding widower and retired handyman who was lonely, too. Soon they were deep in conversation, and Dorothea, who gave her name as "Donna Johansson" began spinning her latest story about how she was recently widowed, had just arrived in town, and was trying to get over the death of her husband. Unfortunately, just after she arrived, a larcenous cabdriver stole all her luggage.[138] She was like a spider, luring her next fly into the trap.

When Willgues mentioned that he was living on a pension, Dorothea told him that she could help him increase his Social Security benefits because she knew what disability he should receive for his various medical problems. Moving quickly, perhaps too quickly, she spoke about wanting a fresh start in a new place. Because they were both alone, maybe they could get together and she could cook a Thanksgiving dinner. They could even consider sharing an apartment together.[139] It was all a little fast for Willgues, but he did make a date to get together with her the next day—though he felt vaguely uneasy, as if something about their encounter wasn't right.

As Willgues settled back to watch TV later, he realized that she looked like the woman he had seen on TV earlier that morning—the woman who was the subject of a national manhunt. Unsure, he called the CBS news bureau in Los Angeles, and a few hours later, CBS assignment editor Gene Silver, convinced that the "Donna" Willgues met was Dorothea, called the police. First Silver assembled a camera crew, and they were there waiting when the police arrived at Dorothea's room at the Royal Viking Motel around 10:30 p.m. She answered the door quietly, giving her name as Donna Johansson. But in moments, after the police checked her driver's license, which had her proper name and 1426 F Street address, she was under arrest and in the back of a patrol car in handcuffs, and the CBS camera crew filmed it all.[140]

Very early Thursday morning, John Cabrera, who had started the digging at Dorothea's house, was in Los Angeles with another detective to escort her back to Sacramento. Because commercial flights wouldn't run until several hours later, they used a jet chartered by Sacramento's NBC affiliate KRCA-TV and the *Sacramento Bee*, who invited the police to join them in return for the first scoop on the Puente story. They agreed not to ask Dorothea about the case, and the detectives gave Puente the usual Miranda warning, but she did state what would be the centerpiece of her defense: "I cashed the checks, yes. . . . But I have not killed anyone." She added, "I used to be a very good person at one time."[141] After that, she had nothing more to say for some time.

With Puente finally in jail, the case was in the hands of the district attorney, defense lawyers, and psychologists. The end game went on for about five years as the prosecution sorted out its evidence and the defense filed motion after motion, winning only one major one—the right to transfer the case out of county because of all the publicity. The new venue was Monterey County—and it took until February 1993 (about four years) to finally try the case.

It was a hard case to try because it was all strictly circumstantial evidence. Despite all the bodies dug up from her yard, no one had actually seen Dorothea either kill the victims or bury the bodies. The prosecution believed that perhaps Bert Montoya might have helped her bury the six older, very decomposed bodies. But then, of course, he was dead, perhaps because he knew too much. At the same time, the prosecution had two other victims to add to the death toll. One was Ruth Monroe, whose 1982 case was not well investigated at the time. The other charge was for drugging and killing a former prospective husband, Everson Gillmouth, a lonely widower who had last told his sister Reba Nicklous in Oregon in August 1985 that he was going to live with Dorothea and hoped to marry her if things went well. A few weeks later he disappeared—until he turned up in a box on the side of the Sacramento River in rural Sutter County on January 1, 1986.[142] At the time, with no ID, no missing person's report, and no matching prints, he was another John Doe until Reba read about the Puente investigation and called the police.

It was hard to pull this huge mountain of evidence together so it made sense. Through the long trial that went on for six months, prosecutor John O'Mara urged the jurors to look at the totality of the circumstances to show that these people didn't die naturally. They were bound up, taken from the house, and buried. He pointed out that Dorothea already had control over their money, so she didn't have to kill them for that. But she killed those who became sick or troublesome, and the strong ones either managed to endure or she kicked them out of the house.[143] She wanted their money so she could live the gracious lifestyle she had invented for herself. That made her feel important; it gave her a sense of worth. She built her success and her charitable works on the money and lives of the forgotten people who were society's cast-offs. But all her good works, all her charity, was no excuse. She was a vain and high living "stone-cold killer," a person who killed with no feeling, with no remorse.[144]

The defense painted quite a different picture. This was a woman who "tenderly cared for" the down-and-out people who "nobody cared about." She was the one who "provided food, a warm, clean place to stay, laundry services, clothes, and furnished areas." Unfortunately, despite her care, some of them died of natural causes. Afraid of being caught and having her parole revoked for running the boarding house, she buried them in her yard. She stole their checks, nut that didn't make her a killer, just a thief.[145] "Dorothea Puente has a touch of larceny in her heart," Kevin Clymo, one of her defense attorneys, said in his opening statement. "But greed doesn't make her an evil serial killer."[146]

Prosecutor O'Mara offered reams of evidence about how Dorothea had taken Social Security payments, forged checks, failed to report deaths to the police or paramedics, and kept taking the money. He showed how she documented how much she was collecting from each dead person she knew was buried in the ground, much like the prosecutor in the Juan Corona case showed how he kept lists of the victims who turned up dead. "Follow the money," O'Mara emphasized. "When you find money, you'll find Dorothea Puente. She followed the money."[147]

Then O'Mara highlighted the odd juxtaposition of appearances, the "outward lie" and the "inner truth." This is what made the case so puzzling and made Dorothea Puente an enigma. On the surface, even her house, like herself, presented a "visual and logical contradiction." To all appearances, her home was a "quant Victorian house with beautiful, lush gardens beside it, a wrought-iron fence, brick pillars, decorations on the front door."[148] It had an inviting, homey presence. At the same time, Puente's outer kindly appearance didn't fit with her "inner anger, cruelty, and coldness." If the jurors could see past that, they could see the inner truth, in which "she wanted to live in a style she could not afford. She wanted to present herself as a woman of substance, of power. To do this she needed their money." So she got rid of the "sickest, unruliest, most abandoned tenants." O'Mara concluded with a final image of the case, quoting from Henry David Thoreau: "Look at the totality of the evidence. Some circumstantial evidence is very strong, as when you find a trout in the milk."[149] Through the long trial, Puente herself contributed to the enigma by sitting quietly and icily, almost like a stone statue, in her prim, grandmotherly dress with her white hair.

On the other hand, Clymo left the jurors with his own Thoreau story about coming on the tracks of a fox near a rabbit that had been killed and eaten in the woods. At first, he thought the culprit was the fox. When he looked more closely, he realized the true killer was a predatory bird, an owl, and the fox had merely come upon the bird as it was eating its kill.[150]

Was Dorothea the trout or the fox? After the trial ended on July 15, 1993, it took the jurors over a month to come back, and at one point, they nearly dead-locked because of one hold-out who had difficulty making a decision. Finally, on August 25, after nearly six weeks of contentious deliberations, the jury came forward with its verdict. They found Dorothea guilty on three counts of murder: for Dorothy Miller, Leona Carpenter, and Benjamin Fink, though it was hard to pick out exactly why the jurors settled on these three victims. About the best O'Mara could come up with was that these verdicts were compromises to get a reluctant juror to at agree to convict on something. Judge Michael J. Virga made the sentencing decision on December 10, 1993—life without possibility of parole. Puente remains in prison today.

THE CASE OF DAVID BROWN

Garden Grove, California, 1985–88

On the surface it seemed that investigators Fred McLean and Jay Newell had an open-and-shut case as they investigated Linda Brown's murder at the well-furnished suburban house in Garden Grove, California, on March 19, 1985. The police found Linda Brown on her bed in her nightgown, lying in a pool of blood, still gurgling from two shots in the chest and lungs. A couple of hours later they found her fourteen-year-old stepdaughter, Cinnamon, with a note that said, "Dear God, please forgive me. I didn't mean to hurt her." At the police station, Cinnamon had described how she had done the crime, holding the gun and shooting twice, explaining that she very much loved her father and was angry because her stepmother had kicked her out of the house and made her live in a trailer. After she sunk into a coma and recovered, she said she couldn't remember anything about the night of the murder. At her trial, she was readily convicted and sent to the Ventura School for Girls, where she was a model prisoner, taking college courses and looking like a beautiful secretary or receptionist in an office.

Somehow, even as everything fell into place, both Newell and McLean felt that the case didn't quite feel right; something was wrong. For Newell, after the case was officially closed, it became something of an obsession. When he continued to investigate, the story of what really happened and why was shocking. In fact, Newell and McLean nearly lost their lives trying to find the truth.

At the time the case began, Garden Grove, located in the heart of Orange County, seemed an unlikely place for a murder involving mystery and intrigue. In the 1980s, it was a place of thriving orange groves and vineyards, and it was being transformed by a vibrant new computer industry into an area of prosperous suburban homes. It is very close to Disneyland, an area that spelled innocent family entertainment, and the town was known for its conservative Republican politics and its young, upwardly mobile, high-tech, and sometimes very wealthy population.

Nationally, it was the height of the Reagan years in Washington—the president had just begun his second term after a landslide victory, and the excitement of success, achievement, and opportunity in boom times was in the air. Indeed, Sylvester Stallone's successful Rambo franchise, crowned by *Rambo: First Blood, Part II*, released that year, was quite a symbol of the power of the individual to scale the heights, getting rid of any enemies with a blast of gunfire, and then live happily in the end. There was a grim underside to all of this emphasis on success and hard work in the growing number of homeless individuals, disrupted family life, and scandals of corrupt businessmen who went too far in the name of greed and were involved in stock and banking excesses. The emphasis on presenting a successful image, looking good, and appearing powerful ruled the day—there were even a growing number of workshops and success gurus doing programs on topics like Dress for Success that helped anyone learn to create the right image to move ahead. In the focus on success and good appearances, sometimes truth got lost.

This was this kind of contradiction between appearance and reality, image and truth, that bothered Newell about the Cinnamon Brown case. Even though she confessed and was readily convicted, she didn't seem like a killer. Even the psychological tests she took in prison, like the Minnesota Multi-Phasic Indicator, showed she had no tendencies for violence, no apparent anger that might lead to homicide, although she did show a tendency to lie. What was she hiding or covering up? Newell felt driven to find out; he had to know.

The original case began with a radio call at about 3:30 a.m. on March 19, when Garden Grove patrol office Darrow Halligan got a radio call for a "possible 187" on Ocean Breeze Drive. When he arrived a few minutes later, the house was unusually quiet, and the dispatcher assured him the suspect wasn't in the house according to the informant. He arranged to meet the informant at the front door. A few minutes later, as he walked up to the house, a short, stocky man opened the door. Next to him was a young blonde woman holding a crying baby and crying hysterically herself. The man appeared tense and teary-eyed, too, although his first comment surprised Halligan. "I think my wife's been shot," he said. "She's in the bedroom. I'm afraid to go look, officer. Would you?"[151] It was a puzzling remark, making Halligan wonder why the man would think his wife had been shot if he hadn't even seen her.

In any case, Halligan went on through the house holding his flashlight, while the man and woman, at his request, waited on the living room couch. After he pushed through the half-closed door into the bedroom, he heard the sound of gurgling. When he shined his light on the bed, not wanting to turn on the light and perhaps disturb any fingerprints on the switch, he saw a woman with long blonde hair lying on her back with her right arm hanging over the side of the bed, her left hand held up toward her ear. He saw a pool of blood on her chest that he was sure came from her lungs.[152] She was still alive, but only barely. In a few more minutes, paramedics arrived to take her to the hospital emergency room. At the same time, other police officers, including Sergeant Dale Farley, who took charge of the crime scene, arrived.

At 4:30 a.m., homicide investigator Fred McLean got the call to take over as the primary investigator of the murder of the young woman who died in the hospital. The medical team couldn't save her, and it was very clear how she died—two bullet wounds in her chest. McLean soon had the name of the chief suspect and probable reason, but he felt from the beginning that something wasn't quite right. After eighteen years on the force, he had come to sense such things, though homicide investigators were supposed to just go on the evidence, just the facts.

McLean began with a quick overview through the Brown house, noting that it seemed to be packed with new furniture, mostly solid but ordinary furnishings.[153] There also appeared to be lots of small knickknacks, including a shelf with dozens of ceramic unicorns, and numerous family pictures. Among the unusual things he noticed was three empty plastic prescription vials with their lids off, and next to them an empty glass. After noting their labels, indicating the vials contained Darvocet-N (a painkiller) and Dyazide (a diuretic), prescribed for David Brown, he bagged the vials and glass as possible evidence. It seemed curious to have open and empty vials in a laundry room.

McLean got a brief rundown from Farley, learning that the husband had been out and came back after the shooting occurred. Now the husband and girl with him, Patti Bailey, thought Brown's fourteen-year-old daughter Cinnamon did it, because Patti told one officer she saw someone who looked like Cinnamon go out the back door after she heard gunshots. But Cinnamon was gone, and McLean already thought it strange, since fourteen-year-old girls rarely used guns to get what they wanted or if they were angry. Temper outbursts maybe, but not guns.[154]

Other investigators gathered physical and trace evidence, like fingerprints and fibers, though most of this would not be useful if the shooter was someone in the household. McLean went to interview David Brown. He was sitting slumped in the living room, as if devastated by his wife's murder, but when he spoke about his daughter as the possible shooter, he seemed strangely matter-of-fact, as if resigned to the fact she had done it.

In detail, he explained what he remembered of the night before. Though he looked older, with a somewhat scarred face from teenage acne, Brown was only thirty-two, and he had become quite successful at running his own data recovery business. He had developed a special process that enabled him to retrieve data and had numerous corporate clients. His dead wife, Linda, he explained, helped him run the business. The previous day, they had planned to go to the desert on a picnic, but after the rain led them to change their plans, they spent much of the day playing Uno, a favorite card game, with his family. But Linda had become upset, he recalled, and there was some kind of fight between her and Cinnamon, who didn't get along very well. That's why, Brown explained, Cinnamon had been living in a small travel trailer in the back yard for about three weeks. Due to their continuing problems, his wife had "kicked Cinnamon out" of the house.[155] He complained that Cinnamon wouldn't help with household chores and didn't get along with Linda's younger sister, Patti, either. Presumably those were the reasons that Cinnamon might want to kill Linda, he seemed to be suggesting.

David noted he had had an argument earlier that evening with Linda himself, over whether to let their baby daughter, Krystal, cry—David, like his mother who had been visiting, thought she should pick the baby up right away, but Linda didn't think she should. After they made up and went to bed, he had still been upset and went for a drive that night, stopping off at the nearby store to pick up a few comic books, and then driving onto the beach and stopping at a restaurant. About an hour later, when he returned, he said, Patti greeted him at the door, holding the baby, and crying hysterically, as she told him that she thought Linda was dead and Cinnamon was perhaps the one who killed her.[156]

McLean then spoke to Patti, who at age seventeen looked amazingly like her dead older sister. She had the same long blonde hair, pale skin, thin waist, large bust—very much the image of a clean-cut Valley Girl. Her story seemed to parallel David's, as she described how Cinnamon had moved back and forth between their house and the home of her mother, David's first wife, Brenda. She confirmed that for months Cinnamon had been angry and moody, fighting with everyone in the family about doing chores and over household rules. In fact, Patti reported, Cinnamon had become so moody she had even talked about killing herself with a gun two months earlier in January. In February, Linda had kicked her out and made her stay in the trailer. Though she came in to eat and watch TV, mostly she stayed in the trailer.[157] Patti also described how she had been awakened around 2:20 by a gunshot and saw Cinnamon standing next to her bed. Then she saw Cinnamon suddenly run from her room.[158] That's why she thought Cinnamon must have killed Linda. After David returned home, he had asked her to check the trailer, but Cinnamon wasn't there. After David had called his father, Arthur, he had called the police.

Where was Cinnamon? Neither David nor Patti knew. Just to be sure they had been telling the truth about not doing any shooting themselves, McLean asked two investigators to conduct a gunshot residue test on them by swabbing their hands with cotton swabs.[159] The test over, McLean joined two other investigators in the backyard to look for Cinnamon. She wasn't in the trailer, as Patti had said; but as the officers searched around the backyard, shortly before 7 a.m., McLean noticed the two doghouses encircled by a pen near the trailer and nearby the four dogs were barking loudly. It struck him at once that the dogs would have been likely to bark and be heard during the night if the killer had been a stranger; yet they had apparently been quiet. But now they were barking.[160]

He looked closely, and discovered that Cinnamon was lying semiconscious, curled up in a fetal position, in the larger of the doghouses. She was lying in a pool of her own vomit, and around her, he noticed, were dozens of orange-tinted capsules. Unsure if she was even alive, McLean called out to her, softly calling her name. She roused slightly, and he reached out his hand to her. As she weakly grasped his hand, he helped pull her out of the doghouse. She seemed obviously very sick, cold, and drowsy, as she shivered in his arms, clinging to him like he had just saved her. He was immediately struck by how little she seemed like an angry, fearless killer who had just emptied two gun shots into her stepmother.

He noticed that Cinnamon was holding a piece of pink construction paper tightly in the fingers of her right hand. He pried her fingers apart and noticed some writing in the round, careful strokes of a child: "Dear God, please forgive me. I didn't mean to hurt her," the note read. It was as if Cinnamon was holding a signed confession to Linda's murder. Something still bothered McLean about the whole scenario. The next step was to talk to Cinnamon as soon as he could and find out what she knew.

The session began shortly after 7 a.m. at the Garden Grove Police Station. First, Steve Sanders, a detective who had spoken to her about five months ago at her high school when she reported a flasher, introduced himself. She managed to say she remembered him and then complained of a terrible headache and vomited a bright orange material into a wastebasket. To see if she had recently fired a gun, she was given the same residue test he had earlier administrated to David and Patti. A team of paramedics examined her and questioned her about what she had taken. Cinnamon explained how she had taken the three bottles of pills, perhaps 260 of them, around 2:30 or 3 a.m. After McLean joined them and showed the list of medications he had bagged into evidence, it seemed apparent that if Cinnamon hadn't vomited as much as she had, she would have been dead long since.

For now though, she seemed stable, but very sick. Strangely, in the midst of describing how and when she took the pills and how tired and light-headed she felt, she asked, "Is my dad all right?" It seemed such a puzzling thing to be more worried about her father than herself when she was so sick. After Sanders reassured her that her father and Patti as well were fine, she wanted to know about Linda. "How's Linda?" she asked.[161] If she had fired the gun, it seemed now that she didn't fully understand what had happened, what she had done.

After Cinnamon changed out of her vomit-stained sweatsuit and put on a prison jumpsuit, McLean and Sanders read her Miranda rights and began questioning her. It was an odd interview. Cinnamon responded woozily, frequently complaining of being tired and drifting off. When they asked if she knew why she was here, she responded, "'Cause I hurt Linda." She admitted she shot Linda, too. But when McLean told her that Linda was dead, she seemed genuinely shocked.[162] However, she went on to state that she had fired three shots, "One was in the room with Patti, and the other two were with Linda," explaining that she had shot the gun once in Patti's room because the trigger got stuck. She also echoed the problems that David and Patti had reported earlier—fights with her mother who yelled at her for being a brat, a conflict with Linda resulting in being ordered to leave the house or Linda would kill her, though she couldn't say exactly what she and Linda argued about. Several times she talked about how she loved her father "very, very much."[163]

After about a half hour of questioning, Cinnamon began fading into unconsciousness. She was rushed to the Garden Grove Medical Center, where paramedics hooked her up to a heart monitor and IV and tried to keep her alive. The officer who accompanied her to the hospital, Pamela French, sat by her bedside and noted how from time to time that Cinnamon seemed to mumble some random remarks. They sounded almost robot-like, as if they had been programmed into her subconscious. "Had an accident . . . killed my stepmother . . . didn't do it on purpose, didn't mean to . . . She was hurting me . . . She hated me . . . She wanted to kill me . . . She wanted me out of the house."[164]

Around noon, Cinnamon slipped away entirely in unconsciousness. So far, everything she said seemed only to confirm what the investigators had learned so far—she had fired the gun and killed her mother, feeling angry and resentful; her own father seemed resigned that that's exactly what happened, just as Patti had said. The additional evidence at the crime scene certainly confirmed her story about the gunshots. The investigators dug a .38-caliber bullet from the wall above Patti's bed, and the medical pathologists reported that there were two .38-caliber bullets in Linda's body.[165] By all accounts it seemed to be a simple case of a jealous teenager who resented her stepmother, felt hated and rejected, and disliked her overly restrictive rules. One day she simply snapped and shot back with a gun.[166]

The detectives simply had to gather additional evidence needed to support her confession, because legally a confession by itself was never enough. Since there were three gunshots, a gun residue test could show that Cinnamon had fired a gun recently (and that David and Patti hadn't), providing the needed corroborating evidence, but the GSR test came back negative. So it was the kind of case where one of the district attorney's investigators, Jay Newell, began to wonder if things were really as they seemed. He stayed on the case even after it was officially over and closed. For now the case seemed open and shut; it was just a question of gathering the necessary evidence to bring the case to trial.

Newell came into the case after it was assigned to a deputy district attorney, Dick Frederickson, who handled the prosecution against Cinnamon. Newell was a thirty-nine-year-old veteran of law enforcement who some compared to a pit bull, because he was so tenacious. His job was to work with police investigators on the case.

The results of the forensic tests were still being determined. McLean and Sanders started asking questions about Cinnamon and the Brown family, which they described in their reports, and Newell read them. The more he reviewed the reports, the more he started having questions, like McLean and Sanders did. The reports just didn't square with the picture of a rebellious teen who hated her stepmother.

As McLean and Sanders learned, some of Cinnamon's school friends described her as a happy teenager who got along well with her stepmother. What she mainly complained about was a father who was overly strict and repeatedly grounded her for even minor offenses, such as getting home from school a few minutes late or talking back.[167] She might pull "pranks, just silly stuff," one friend said. "But she really minds at home." From time to time, after a fight with a her father, she might go out to the trailer to sleep, or he might lock her in the back yard (with the trailer) if she was on restriction over the weekends.[168]

Cinnamon's natural mother, Brenda, whom she lived with from time to time, also had some strange things to say. Brenda noted that a few weeks before the shooting, her daughter said that David and Linda weren't getting along well. She also said that David and Patti said they overheard Linda on the phone, plotting with her twin brother, Alan, to "get rid of David." Brenda also reported that Cinnamon told her, "Linda was afraid David might leave her for Patti." David said he was thinking of hiring a private detective to check up on Linda.[169] McLean wondered if this might have been some fantastic story Cinnamon had simply made up, perhaps seeking attention, as teenagers sometimes do. He also wondered about Brenda's comment that David had asked her to describe Cinnamon as "flaky, suicidal, and out of control," as both he and Patti had described her in earlier interviews. Was he trying to protect her by building a "not guilty by reason of insanity" defense?[170] Or was something else going on?

It also seemed odd that just a few weeks before the murder, David had pulled both Cinnamon and Patti out of their high school, claiming the school wasn't safe and saying that he would send Cinnamon to another nearby school and that Patti would be moving to Nebraska. However, when McLean was interviewing David, he never mentioned Nebraska and said he had decided to hire a tutor and have Patti learn at home, because she wasn't doing well at the high school. He never did hire a tutor. Instead, Patti spent nearly all day, every day, at the house.

McLean also learned that Linda was the one person who knew almost everything about David's data recovery business. When he asked about insurance, David mentioned that he had once had a million-dollar police on Linda but had dropped it and had only gotten a new small policy on her.[171]

What seemed so strange to Newell, when reviewing the reports, was that the more information turned up about Cinnamon, the less she seemed to have a motive to murder her stepmother. Yet she was the only one the evidence seemed to point to, particularly with her confession that she had fired the gun and was the only one to blame.

It seemed the prosecution would be facing one of Orange County's top defense attorneys, Al Forgette. David Brown seemed determined to do the best he could to keep Cinnamon out of prison by using an insanity defense. After talking to her for two hours on March 20, a day after the shooting, Dr. Seatwright Anderson determined that she was so depressed she didn't know the nature or the quality of the murder she had committed—a good basis for insanity under the M'Naughten rule used in California. Oddly, though, she never spoke about wanting to kill Linda, and she was most concerned about keeping her father's love. Would he still love her after she had killed Linda? Shortly after she spoke with Dr. Anderson and had a meeting with her father, Cinnamon couldn't remember anything more about what happened the night of the shooting. Doctors and investigators repeatedly questioned her, but it was as if her memory had suddenly disappeared, like a door had closed to shut out the horrible events that occurred that night.[172] Dr. Anderson stated in his diagnosis that she had "psychogenic amnesia," plus she didn't even seem to recognize him. She just wanted to go home.

Cinnamon remained in Juvenile Hall as the preparations for her trial went on, and her father came to visit her from time to time. He kept reassuring her that the defense was doing everything to help her and that as a juvenile the courts would go easy on her. She remained unaware of the major changes that occurred at home. For one thing, David and Patti had moved, along with baby Krystal, to a new house in Orange, a city just a short ways from Garden Grove. Patti had essentially replaced Linda in David's life. Not only did she look very much like Linda, she now wore her dead sister's clothes and jewelry and was with David almost constantly—at home and when he did things for the business. She replaced Linda's pictures with her own. David had told McLean that he had only one small policy on Linda, but he got death benefit checks from four insurance companies—three paid in full, double indemnity (the fourth, where David had only paid the first premium, negotiated a partial settlement). Altogether, David obtained about $850,000.[173] It helped him buy an even nicer house in Anaheim after Cinnamon's trial.

The trial itself was almost a foregone conclusion. All the evidence, all the testimony pointed squarely at Cinnamon. Her defense attorney managed to get her original confession to McLean thrown out on the grounds she was in no condition to understand her Miranda rights because she was on the verge of losing consciousness. It turned out she had made another confession to one of the medical assistants, who had written down this information. So though the residue test on her hands came back negative, which could be because she had been lying in her own vomit and urine for several hours before the test, the confession provided the backbone of the state's case.[174] The key witness against her, Patti, largely confirmed her original story about Cinnamon's arguments with Linda in the weeks before the murder, and David Brown's testimony, read into the record, corroborated this, too. Oddly, David did not actually testify, pleading ill health. He often used reasons of poor health to get out of things he didn't want to do in the past. Perhaps he had a good reason for doing so this time, too—not wanting to testify against his daughter and affirm her guilt in court.[175] After all, why do anything to anger or alienate her? Cinnamon was disappointed at not seeing him there, supporting her.[176] It was the first of many disappointments that contributed to a break in discovering what really happened.

On August 12, 1985, the trial was over. Judge Robert Fitzgerald at the Orange County Courthouse in Santa Ana, deciding the case because Cinnamon was a juvenile, determined that she had killed Linda with "premeditation and deliberation, with malice aforethought," and was therefore guilty of murder in the first degree.[177] He determined in the penalty phase that though she was depressed, she still was sane. On September 13, he sentenced her to twenty-four years to life. As a juvenile she might possibly get out in a little as six years, but otherwise she would most probably serve until she was age twenty-five and then be placed on parole.[178]

Under most circumstances, that would have been the end of the case: a teenager, thinking she might be treated lightly because of her age by the criminal justice system, was sentenced to serve the longest sentence possible. The single confessed killer in the case had been tried and brought to justice.

But Newell still felt bothered by the case. When he spoke to McLean, he felt the same way, just as he had from the beginning. Somehow all the pieces didn't quite fit, especially when McLean ran into David Brown's sister, Susan Salcido, who was with Brenda outside the courthouse after Cinnamon was sentenced. Susan spoke darkly about her suspicions. She felt Cinnamon was living in the trailer not because Linda kicked her out of the house but because Patti wanted her own room in the house. Patti and David were always together after Linda died. She also pointed out that David had always liked to manage events, and thought it was suspicious that he should ask her as well as Brenda to describe Cinnamon as "disturbed, possibly suicidal." In any event, Susan felt things were peculiar, especially because Patti still lived with David.[179] Her comments added to the lingering concerns that McLean and Newell felt.

But where could they go with their concerns? What could they do? Though McLean had other responsibilities to deal with now, Newell decided to keep pursuing the matter on his own. He wasn't sure what he would find or where the investigation would lead. But he felt compelled to keep looking. He did so, even though his search nearly led to his own murder and to more besides.

Newell began to investigate the Brown case on his own time. He started by interviewing everyone that knew David, including ex-wives, relatives, and family friends. He also checked public records. Soon he began to discover some curious facts. Only three weeks after Cinnamon's trial concluded, David bought a luxurious house in Anaheim—a beautiful, Tudor-style house with a swimming pool up in the hills overlooking a canyon. It cost him $330,000—paid in cash.[180] Apparently, the insurance money he got helped close the deal.

As Newell learned, David had all sorts of health problems he had been treated for—including high blood pressure, heart trouble, headaches, depression, allergies, stomach problems, and more. He had also been in at least seventeen documented auto accidents. He had gotten nice insurance settlements for these, too, which he used to either replace or get better cars.[181] David did seem to have the magic touch when it came to insurance.

Newell also discovered from the Department of Motor Vehicles that in two and a half years—between the time Cinnamon was found guilty in August 1985 and the spring of 1988—David bought fourteen expensive cars and trucks, including a $60,000 motor home, a $70,000 Mercedes convertible, and several Ford Broncos, Nissan Sentras, and station wagons.

By contrast, before Linda's death, David had experienced various financial problems, including a lien when he didn't pay his federal taxes. Starting in 1983, things began to improve as his data recovery business Linda took off. By 1983 his income was $124,000; in 1984, it was over $170,000. If he was having trouble with Linda and wanted to divorce her, Newell reasoned, it might not go well for him financially. Under California's community property laws, he would have to give her half his business. But what if he didn't have to divorce her? Newell could imagine the possibilities. But if David had the motive, why did all the evidence point to Cinnamon—why would she take the blame?

Newell probed into David's childhood and earlier marriages. Among other things, he noticed that early on David liked to play the role of the rescuer and be in charge as he did with Brenda, his first wife, taking her out of a desperately unhappy home in a lower income abusive family.[182] When Cinnamon was born, he had always been the fun, attentive parent. Importantly, according to Ann Rule, from the beginning of her life, David programmed Cinnamon to believe he was "the most wonderful, funniest, most powerful man in the world. She adored him."[183] This adoration proved central in helping Newell understand what was going on.

Besides being the protector, Newell discovered, David also was very jealous and possessive. Starting with Brenda, he wanted to keep women dependent on him. He didn't even want Brenda to drive and got angry when she had lunch with co-workers, but felt he could freely see other women himself.[184] It was a pattern he continued with other women—and as Newell noticed, his sexual ideal continued to be teenage girls, like Brenda had been when they first got married. Not only did they look lithe, they were more docile and readily looked up to him; he could teach them and train them. They didn't have the independence and maturity of older women.[185] In fact, that's when he first met Linda—when he was cheating on his first wife with another woman. Linda lived two houses down the block. She was only thirteen or fourteen at the time, one of a large, low-income welfare family with eleven brothers and sisters. Like Brenda, Linda looked on him as her ticket out. They began dating when she was fifteen and married when she was seventeen. After a brief divorce a few months later, David decided he wanted to remarry her after all and did so in December 1981. He also began his successful company around then. Soon after, they remarried, Patti moved in. It was something of a strange arrangement, because Cinnamon was only two years younger than Patti, and Patti began to spend more time in David's household than Cinnamon did, when she began to bounce back and forth between Brenda's and David's homes.[186] Also, it appeared that Patti came to develop a strong crush on David, which didn't bother Linda at first. As Patti turned from a kid into a teenager around the same time that Linda got fat from her pregnancy in the summer of 1984, Linda began to be uncomfortable about the situation, as Brenda observed and told Newell.[187] Among other things, it bothered her that David used to take her almost everywhere with him—but now he sometimes went to work without her and sometimes took Patti instead.[188] Her mother, Ethel Bailey, said Linda told her several times she wished that Patti would move back home, but David didn't want her to go.[189] Linda tried to dismiss any apparent disharmony. She loved her new baby, Krystal. So the situation continued. To Newell, it seemed like a gradually disintegrating marriage with the younger sister stepping into the role of the older sister.

Apparently, as Newell learned later, there was a day in September 1984 when the family had stopped at a K-mart to do some shopping. Linda stayed out in the car with Krystal to change her diaper; David, Patti, and Cinnamon went inside. Cinnamon went off to look for a tape, and after she found the one she wanted, she found her father with Patti in the clothing department. They were in a corner near the racks of dresses, and she was shocked to see them locked in a passionate kiss. After she ran off, David came running after her and tried to explain the kiss as an accident. He got her to promise to say nothing about what she saw.[190] But it bothered her for a long time. She even had nightmares about it, and then tried to repress the memory. Finally, Cinnamon trusted Newell enough and felt angry enough to talk.

Cinnamon continued to remain in prison, and she became a model prisoner, taking classes to finish high school. She also became a part-time reservation clerk for several airlines, working at a reservation center within the prison and earning a little pin money for her efforts. For his part, David Brown continued to give her a generous allowance to make purchases at the prison commissary, and she was allowed to charge mail-order purchases to his credit card. Gradually, his visits decreased from alternate Saturdays to every month or so, due to his health problems, work, and family obligations, he claimed. Of course, he kept promising, "I'm doing all I can to get you out." There were a lot of things he kept from Cinnamon, including his relationship with Patti. Cinnamon had no way to call him directly. The only way she could reach him was by calling his answering service and leaving a message or by writing to his office, then wait for his eventual reply.[191] It was a way he could keep her hoping and hooked in emotional dependence on him. It enabled him to go on with his life, too—a life that included living quite well in a beautiful new home with many expensive cars. Close by his side, much as Linda had been, was Patti.

Curiously, David had married Patti in Las Vegas on July 1, 1986, although Newell didn't learn about this until much later in his investigation. Nobody else in the Brown family knew about it either. It was conducted as a secret ceremony, without any rings or announcement or honeymoon—more to make Patti feel content that she was finally David's wife, presumably secure in his love. David had even put false information on the marriage license application, beyond what was on his driver's license, thinking he might be able to deny it was a legal marriage later. He required Patti to sign a prenuptial agreement that essentially left her with only a 1955 MG and the future proceeds (if any) from two personal injury accidents she had had while in the car with David.[192] He also swore Patti to secrecy. After all, their own families didn't approve of their closeness. It might not look right for a man to marry his sister-in-law so soon after his wife had been murdered.[193] Certainly, Cinnamon couldn't know, especially after she got so upset when seeing them kiss at the K-mart. This had to be their special secret. Otherwise, it was too dangerous—especially if Cinnamon knew the truth.

As Newell continued to gather information about David's background, particularly his insurance claims and real estate and car purchases, he got a request in January 1987 to check on some inconsistencies in Cinnamon's parole file. The examiners were wondering why she seemed to be adjusting so well, though her memory about the crime was still so fuzzy, and the therapist felt she would never be able to move forward until she was willing to deal with what happened that fateful night. There was one other thing that puzzled the examiners. When her grandfather came to visit, he told her he knew who had really killed Linda, and he would tell when the time was right. Apparently, now was not that time.[194] Accordingly, one of Cinnamon's parole agents asked the district attorney's office in Orange County to interview Arthur Brown, and Dick Frederickson asked Newell to look into the matter.

On January 28, 1987, Newell did so, driving up to David Brown's house, where Arthur and his wife, Manuel, were living. When he arrived, he saw Arthur in the yard and was relieved that David was not home. He explained that he was checking on something Arthur had said to Cinnamon, and he could tell he was very nervous as they spoke. Arthur told Newell he didn't think Cinnamon had anything to do with the killing and that he felt he knew who really planned it. In fact, he heard Patti talking about how she heard Linda talking on the phone with her twin to do away with David and take his business, but she wouldn't let that happen even if she had to do it herself.[195] Two weeks later, Linda was killed. Did this mean that Patti was really the killer?

Before Arthur could say any more, David's car came into view, and Arthur became obviously very agitated, telling Newell he was afraid he would lose his son and granddaughters if said too much. Newell told him to just say he was a real estate agent looking at property at the block, and David seemed to buy his story. He even spoke about wanting to make more money in real estate. Unfortunately, later that night, Arthur admitted to David that he really had been talking to Newell at the district attorney's office, not a real estate agent.

This was the beginning of a kind of cat-and-mouse game that led to attempted murder. Besides yelling at Arthur, charging him with possibly endangering the whole family by talking to the police, David told Patti to burn any sign of their marriage—notably their marriage certificate and prenuptial agreement, though the original was still on file in Las Vegas and his lawyer had copy of the prenup. He told Patti not to leave the house at any time without him.[196] He didn't even want her to talk to her own family. He gave her a beeper, so he could always check on her—and he did, calling when he left the house to make sure she was still there. It was like she had become a prisoner in her own home, as much as Cinnamon was in prison.

Making things even more uncomfortable, Patti got pregnant. When David insisted on an abortion, she refused. As her pregnancy became too obvious to ignore, he came up with a solution—he invented a purported father named Doug, a guy of Greek ancestry who drove a sports car. David even had a bouquet of flowers with a card signed Doug delivered to the house. Although it might have seemed unlikely that Patti could have possibly had a baby with anyone else since she was confined to the house and under heavy watch by David, the Browns and Baileys quietly went along with his ploy. No one dared to openly confront David, as much as they might suspect or be certain of the truth.[197] On September 29, 1987, Patti's daughter, Heather, was born. Patti felt her first connection of love and caring for someone other than David, but Heather's birth drove David farther away from her—just as the birth of Krystal had driven David away from Linda. He liked his women young and immature. David tried to get several hundred thousand dollars in insurance on Heather but was turned down by several agents who thought it was too much insurance for a new baby.[198]

Then came the big break in the case. It occurred shortly after David's company was doing better than ever—earning more than $250 million in 1987. David decided to buy an even larger house near the one in Anaheim Hills where he had been living—one that had a guesthouse, so his parents could live there—giving him more privacy, though they were still in his house, under his control.

At this point, Newell decided to try a new strategy after reading Cinnamon's latest psychiatric report presented at her parole hearing. He noticed that the doctor suspected that Cinnamon, now seventeen, was faking her amnesia because she hinted in her conversation with him that she wasn't responsible for the shooting, was angry about still being in prison, and was angry at whoever was responsible for killing Linda.[199] Though Newell couldn't legally approach Cinnamon himself without asking for a parent's permission, and David certainly wouldn't give it, he could try to get her to start speaking to her parole officer. Maybe he could do something to get her angry enough to speak.

Newell took some pictures of the beautiful new home where David and Patti lived, as well as the old one he still owned in the Anaheim Hills. He took the prints to Cinnamon's parole officer Carlos Rodriguez, and urged him to let Cinnamon know just how David was living in luxury with Patti. She should know about Patti's new baby—although perhaps she already did, because Brenda had stayed in touch with her daughter and visited her from time to time. Apparently, her parole officer told Newell, Cinnamon had been asking questions about Patti's baby. She seemed to be especially disturbed by it, but apparently hadn't been able to ask her father directly. He didn't come very much anymore, and she still couldn't contact him directly, though he kept sending funds to her account at the commissary.[200]

A few weeks later, on July 19, 1988, shortly after she turned eighteen, Cinnamon called Newell herself. Learning about Patti's baby had been the ultimate betrayal for her. She still loved her father, but she realized he had manipulated her and used her. She felt abandoned by him too, though also scared of what he could do. It was finally time to talk.

Rodriguez put her call through to Newell, saying she wanted to talk about her case. With Frederickson on the extension, for the first time Newell heard Cinnamon begin to open up about what really happened. Before she talked, she wanted to be sure she would have some protection from her father. With that reassurance, Cinnamon began her story that blew the case out of the water. "He was in the wrong for what he did, and I was too young to realize it. I know now that's time for him to take the responsibility for the crime that's taken place . . . I knew what was going to happen, but I didn't actually do the murder."[201] At first, Cinnamon didn't want to admit she had fired the gun, because she was upset and ashamed at what she had done. Finally, she admitted it. Her willingness to talk set in motion a series of events that led to a trial that at last revealed the truth.

As Cinnamon described it, the plan to kill Linda had been set in motion seven or eight months before the murder took place. It started with a story that Patti had overheard Linda plotting to kill David for his business, and David told Patti and Cinnamon that they would have to get rid of Linda. He didn't have the ability to do it himself—he couldn't stand violence and didn't have the health to do it. So Patti or Cinnamon would need to do it. If they didn't, David would leave the family to protect himself, which would mean abandoning Cinnamon, too, and for her, that was the worst threat of all. The thought of David leaving was devastating for her. His hook was that she would do it "if you love me." Cinnamon loved her father so much that she would do almost anything for him, even kill.

Over the months, David helped Patti and Cinnamon accept the idea that they would do it. Their were repeated discussions about how they would go about killing Linda. One idea was to push her out of the door of the car while they were on the freeway. Another option was to get her to take a bath and put an electrical appliance in with her—but Linda always took showers. They also discussed poison. Again and again, Cinnamon heard the message from David and Patti that killing Linda was the only way out—the only way to save David and keep the rest of the family together.[202] Finally, though Cinnamon didn't really want to do it, she agreed to help. David's repeated message had finally worn her down, especially when he told her, "If you love me, you'll trust me. Just believe what I say. I'm your father. I know what's best."[203]

On March 19, after a family trip to the mountains when there was a plan for Cinnamon to shoot Linda that didn't happen, the fateful night arrived. After dinner, the family sat around in the living room playing Uno. When Linda went off to take a shower, David told Patti and Cinnamon that this was the night. "We have to do it. Any day now, she can kill me. Do you want her to kill me? It has to be done." After reminding Cinnamon, "if you really love me, you'll do it," David put the plan in motion.

A few days before, Cinnamon had written several suicide notes, and David chose one of them, telling her to get rid of the others. At around 2 a.m., while Linda was sleeping, David came into the room where she and Patti were sleeping, woke them up, and told Cinnamon it was time to act. He led her into the kitchen, where he asked her to take the pills from three bottles. This way, it would look like she tried to kill herself.[204] (David later insisted this was just a phony suicide attempt, but in fact, the pills had been more than enough to kill her had she not vomited.) Cinnamon said that as her father instructed, she went to the larger of two doghouses in the backyard, heard David leave in his car, and then heard the shots. He came back to the doghouse later and reminded her to say she did it, because as a juvenile, he claimed, she wouldn't get in trouble. They would go easy on her, and she would soon be home. Soon after she spoke to the psychiatrist while recovering from her overdose, her father visited her in the hospital and told her that her lawyer advised her not to remember what happened the night Linda was killed. She cooperatively claimed she could no longer remember anything. She continued to maintain that position until she finally called Newell, saying she was ready to talk.[205] The reason she did so was because she realized her father had repeatedly lied to her. He hadn't sent Patti away as he promised. He had been living the good life while claiming he was too sick to visit her in jail. The final straw came when she learned that he was the father of Patti's baby. She felt betrayed and abandoned and ready to start telling the truth.[206]

The story that Cinnamon told Newell was close to the truth, but not quite, because she wasn't ready to admit that she had pulled the trigger herself. Her story suggested that Patti was actually the one who fired the gun, though Cinnamon wasn't accusing her directly. I was close enough to get the investigation of the case reopened.

Newell had to find a district attorney willing to reopen the case, and after he convinced Jeoff Robinson, then in charge of prosecuting all Garden Grove homicides, he got the go-ahead to pursue the matter. To bring any charges, he needed more than just Cinnamon's story. Fortunately, Newell also convinced Fred McLean's supervisor to put him back on the case. A few weeks later, Cinnamon was telling the story in more detail to both Newell and McLean.

After that, the investigation moved ahead quickly. Newell and McLean arranged for Cinnamon to talk to her father while wearing a wire. She asked David to come to talk to her quickly at the prison school because the parole board informed her she would have to either tell them about Linda's murder or stay in prison for four to seven more years. What should she tell them?

Nervous but not suspecting a thing, David came to see her, and as they sat on the lawn, he began telling her the usual lies about how ill he had been, how badly things had been going at home, and his continuing struggle to get her out. As Newell and McLean had asked her to do, Cinnamon asked David questions about why Linda had to die, and David began to spin various stories that eventually helped put him away when Robinson played them for the jury. Among other things, he spoke about how the Mafia had wanted his business, leading Linda and her twin brother to try to kill him. When Cinnamon seemed unconvinced, he suggested it was because Linda wanted to kick Cinnamon out of the house, though that wasn't the reason she left for the trailer, said Cinnamon. Patti wanted the room.

When it seemed that Cinnamon wasn't buying his various excuses, David proposed that he would have Patti confess she had killed Linda so Cinnamon could leave and Patti could go to prison instead. Why couldn't David simply tell the truth, Cinnamon asked. He resisted, "Tell the truth and go to jail."[207] The words helped spell David's own prison sentence, and he continued with still more lies about others who might have killed Linda, about how there was no insurance because the policies were canceled after Linda died, and how he was afraid of Patti killing him, because if Cinnamon hadn't killed Linda, Patti must have. The conversation helped the detectives realize how David had been able to use his powers of manipulation and control to whoever killed Linda to do so as his puppet.[208] They still weren't sure exactly who killed Linda, because Cinnamon still claimed to be outside in the doghouse when the shots were fired, but they were sure David had been behind the planning and plotting. Perhaps it was Patti, since she was the only one left in the house.

The taped conversation was enough to suggest a motive for David or Patti. With Linda gone, they could be together—and because it seemed certain that Heather was their baby, that certainly helped tie them together. After McLean discovered there were four life insurance policies on Linda's life, money was clearly a motive, too.

Finally, Robinson could make the reopened investigation official. On September 21, 1988, he filed murder and conspiracy to commit murder charges against David and Patti, and the next day, Newell, McLean, and two patrol officers arrested them. At his interrogation with Newell and McLean, David gave varying contradictory versions of what happened that night. Patti first tried to deny any sort of sexual relationship with David, but then, after she heard him talking about taking Cinnamon's place and Newell suggested she had killed Linda and tried to kill Cinnamon, she asked for a lawyer. Eventually she became willing to talk about what happened that night and testify against David.

As he languished in jail, realizing that Patti's testimony against him would be damning, David began writing to her, trying to reassure her of his love, while still denying that he was Heather's father. This was David's big mistake, and it led Patti to agreeing to testify against him, just as his failure to support Cinnamon led her to realize his betrayal and talk against him, too.

But if Cinnamon testified, she had to tell the full truth, or she wouldn't be believed because she was already a convicted murderer. As Newell explained, her story about being in the doghouse and just hearing the shots didn't quite fit, because there was no evidence that Patti or David actually killed Linda. Finally, Cinnamon told the truth about the last piece of the puzzle. She *had* fired the shots herself—though she was too ashamed to admit it. After she had taken the pills as David requested, he said he was going to leave for an hour or two and he expected Linda to be dead and the girls would have to do it. Before he left, he handed Cinnamon a pillow and told her to put it over the gun to muffle the sound of the shot. After he left, as Cinnamon walked back into the bedroom she shared with Patti, Patti gave her a .38 revolver, showed her where to put the pillow. With the hammer cocked, Cinnamon went into Linda's bedroom with the gun. After she fired, wounding Linda, the pillow got stuck in the trigger. She ran back into Patti's room, and Patti helped her get the pillow unstuck, though it went off in the process, hitting the tapestry on the wall above the bed. Cinnamon went back and fired the second shot into Linda. Afterward, as planned, she went to the doghouse. What Cinnamon didn't realize until she actually testified on the stand is that the drug overdose she had taken was not meant to simply look like a suicide attempt—it was actually meant to kill her. In one of his taped statements, David talked about her just taking a combination of harmless drugs like Tylenol—in fact the drugs she had taken would have certainly killed her had she not vomited them up. David had meant to throw her away, too.

Before the trial went on, David, increasingly desperate and seeing that Patti was going to testify against him, tried to arrange for a hit man to kill Patti, as well as Newell and McLean. He arranged for a burly six-footer named Richard Steinhart, who was being held in jail as a material witness in a murder and counterfeiting case, to do the hit, promising to pay him around $500,000. But Steinhart heard of a jailhouse snitch talking about the planned hit, so he decided to go to the authorities himself. Like Cinnamon had, he wore a wire as he talked to David about the plot, and later led David to think the hits were done. "You did great . . . I love you," David said at the end, when he thought the proposed victims were dead.[209] At his trial, the jurors heard about the hit that went awry, too.

In the end, at his trial, which began on April 30, 1990, the jury heard in David's own words how he had repeatedly lied, manipulated others, and was ready to throw away members of his own family to live the good life he wanted. Because the prosecutor hadn't sought the death penalty, David was sentenced to life in prison without the possibility of parole. Otherwise, the judge might have likely given him death, telling him at his sentencing: "You're a scary person. . . . You don't look like Charlie Manson . . . but . . . you're a master manipulator. . . . If Cinnamon had gone under, you would have walked away. Mr. Brown, you make Charlie Manson look like a piker."[210]

Meanwhile, Patti pleaded guilty to murder and conspiracy and received a life sentence. As a juvenile, she would probably be released on parole at age twenty-five. As for Cinnamon, after repeated appeals, with support from Newell and Robinson, she was paroled at age twenty-one in February 1992. In fact, according to Ann Rule's newsletter, Cinnamon and Patti Brown have been free for over a decade. After living with a family in Orange County for about six months, Cinnamon married and had a child, though her husband committed suicide in 2007. As for Patti, after she was paroled from prison, she married a prison guard, gave birth to twin boys, and regained custody of her daughter, Heather, who was fathered by David. But like Manson, David Brown is still in prison. If it wasn't for Cinnamon's unexpected survival and Newell's persistent investigation, Brown probably would have gotten away with murder, and perhaps still be living the good life.

Chapter 4

The 1990s

THE HISTORY OF homicide investigation in the 1990s has been marked by major technological advances that are still going on today. There seem to be several major trends in a decade marked by a technological revolution that has created a truly global society linked by computers and the World Wide Web in a digital age.

First, although murder and other crime rates have reportedly declined nationally in the 1990s, partly because the population has grown older and most killers are under age forty, the killings that have occurred were often more violent, more bizarre, and committed by younger killers. As historian of homicides Roger Lane writes, "Historically the settled middle class has only at rare times worried about murder, mostly a matter for other folks. But this is one of those times: even as homicides by ordinary adults are falling in number, the most troubling kinds have been rising, from ideological bombings and serial killings to the more common murders by strangers, criminals, and deeply alienated teenagers."[1]

Second, murder was front page news more than ever, a trend that continues today, especially when committed by high-profile celebrities, involves an unusual method or large number of victims, or hits a seemingly respectable well-educated individual or conservative town where the crime seems out of the ordinary. In fact, in the 1990s and today, murder has become more than news; it has turned into a kind of real-life soap opera entertainment, a little like public hangings used to be in the nineteenth century. Such dramas have become the staples of Court TV, docudramas on the History Channel, reports on entertainment news programs like *20/20* and *Dateline*, interviews on late-night programs like *Larry King Live*, and other features.

This interest in following real cases led to a continuing outpouring of true crime books about high-profile and interesting cases from the 1990s, as well as a growing number of anthologies, encyclopedias, and collections. Among them are *The Encyclopedia of Serial Killers* by Brian Lane and Wilfred Gregg (published in various editions between 1992 and 1994), *Bloodletters and Badmen* by Jay Robert Nash (1995), *Signature Killers* by Robert D. Keppel (1997), and *The A to Z Encyclopedia of Serial Killers* by Harold Schechter with David Everitt (1996). At the same time, some of the most noted serial killers have gotten one or more books written about them—continuing a trend that took off in the 1970s and expanded in the 1980s. O. J. Simpson had more than forty books written about his own trial, which hit the news on June 12, 1994. As recently as 2007, Simpson was the center of a controversy over a book to be published by Regan Books called *If I Did It*, in which he "hypothesizes" how he might have killed his ex-wife, Nicole Brown Simpson, and her friend, Ronald Goldman. The book was canceled by the ensuing uproar over the bad taste of a "confessional" book by someone commonly believed to have gotten away with murder, but has just resurfaced with another publisher after a lawsuit by the Goldmans to get any profits from the book assigned to them, not to Simpson. Even today, the JonBenét Ramsey murder case continues to fascinate the public with revisions upon revisions of what really happened. A recent turn in the saga was a false confession by accused child molester John Mark Karr, followed by reports of evidence showing that the Ramseys were not guilty after all, though they were commonly believed to have gotten away with murder.

As for other noted killers or suspects who have been featured in books, among the most notable are the Unabomber, Ted Kaczynski (*Unabomber: The Trail of America's Most Wanted Serial Killer* by John Douglas and Mark Olshaker, 1996); the Gainesville Killer, Danny Rolling, in Florida who was executed in 2007 (*The Making of a Serial Killer* by Danny Rolling and Sondra London, 1996); Jeffrey Dahmer in Wisconsin (*The Milwaukee Murders* by Don Davis, 1992; *Step Into My Parlor: The Chilling Story of Serial Killer Jeffrey Dahmer* by Edward Baumann, 1991; *Of Men and Monsters: Jeffrey Dahmer and the Construction of the Serial Killer* by Richard Tithecott, 1997); Joel Rifkin in the Long Island and New York City area (*Garden of Graves* by Maria Eftimiades, 1994); and many more.

In the 1990s and today, more than ever before, serial and other noted killers have become a kind of entrepreneurial industry, sparking the creation of such products as serial killer trading cards, T-shirts with the pictures of famous killers or suspects from Charlie Manson to O. J. Simpson, and records and artworks created in prison by convicted killers. Moreover, new technology has contributed to the growing interest in this phenomenon in the form of Internet news groups and online forums devoted to the topic and Web sites with information about serial killers. Among them is the serial killers site by Sondra London, who collaborated with Gainesville killer Danny Rolling, on one book, *The Making of a Serial Killer*, and has books with or about other killers on the way. Paradoxically, as much as the TV hosts who have interviewed her may have sounded appalled, they contributed to promoting her book with Rolling and making the public more aware of her Web site. Meanwhile, some killers have even gotten their own Web sites, either created themselves from prison or operated by fans, including sites dedicated to Manson. In fact, the growth of serial killing in the early 1990s led two historians of homicide, Ronald M. Holmes and Stephen T. Holmes, who wrote *Murder in America* in 1994 to declare, "Serial murder may be the crime of the 1990s," pointing out that "stories of serial killings have long been rampant in the media, especially since the middle 1970s, and serial murder has become a part of North America's consciousness."[2]

Such attention has given the high-profile killer a kind of notorious glamour. We decry it as evil on one hand but celebrate it with a dark fascination on the other hand. In turn, this mix not only encourages the killer featured in the press but inspires imitators. This is even more combustible when considering other factors in society that have contributed to the boom in these high-profile, violent, and often sexually driven killers at a time when otherwise ordinary homicides are down.

Both in the 1990s and today, there seem to be far more rage-driven killings than ever for all sorts of reasons—from the anonymous road rage killing to hits against business partners and lovers to drive-by shootings in the inner cities. The formal statistics are still being compiled. One can see the growing number of articles in the newspapers and news magazines as well as the growing concern on TV news and talk shows. The phenomena seems to be related to a general breakdown in traditional standards of civility and community institutions, coupled with a continuing emphasis on money, power, and celebrity—along with doing what's practical, expedient, and self-serving, rather than what is considered ethical and moral.

According to Lane, some of this response in the lower income inner-city neighborhoods is due to a set of values called the "code of the streets," in which status rests partly on owning what's considered fashionable. Especially important is being accorded the proper respect or "deference" one deserves, or one should fight for one's honor.[3] Although this code might be associated mostly with the inner cities, it would seem that it has been behind a growing number of other killings, from road rage that turns to homicide to school and prayer meeting killings by alienated teens to the kind of feminist rage that led serial killer Aileen Wuornos to lure and kill men who thought they were picking her up as a prostitute on the highways.

The ability to combat homicides with improved investigative techniques increased over the 1990s. The reliability and acceptability of DNA evidence has been especially significant. In the late 1980s, DNA was increasingly introduced in the courtroom.[4] In 1989, Judge Gerald Sheindlin of the Criminal Courts in the Bronx, New York presided over the first double murder trial that raised serious questions about the standards for the admissibility of DNA, which helped provide the guidelines that would be used in subsequent cases involving such evidence in the 1990s. In the *People v. Castro* case, Sheindlin ruled the DNA inadmissible on the grounds that the DNA hadn't been properly analyzed by the lab (although Castro admitted it really was his blood on the watch of the murder victim after he pled guilty since there was other evidence that could be used against him).[5] After the case, in fall 1989, the National Association of Criminal Defense Lawyers established a DNA Task Force led by Barry Scheck and Peter Neufeld, who tried to argue against using DNA in the courtroom,[6] although ironically, Scheck later sought to use DNA to exclude suspects in rape and homicide projects in what came to be known as the Innocence Project. By 1992, the scientific community was weighing in on the side of DNA, reflected in a report published by the National Research Council noting that DNA testing was generally accepted in the scientific community, with the proper methodology used in the labs for testing.[7]

The big question though, was whether it would be accepted by a jury and the general public. In the O. J. Simpson case, the introduction of DNA evidence using blood that Simpson had allegedly left at the murder scene was something of a watershed. For several mind-numbing weeks, the prosecution provided the jury—and the American public glued to the case on Court TV and the nightly news—with a lesson in DNA science. The basic message was that the DNA evidence was amazingly accurate—like a genetic fingerprint, with astronomical odds against someone else leaving the same DNA traces. The lab technicians were able to use various duplicating and magnifying techniques so that even a tiny bit of blood was enough to leave this DNA fingerprint. At the time, the use of this evidence was still controversial—and Judge Lance Ito had one of many hearings on whether DNA was scientifically established enough to be admissible, which he decided it was. Even then, the jury found the presentation of the evidence hard to follow and ended up not being convinced for various reasons—from not understanding it to believing there could have been lab contamination or evidence switching, despite careful lab procedures and independent testing.

The public debate that followed the use of the DNA evidence at the trial contributed to its growing acceptance in the future. Since then, DNA testing of blood, sperm, and other biological evidence has become a routine part of every investigation. There may be questions about the procedures used, but they gained general acceptance as being as indicative as a fingerprint of a suspect's guilt. And today, with shows like *CSI*, DNA and other modern technologies have become part of everyday conversation.

Another trend has been the increased use of profiling and other psychological techniques to identify patterns in multiple killings and guide investigators in the type of person to zero in on as a suspect. Much of the pioneering work was done by the FBI's Behavioral Sciences Unit in Quantico, as described by John Douglas, Robert Ressler, and others who helped develop and expand this approach. In the 1990s, this technique spread widely, with further refinements in classifying different types of killers and their methods—a response that paralleled the growing diversity in the kinds of homicides committed as the number of sexually motivated and serial killers expanded. Increasingly, as described by Robert Keppel, the chief criminal investigator for the Washington State attorney general's office, in *Signature Killers*, investigators have looked beyond the kind of common behavioral patterns that made up a killer's modus operandi to the underlying psychological dynamics that created a more personal signature or identifying mark providing important insights that might help lead to capture. Keppel writes:

> We know, at last, what makes signature killers tick and how they got that way. Since their careers and lifestyles have an overall similarity, no matter what their respective MO's, somewhere in this research must like the core something that all signature killers share, the answer to why these people made the choice to kill. By piecing together the circumstantial evidence that accumulates around signature killer cases like seaweed on a fishing boat's hull and matching the evidence to the histories of other cases and my own interviews with signature killers, we've come up with some pretty good explanations for how their behavior develops and where it goes when it reaches the end of the continuum of violence.[8]

As Keppel points out, the process begins with an early anger that grows and takes various forms until it is finally expressed.[9] Although no two signature criminals are identical in their motivations or methods, certain prototypical events tend to start and fuel the process, and they help explain how the killers make their choices.[10] Such information is often used by psychiatrists and psychologists in helping explain why a defendant committed the crime as part of a defense to mitigate the sentence or argue not guilty by reason of insanity. It can also help the investigator in trying to understand the dynamics of motivation in building a case against a suspect.

Other researchers have developed assorted models for helping understand the phases involved in serial killing, as well as typologies of serial killers. Again, such information can be used not only to better understand but to prevent or capture such killers. For example, Ronald Holmes and Stephen Holmes note that a growing number of researchers have accepted a five-phase model that starts with a fantasy (whether sexual, acquisitive, or demonic) and is then typically followed by a period of stalking—and usually depersonalizing—the victim. Then comes the abduction—or a blitz type of attack in the case of the disorganized offender. After the murder of the victim in the fourth phase, the killer engages in disposal of the body, either at the site where the murder occurred or in another location. As for typologies, researchers have commonly identified four or five main types of serial murderers—including the visionary killer (who is impelled to murder because he heard voices or saw visions), the mission killer (who has a conscious goal to eliminate a certain identifiable group of people), the hedonistic killer (who kills for the thrill because he enjoys it, often due to a sexual motive), the power/control killer (who receives gratification from controlling his victim), and the predator (who is attracted to the "hunt" as a kind of recreation).[11] This kind of intensive analysis of killers was new in the late 1980s and expanded in the 1990s and continues today—a response to the growing number of serial killers on the loose.

Another investigative tool in the 1990s arsenal has been the expansion of information collection and databases. In the late 1980s, the Violent Criminal Apprehension Program (VICAP) started to collect information about unsolved crimes from different jurisdictions, and police departments all over the country were asked to submit detailed information about offenses. Eventually the form grew to 15 pages of almost 200 questions. These data were analyzed by the National Center for the Analysis of Violent Crime (NCAVC) under the auspices of the Behavioral Science Unit of the FBI.[12] In the 1990s, this program proved to be very useful in providing an expanding national database.

In addition, in the 1990s and continuing today, local police departments became increasingly computerized and linked to national networks. In many cities, like Oakland, California, some patrol and investigator cars now have what are called digi or computer units. Instead of calling in names of suspects or vehicles for dispatchers at headquarters to refer for checking, the officers can do the checking themselves.[13]

In the 1990s, the media increasingly played a role, not only in reporting about, sensationalizing, and popularizing high-profile cases but by contributing to the investigative process by calling on citizens to provide information and leads. Certainly this has been done in the past by the newspapers, radio stations, and TV news programs in highly publicized cases. However, in the 1990s there are even more outlets seeking public input, including programs like *America's Most Wanted* (begun in 1988), which features stories of wanted criminals and asks for tips from citizens. As the publicity given to a growing number of cases has increased, these shows have generated more tips and information from the public. There are additional media sources provided through the Internet—another source for sharing information and leads, as well as publicizing cases.

In short, just as homicide has gone global in the way it was publicized and promoted, so have investigative techniques, using not only national but international databases of information and the assistance of a widely dispersed public. These trends can be expected to continue and further intensify as new technologies and scientific techniques have continued to revolutionalize modern investigations and as the power of the Internet, through search engines and social networking sites from Google and Yahoo to MySpace and YouTube continue to erode privacy and expose information about anyone to the light of day.

To some extent, homicide has continued to remain the most local of crimes, because it often results from conflicts within the family or intimate social networks, arising out of feelings of rage, jealousy, greed, revenge, and other motivations. At the same time, some murders have become increasingly impersonal, as alienated, mobile individuals have turned their feelings against strangers or society as a whole. Such changes in the pattern of homicide have made the modern killer in the 1990s and today more difficult to catch in some ways—they are more alien and unknown, their reasons for killing more obscure, their motivations and ties to their victims less understood, all of which make their crimes that much more baffling. Fortunately, the techniques of investigation have evolved as well, providing the modern investigator with a much greater arsenal of techniques—from databases and more sophisticated psychological analysis to DNA as well as connections with investigators all over the world—that can help track down the most elusive killers.

Inevitably, some have still managed to elude capture—or there have been problems in using the evidence against them in the courtroom to obtain a conviction, though they are likely guilty of the crime. Overall, the history of homicide over the 20th century indicates a growing sophistication in investigative techniques and ability to use these techniques effectively. At the turn of the century, there was limited ability to conduct any sort of homicide investigation; often the police didn't even try if the members of the community didn't immediately know who the perpetrator was. Today, the slightest bit of evidence—a strand of a hair, a bit of fiber, a drop of blood or semen, a fingerprint left in passing—can reveal a killer, and extensive databases that link police departments all over the nation and to other countries can help track a killer down. Anonymous computer addresses still leave a trail for the modern-day computer detectives. Despite a breakdown in local communities, it becomes very difficult to hide.

Thus, as we progress through this new century, investigators of homicides and other crimes stand poised to make even more breakthroughs. It will be interesting to see the developments that this century of homicide investigation brings.

Following are some representative cases from the 1990s showing trends and investigative developments.

THE CASE OF CHARLES STUART

Boston, 1989–90

When the call came into the Massachusetts State Police from a cellular phone on October 23, 1989, at 8:35 p.m., it seemed like another ordinary, though serious call for help from a motorist calling from a bad area of the city. Because the call originated from a cellular phone, it first went to the State Police Communications Center, located near Boston University, rather than directly to the Boston Police, and civilian dispatcher Gary McLaughlin took the call. Immediately, he heard the wheezing, grunting sound of tortured breathing, and then a male voiced sobbed brokenly, "My wife's been shot. I've been shot."[14]

At first, the man couldn't say where he was calling from. A second dispatcher, Gary Moran, and shift commander Sergeant Daniel Grabowski got on the line to try to help, as a tape recorded the call. For the next few minutes, the man vaguely described how he had gotten in the car at Huntington Avenue, which at least let them know he was calling from the Boston area. Beyond that he was uncertain, describing what happened only vaguely. "I don't know," he said, his voice starting to sound panicky. "He drove us . . . He made us go to an abandoned area."[15]

As McLaughlin tried to pinpoint where he was to send help, Grabowski quickly called the Boston Police Department on a separate line to let them know a motorist was in trouble, and Moran sent out a call on the city police's emergency radio channel.

It took nearly fifteen minutes to gradually learn enough information to find out where the caller was. At first, all he could say was he was in a blue Toyota Cressida, his wife had been shot in the head, the person who had shot him had taken off and taken the keys, but he had a spare set in the car. Finally, after he started the car again, and police cars were driving in the general area trying to find him, he announced the name of the street where he was just pulling over—Tremont Street. Soon after he announced, "I'm going to pass out, and my wife has stopped gurgling. She's stopped breathing." There was the sound of a siren in the background, and soon police had located his car.

Officer Wayne Rock drove his patrol car beside the blue Toyota that was now parked near a dilapidated low-income housing project. When he opened the door, Rock saw the grim scene. A very pregnant woman was slumped over, bleeding heavily from a bullet wound in her head, and her husband seemed barely conscious and badly wounded in the driver's seat beside her. Moments later, an ambulance roared up and took the woman, Carol Stuart, to Brigham and Women's Hospital. Soon after a second ambulance picked up her husband, Chuck Stuart, and took him to Boston City Hospital.

Ostensibly it seemed like a violent robbery that turned into a shooting, just as Stuart claimed it was. It appeared that he and his wife were a successful suburban couple living a charmed, picture-perfect life, who were tragically waylaid just after they had been to a childbirthing class. The area where Chuck reported being attacked was considered one of the most violent, dangerous areas of the city—Mission Hill. But in the weeks ahead, the incident snowballed as the story captured the nation, turned into a debate about racial bias and justice in America, and threatened to turn Boston politics upside down.

The story exploded as it did because initially there seemed no reason to doubt what Charles Stuart said. Plus the incident was captured by the media because the night that Stuart was brought to the hospital, a camera crew from the TV program *Rescue 911* had been following the Boston paramedic team that arrived to take them to the hospital. There was compelling footage aired on national TV when the news of the story broke the following night. Thereafter, the story became almost a nightly soap opera, as people wondered first whether Carol, her baby, and Chuck would live—and then whether the police would find the savage killer who had torn apart the lives of this suburban couple.

The news of the story broke with a brief front-page story in the *Boston Globe* that announced: "Couple Shot After Leaving Hospital: Baby Delivered,"[16] and then gained further appeal when the broadcast news played a copy of the tape of Stuart's panicked call to 911. The transcript of the call was published in many major newspapers.[17] Soon the tape from the *Rescue 911* crew was added to the media mix. By October 25—two days after the shooting—the story had gone national, appearing in *People*, *Newsweek*, *Time*, and other major news media.

In turn, Chuck's account of the robbery, given from his hospital bed where he was fitted with a colostomy bag since the shot through his side had torn through his intestine, helped fuel the story. He described it when he first began talking to detectives who spoke to him in the hospital on October 24. He and Carol had just left the Brigham and Women's Hospital where they went for childbirth classes and had stopped at a traffic light a few blocks away. As they waited, a black man with a silver pistol suddenly jumped into the back of their Toyota, told them he planned to rob them, and told Chuck to turn left and drive straight ahead. According to Chuck, he spoke in a raspy voice and said ominously, "Don't look in the rearview mirror." He directed Chuck to drive into the dangerous high-crime area near the large Bromley-Heath housing project, and told him to pull over and stop at a deserted corner, where he demanded the car keys, money, and jewelry. In detail, Stuart described the various items, which included Carol's handbag with about $100 in cash in her wallet and two of her rings—one a ruby dinner ring with small diamonds, the other her engagement ring with a 1.5-carat diamond. Stuart handed over an expensive Seiko gold watch.[18] Then, according to Stuart, the gunman became angry because Chuck claimed he didn't carry a wallet, shot Carol in the head, and then after Chuck ducked a shot in the head, leaned over the seat and shot a bullet into Chuck's side, after which he fled into the dark night.[19] Though he had taken the keys, Stuart said, he had an extra set of keys so he could start the car; though the gunman said not to look at him, he had been able to see him clearly so he could give the police a detailed description.

This description turned the story into a racial and political hot potato, as the police began their search for the gunman and soon found a few likely suspects, The controversy about racism and police bias and brutality that dogged the case soon followed.

As Stuart described the killer, the man was brown-skinned, between the ages of twenty-eight and thirty-four, about five feet ten inches tall, and thin, perhaps 150–60 pounds. He had a patchy beard and wore a short Afro.[20] He had a raspy, gravelly voice. He wore a dark shirt and black sweatsuit with two or three red stripes and a black baseball cap. He held the gun in his right hand and seemed very nervous. At the time, the police never thought to question Stuart's description, even though he had presumably seen the man in the darkness for only a short time and for much of this time was looking forward. "Don't look in the rearview mirror," the man had allegedly said. There seemed no reason to question his story, because he had been wounded gravely and almost died himself. He seemed to be an attentive husband in a good marriage with a child he seemingly wanted very much due in just two months. Both he and his wife were successful, drawing in relatively large incomes—she as a tax lawyer, he as the manager of a prestigious furrier. Why should there be any reason to doubt his story?

If anything, his story fueled a growing concern with the rising use of guns in killing. Soon after the story broke on October 24, Boston mayor Raymond Flynn and Police Commissioner Francis "Mickey" Roache met with members of both Carol's and Chuck's families and held a press conference to announce that they would do all they could to catch the gunman. He cast the search in terms of a public outrage against violent criminals, which began the process of making the case political, stating, "I demand that the Boston Police Department continue to be extremely aggressive in cracking down on people who are using guns and killing innocent people. . . . We will use every lawful tool to support our police officers in cracking down on gun-wielding criminals."[21] The attack and his statement helped fuel a concern with crime generally, not only in the Mission Hill area but throughout Boston—and throughout the whole United States. It fed into the fear of the black perpetrator—an image based in some truth, in that proportionately there were a high percentage of African Americans involved in violent crimes, particularly in the inner cities. But the case helped magnify the fear, and for a long time, the fear contributed to the belief in Stuart's story. It fit the popular image in the public mind—and politicians jumped on it to promote various agendas from gun control to reinstating the death penalty (for example, Republican party leaders thought it would help them restore this).[22] So the story grew.

Initially, the media played up stories of Chuck and Carol Stuart as an ideal couple while demonizing the black perpetrator. Besides quotes from family, friends, and business associates praising Chuck and Carol, the press kept the public on edge over whether their baby, Christopher, born prematurely from a cesarean section, would survive. When the baby died, there was a public mourning for an even greater tragedy,[23] especially as the public learned about how wonderful Chuck and Carol were. For example, Stuart's boss, Ted Kakas, described how Chuck "collected donations for orphans every Christmas and at Thanksgiving organized a food collection program for the needy."[24]

Stuart was described as a kind of Horatio Alger figure who worked his way up to where he was. Raised in an Irish family in Revere, a suburb of Boston, he had gone to parochial school. As a teenager he had gone on to vocational school, where he was especially interested in cooking. After graduating, he began working as a cook at a hotel that became the Sheraton-Tara in Danvers, north of Boston. On his next job, as a cook at the Driftwood Restaurant in Revere in 1979, he met Carol, who was halfway through law school at the time. Despite the disparity in their academic backgrounds, the relationship took off, and a couple of years later, in 1981, as Carol began working as an accountant for the Arthur Young Company in Boston, Chuck began his own upward climb by landing a job as a management trainee at Kakas & Sons, the premier furrier in Boston. Though he had lied on his job application, claiming he had gone to

Brown University on a football scholarship (though Brown didn't give such scholarships and he never went there), the Kakas brothers never checked, and Stuart thrived in his new position. By the late 1980s, he had become the store's general manager, and Carol had moved up the professional ladder to become a tax attorney at Cahners Publishing.[25] Both were doing well, and by the late 1980s, they had bought a large split-level house with a pool in the Boston suburb of Reading.[26] And they lived a typical yuppie lifestyle that included expensive clothing, fitness routines, pool parties, eating in restaurants, vacations in Europe.[27] After Carol got pregnant, Charles acted like the delighted father looking forward to the birth of the baby around Christmas 1989. He joined his wife going to childbirth classes to help her prepare for the birth. Certainly the marriage seemed strong and solid.

Stuart penned a heartfelt farewell message to his wife in his hospital room on October 26, and it was read to mourners at Carol's funeral, attended by 800 people, including the Boston mayor and chief of police and Massachusetts Governor Michael Dukakis. The press and public was even more sympathetic and supportive.[28] Chuck wrote, in tear-jerking prose:

> Good night, sweet wife, my love. Now you sleep away from me. I will never again know the feeling of your hand in mine, but I will always feel you. I miss you and I love you. God has called you to His hands, not to take you away from me but to bring you away from the cruelty and the violence that fill this world.[29]

A grieving nation felt his pain again when, after seventeen days, his premature newborn son, Christopher, who weighed only three pounds and thirteen ounces, died. After two operations to save his own life, Stuart asked to be taken to another hospital so he could cradle his dying baby in his arms.[30]

As Stuart recovered and Carol and Christopher were laid to rest, the hunt for the presumed killer went on. The police and public didn't know that Stuart's younger brother, Matthew, who worked as a paint mixer and had a reputation as a heavy drinker, occasional coke user, and hell raiser, had gone to their firefighter brother, Michael, on Thursday, October 26, three days after the shooting, to tell him an odd story about Carol's murder. As later revealed through Michael's attorney, Matthew had confided that "Chuck was personally, directly involved in Carol's murder, and Matthew was involved too in a less direct way."[31] A few days later, Matthew flew to California and remained there for more than two months. In early January 1990, Matthew finally decided to go the district attorney and describe some of what he knew about the case.

The police were taking Chuck's story very seriously, especially because his wounds seemed so grave. The day after the shooting, searchers had found the keys to the Toyota in the empty lot where Stuart claimed the shooting had occurred.[32] There was no reason to have any doubts.

The police fanned out through Mission Hill, searching the storm drains and sewers for weapons, as well as looking for a suspect. From all accounts, they thought they were searching for a very dangerous, cold-blooded man, who was willing to shoot a very pregnant woman.

The case quickly became political, as Ken Englade describes in his book about the crime *Murder in Boston*. On October 26, at a news conference describing the search for suspects, Police Superintendent Saia asked for stronger federal gun control legislation and urged the state legislature to pass a bill restricting the sale and use of assault weapons.[33] Governor Dukakis and Attorney General James Shanon made their own announcements, asking for additional funding for crime prevention programs.

Meanwhile, members of the black community, such as Louis Elisa, president of Boston's NAACP chapter, were getting involved in the case by criticizing the quick and extensive hunt for a black suspect. As Elisa pointed out, Mayor Flynn's call for the Boston police to apprehend Carol's killer reflected a double standard, because the victims were white suburbanites. Flynn hadn't shown the same concern about the "101 people injured with weapons in Roxbury."[34] This was the beginning of a rallying cry for the black community and others who felt the overly extensive coverage and detective response to the case had occurred because the victims were affluent and white and because the crime happened in the inner city. As one *Boston Globe* reporter wrote, "Elements of race and class had many in Greater Boston debating yesterday why some tragedies loom larger than others, why some lives violently lost bring demands for the death penalty and others yield only private, familial grief."[35] This concern dogged the investigation over the next months—and helped bury the case after its final tragic dénouement shortly after the New Year.

In any event, the widespread attention brought hundreds of mourners to the funeral service for Carol Stuart on October 28 at the Mission Church, where she and Chuck had been married about four years before. Besides family and friends, showing the high-profile nature of the case, the mourners included Governor Dukakis, Mayor Flynn, and Police Commissioner Roache. Even Cardinal Bernard Law was there in his robes, because Carol had been a practicing Catholic. Her murder interested the church as well.[36]

In late October and early November, the police began to locate some likely suspects, which created even more of an uproar from the black community. One who was considered briefly was a prison escapee. A twenty-nine-year-old poorly educated black man named Swanson was picked out as a possibility, since he lived in the Mission Hill project near where the shooting occurred and had recently been in prison for armed robbery.[37] Presumably his name came up as the police searched through records of young black men with criminal records in the area. When the police found him living in an apartment listed under someone else's name—supposedly a friend had said he could live there—they arrested him for breaking and entering. They also found he also owned a black sweatsuit, much like Chuck had described, when they searched the apartment. It had white stripes, though Chuck had mentioned red stripes. It was close enough, and he was hauled off to jail,[38] where he was soon harassed and taunted by guards and other prisoners, even though he wasn't officially charged in the Stuart case. After about three weeks, all charges against Swanson were dropped and he was released from jail, because the police had now found another more likely suspect.[39] Swanson's treatment contributed to the growing anger of the black community of how the police were investigating the case and unfairly singling out and stereotyping black men.

The new suspect was named Willie Bennett, and he had been identified for much the same reason Swanson had been pulled in—because he was a young black man with a record of violent crimes. He had been in prison, and he was a friend of Swanson. Ironically, Bennett had even gone to the apartment where Swanson had been staying to warn him to watch out, since he fit the general profile of the suspect the police were looking for.[40] At age thirty-nine, Bennett had a long history of run-ins with the police. He had dropped out of school in seventh grade and was first arrested in 1964 at age fourteen for robbing parking meters. Over the next few years, he was arrested for a variety of minor crimes, like stealing purses, and in 1973, he had shot a policeman in the leg, resulting in a six-year sentence.[41] After more robberies, in 1981 he escaped from an officer trying to give him a routine traffic ticket by shooting out a patrol car's front tire. He was traced to a friend's apartment months later and finally captured. The result was an even stiffer seven-year sentence for assault and armed robbery.[42] Bennett certainly had a long track record of violence, as well as looking very much like the suspect Stuart had described, including a scruffy beard and raspy voice.

The noose was pulled tighter by a few significant events. For one thing, three weeks before Carol and Chuck were shot, a man with a similar description had robbed a video store in the Brookline neighborhood, not far from Mission Hill.[43] To the police, the storekeeper's description of the robber, including his scruffy beard and raspy voice, suggested it could be the same person as the Stuart gunman. A story was spread by Bennett's fifteen-year-old nephew Joey, who told his friend Dereck Jackson that his uncle Willie had shown him some newspaper clippings about his past brushes with the law and then supposedly boasted that he had done the Stuart shootings, too.[44] In turn, Jackson passed on this information the next day to another friend, Eric Whitney, who passed the story on to his mother, who was seeing a police officer, and told him. He, in turn, passed the story on to one of the detectives investigating the Stuart murder, Detective Peter O'Malley, who asked Jackson and Whitney to come talk to him. Apparently, at this point, Jackson said he thought Joey had just been joking in telling the story. After an intensive interrogation, in which O'Malley threatened Jackson with charges that might result in twenty years in prison, Jackson eventually agreed that yes, he had heard Willie Bennett confess, and Whitney agreed that he had heard Jackson tell.[45] With that information providing sufficient probable cause, O'Malley got a warrant to arrest Bennett and another to search his apartment. By now, O'Malley had found two other people who had incriminating evidence against Bennett—Tony Jackson, who said she overheard Bennett state that "the bullet was not meant for the lady; it was meant for the man," and David Brimage, a high school student, who said Joey Bennett told him his uncle had shot the couple.[46] From O'Malley's point of view, Dereck Jackson's statement was especially telling, because he claimed he heard Bennett state in front of a small group of youths that he had told Stuart to "keep his eyes on the road" and "Do not look in the rearview mirror." What made this so significant, O'Malley thought, is that the police had held back this particular bit of information. It was their way of trying to separate the genuine suspects from those who were implicated because of something they or others learned about the case from the media. Plus, Jackson said he heard Bennett say he was wearing a "black Adidas jumpsuit" when he did the shooting. All this information made O'Malley sure he had his man.[47] He was certain his tough interrogation techniques had finally gotten the story. He never thought to question that maybe his tough questioning had helped bring out the story the police wanted to hear.

On November 11, about two days after Christopher died, O'Malley led simultaneous raids on the apartments of Bennett's girlfriend and his mother and arrested Bennett at his girlfriend's home. After they took him to headquarters, booked him, and placed him in a cell, they held him on armed robbery charges for the video store robbery in Brookline. They didn't charge him with the murders of Carol and Christopher yet, because they lacked physical evidence, including a gun that might tie him to the killings. Bennett said he was with his girlfriend the night of the Stuart shootings. Unfortunately, in an attempt to be helpful, Bennett's two sisters told a reporter he had been with them that night at the Parker Street Lounge, a bar in the heart of the Mission Hill area. Their story, plainly contradicting Bennett's own tale, only made the police even more convinced they had the right man.[48] Stuart helpfully looked at some photos of possible suspects about ten days later and said he had a "strong physical reaction" to Bennett's picture, which helped further convince the police.[49]

In the meantime, there were other developments that helped show that this case was going to be anything but quietly and simply resolved with Bennett's arrest. In fact, it got even crazier and more confusing.

The first volley came from Bennett's family, who claimed he was "being framed because of his long criminal record and his history of violence."[50] Yet in light of the contradictory stories told by Bennett's girlfriend and his sisters about where he was on that night, it was hard to support a claim of bias. The police had the statements from Dereck Jackson, Eric Whitney, Tony Jackson, and David Brimage about Bennett's story. When the victims of the video store robbery identified Bennett at a line-up as the man who held him up, that further firmed up the police resolve they had the right man.[51]

The controversy over Bennett's arrest on racial grounds was starting to build, with some civil rights leaders and community activists complaining because the newspapers described the man alleged to have shot the Stuarts as a black man, whereas one *Globe* columnist noted that the newspaper had at one point left out the racial description of the alleged attacker, which he felt was wrong and misleading, since the information was relevant.[52] This racial controversy soon heated up even more.

On November 15, the launching of a Suffolk County grand jury investigation into the shooting helped complicate and inflame the situation even more, in part because some of the information leaked out of the normally secret proceedings. Among other things, both Dereck Jackson and Eric Whitney told and then sought to recant their story about Bennett's confession. Jackson's lawyer even set up a meeting with O'Malley and an assistant district attorney, at which Whitney said he never heard Bennett confess he shot the Stuarts, and he went back to the grand jury to tell them that, saying he didn't want Bennett to go to jail because of his false testimony.[53] Both Dereck Jackson and Eric Whitney told the *Boston Globe* that they had felt pressured by O'Malley to provide information he wanted to hear against Bennett.[54] It's not really clear what happened, because the grand jury eventually disbanded without commenting on their statements, nor did the police or district attorney ever comment further or use their statements in filing charges. Bennett was never indicted or charged for the murders of Carol or Christopher Stuart, though he was held on $50,000 bail for the Brookline video store robbery.[55]

In any event, the same day that Jackson was telling the grand jury that he heard about Bennett's confession, Stuart was telling the police that he registered his "strong physical reaction" to Bennett's picture. For the time being, at least publicly, the investigation focusing on Bennett as the primary suspect seemed to be on course.

The first cracks were starting to appear in the case, mostly in the form of rumors and whispers that everything wasn't quite as good as it seemed about the Stuarts' marriage. It wasn't exactly clear where these rumors started, but it seems that one reporter told a detective he heard a report that Chuck had gone to one of his friends from high school a few months before the shooting and asked if he would kill his wife for him. When the detective called the man who was supposedly approached, the man denied having any such conversation.[56] Unofficially there were only bits and pieces of rumors. Outwardly, it seemed likely that Bennett—a man with a clear history of violence, including shooting one policeman and threatening another—had been the gunman just as Stuart said. After all, he fit the description so very closely. For the time being, Stuart was regarded as a hero and attracted public sympathy for the terrible loss of his wife and child and the wound he had suffered. He almost died—and a month after the murder, he was still wearing a colostomy bag. He would probably have to continue to wear it for months.

By early December, Stuart was on the mend. He continued to have numerous visitors, including family members and people from work, including a former co-worker, Debbie Allen, who met Chuck when she was working summers at Kakas & Sons and attended Brown University the rest of the year. Debbie called him almost every day at the hospital, sometimes talking to him for up to half an hour. When she told him she couldn't afford to call him every day as he asked, he gave her his telephone credit card to help pay for the calls.[57] Later, there were questions about Stuart's relationship with Debbie—was it romantic and did that have anything to do with Carol's death? For now, she appeared to be a supportive friend.

Stuart's brothers Michael and Mark often came to visit, sometimes bringing him papers from his safe at home, which included some insurance policies on himself and Carol.[58] Matthew didn't visit because he was in California.

On December 5, Stuart was able to go home, though instead of going to his split-level house in Reading, he moved in with his parents in Revere. He still had to wear his uncomfortable colostomy bag. The media scrutiny had quieted down, and he could start quietly rebuilding his life. One of the first things he did was sign the papers on an $82,000 life insurance policy that Carol had taken out through her employer.[59] He had to go to Boston to sign the papers. It would help as he healed, before he was ready to go back to work.

The police still had Bennett in prison, and the big question the media was asking was whether the district attorney or grand jury would charge him with the Stuart murders and shooting. If so, the police would need to have Stuart's firm ID of Bennett as his attacker, more than his comment that he felt a "strong physical reaction" to the photos he saw. In late December, the Boston police sought to have Stuart come in for a line-up to positively identify Bennett so he could be charged; otherwise, Bennett would be cleared of any suspicion. It took some weeks for Bennett's lawyer to try to prohibit the line-up through a request to the Superior Court judge and then an appeal. On December 28, Supreme Court Judge Neil Lynch approved the line-up. A few hours later, Stuart was at the police headquarters, watching as eight black men of approximately the same age and height were asked to walk before him. No one said anything as he watched closely, and finally, Stuart pointed at Bennett and stated that, "He looks most like the guy."[60] Without talking to reporters, Stuart quickly left, but the word went out that he had given a positive ID. Presumably the case was almost closed. It seemed like an indictment for murder against Bennett would soon be forthcoming.

The case exploded into something else, and it left some with even more questions about what happened that fateful night. What occurred in mid-December is that Matthew came back from California. He had told his girlfriend that he had some role in the Stuart shootings. When he had shared this information with his brother Michael, Michael had kept quiet about Matthew's involvement. But his girlfriend had told her parents, and they had gone to their lawyer on Christmas Eve to ask him what to do, presumably to protect their daughter from being tied into what could be a very messy situation.[61]

As a result, Michael called a family meeting for January 1 or 2 to discuss what to do, because it appeared that Chuck was likely to be revealed as at least a conspirator in the deaths of his wife and son. If the information could no longer be contained, the question was what to do about it. In effect, their response was one of spin or damage control. The morality of whatever Chuck might have done was not the issue.

Apparently, what had led up to this meeting is that Matthew had decided he could no longer keep quiet about what he knew—either because, as he claimed later, he didn't feel comfortable with having an innocent man charged with the shooting, or because he was afraid that his girlfriend was about to spill the beans. It was to his own benefit to come forward before he found himself charged with a crime.[62]

In any event, for whatever reason, Matthew told his brothers and other family members that he planned to go to the district attorney and tell what he knew about the shooting. Matthew went to a local tavern and told two friends how depressed he had been since he had come back from California. "So now I've got to do it," he told them. Once he did what he did, whatever it was, "You'll all know . . . The whole world would know."[63]

The same day members of the family were meeting, Chuck was going around his everyday activities with his colostomy bag. Among other things, he received a $10,000 certified check from the bank, drawing on the $82,000 life insurance settlement he had gotten a few weeks before, and he used it to buy a new car. He traded in the used Toyota that had been involved in the shooting toward the price of the new car, which was about $22,000. Then, he bought a $250 gold brooch, which some speculate was for Debbie Allen's birthday the next day, though she claimed she never got it.[64] He also spent $1,000 for a pair of diamond earrings to give to his mother.

On January 3, Matthew went to the DA's office, accompanied by his lawyer and best friend John "Jack" McMahon. Matthew told his story, which had already been given to the DA's office in a synopsis by his lawyer. The DA's office never officially reported what happened at this meeting. According to Matthew, a few weeks before Chuck and Carol were shot, Chuck approached Matthew to propose a deal. It was an unusual offer, since Chuck hadn't spoken to Matthew for almost two years, but Matthew was willing to listen since he was impressed with the way his brother had made a success of his life.[65]

Chuck told him he needed Matthew's help to rip off an insurance company for some big money by robbing his own house. Presumably, Chuck thought Matthew might do this because he had been involved in a kind of prank about four years earlier when he and a friend, after some heavy drinking, had broken into an unoccupied house in the neighborhood and had been arrested by the police. The incident was dropped because the owners knew the Stuarts. In any case, Chuck made the offer, which included $5,000, to take the property. Matthew said he agreed, although when he slipped into Chuck's house to take the items, Chuck and Carol came home earlier than expected, and so, without taking anything, he hid in the bathroom and then slipped away without being seen.[66]

He didn't get the $5,000 Chuck promised, but a few weeks later, his brother proposed another scheme—this time offering him $10,000 to steal something from Kakas & Sons. Matthew agreed, and this time to prepare for the plan, he met Chuck near the Brigham and Women's Hospital, whereupon Chuck led him on a tour of the neighborhood and then drove him to an isolated spot in the Mission Hill area. Chuck explained he would meet him there the next night between 8:15 and 8:30 p.m. with a package. Matthew should be there in his car with the window open, Chuck would toss the package in, and Matthew's job was to get rid of the package. In return, he would get $10,000.

The next night, October 23, he appeared at that location according to plan. Chuck drove up and asked Matthew to follow him to another location, whereupon he tossed him a small package, told Matthew to get rid of it, and drove away.[67] At this point Carol had presumably already been shot and was slumped over in the car, although Matthew said he didn't notice her; nor did he notice that Chuck was wounded or in pain. He took the package and drove away, and Chuck did the same. After he left the area, Matthew stopped, looked in the package, and saw that it contained various items, which he discarded—the nickel-plated .38 revolver, a woman's purse, and some jewelry and make-up. When he saw the gun, he became nervous and called his friend McMahon. They drove to an isolated area near a railroad trestle that crossed the Pines River. They walked out to bridge, and Matthew took Carol's engagement ring from the pile of jewelry, thinking maybe Chuck might want to have this back, and tossed the purse with the make-up and jewelry into the water. McMahon threw the gun even further away into the river.

One of the prosecutors looked at Matthew skeptically, wondering why they should believe this wild story. Matthew pulled out Carol's engagement ring and put it on the table.[68] In effect, the revelation gave the story at least a ring of truth, although the story might raise many questions—such as why Matthew didn't see Carol in the car or notice that Chuck was wounded, or if Chuck could shoot himself between the first location, where he met Matthew, and the second, where he gave him the bundle, without Matthew seeing this. How could the badly wounded Chuck drive so easily from one location to another and then keep on driving for about fifteen minutes while talking to the dispatcher?[69] There were clearly some holes in Matthew's story that might have been explored further if the case went to trial.

Matthew and his lawyer sought to claim that he was covered from being prosecuted for his role in the cover-up under a special statute in Massachusetts called the blood relative law that was passed in 1784. Though little used, this law basically states that a person can't be prosecuted for harboring a blood relative or helping him conceal a crime, and therefore can't be prosecuted as "an accessory after the fact."[70] If the crime occurred when Carol died in the hospital, or if Matthew did more to help with the crime than he claimed, he wouldn't be covered under the law. This was one of those hard questions that was never explored in light of what happened the next day. It was something no one expected—and it raised many more unanswered questions.

On January 3, Chuck Stuart felt a growing pressure on him because he hadn't been able to persuade Matthew to keep quiet about his story, and his brothers and sister hadn't been able to convince him either. Chuck may not have known exactly what Matthew was going to say, but he knew it would bring problems, including the police coming to him to ask more questions. They might charge Chuck with something.[71]

After he returned home from his shopping trip in his new car, he tried to find a lawyer, initially contacting his family's lawyer, John T. Dawley. But after Dawley turned him down, telling him he already represented his father and mother and giving him a list of other lawyers to contact, Chuck apparently felt a growing sense of desperation. He never hired another lawyer. Instead, later that day he drove across Boston to Braintree, where he checked into the Sheraton-Tara hotel shortly before 10 p.m. without any luggage, asked for a 4:30 a.m. wake-up call, and made one untraced telephone call to a number in Boston.[72] Was the call to arrange a meeting with someone? Or did he call a lawyer without success? No one will ever know, unless whoever he called should come forward. This call is significant in light of what happened the next day.

The last time anyone saw Chuck Stuart alive was at 2 a.m. that night, when he walked into an all-night convenience store near the hotel. The two clerks on duty noticed that he was in an unusually good mood as he browsed around with a big grin on his face. After buying a soda and snack, he apparently returned to his hotel, and at 4:30 in the morning, he left again. At some point, he changed his clothes from the black pullover sweater and black slacks he wore in the convenience store to a pair of blue jeans and a parka, though it's not clear where he did so, since he had checked into the hotel without any luggage.[73] He didn't go home, because by now the police were watching his house in Reading; as to where else he might have gone, no one is saying.

Sometime after he left the hotel and before 7 a.m., Stuart drove to the Tobin Bridge, which is where a state trooper, Jerome Cronin, saw the car with its hood open, the engine running, and its emergency flashers on. No one was in the car. When he looked more closely, he saw Chuck Stuart's driver's license on the front seat and a handwritten note that had been scribbled on a piece of stationery with the Sheraton-Tara letterhead. The letter stated that "Chuck didn't have the strength to continue, loved his family, and had been through hell."[74] He said he had been drained by the allegations against him. He did not actually confess that he had done anything; nor did he state what he intended to do, though the note was widely reported as both a suicide note and a confession.

In any case, after seeing the note, Cronin did a license plate check on the vehicle and found that it was in fact registered to Stuart. Just in case the car had been left to conceal a getaway, the local police commanded a check of outbound flights at the Logan International Airport near Boston.

Soon the hunt was over. A few minutes after 7 a.m., a man called the police to report he thought he saw a body floating in the river, and the watch commanders asked the state police diving team to check.[75] Five hours later the results were in. The divers found Chuck Stuart's body on the bottom of the river, about twenty-five feet down, and they took it to the morgue. It seemed quite clear from the location of the body that Stuart had fallen into the Mystic River from the Tobin Bridge. The few abrasions on the side of his face probably occurred when he hit the water at over 100 miles per hour.[76]

The news of his death went out on the wires and hit the front pages and TV news shows, sending shock waves through the country. All the rumors about the not-so-picture-perfect relationship of Charles and Carol Stuart bubbled to the surface. The news suggested a shocking truth—that Bennett wasn't the killer after all, that Stuart had committed suicide because the police had come to suspect that he was the real killer.

Later that afternoon, a team of divers checking out Matthew's story about the Pines River found the package with Carol's handbag, jewelry, and make-up just where Matthew said he had thrown it. They did not find the gun—but four days later they did, after McMahon described how he had tossed it. All this further confirmed what Chuck had said in his 911 call—that there had been three shots fired that night. When the ballistics report came in a few weeks later, it confirmed that the bullets removed from Carol's and Chuck's wounds were from that gun.[77]

It all seemed very neat and complete. Matthew's story and the evidence clearly showed that Bennett didn't do it and Chuck did, particularly as more stories began to surface about the problems in Stuart's marriage. In particular, it seems that Chuck really didn't want Carol to be pregnant because this meant the end of the good life they enjoyed. Carol would be leaving her high-income job to stay home and care for the child; they would have to cut back on their lifestyle, which included trips to Europe. He wouldn't have the money to pursue his dream of opening a restaurant. When he asked her to have an abortion, Carol refused. Perhaps he had been seeing Debbie Allen on the side, though that possibility is less obvious, and Allen has denied there was any romantic relationship. In any case, after Carol refused the abortion, it seemed Stuart began planning to get rid of her, determined to continue living well and perhaps using life insurance money to do so. Presumably he set up the scheme with Matthew, although in his panicky confusion after shooting Carol, perhaps he shot himself more seriously than he originally planned, nearly killing himself rather than just wounding himself enough to deflect suspicion. He took the gun out of the Kakas & Sons safe, as it turned out, although the owners didn't know this at the time. That's what Jay Kakas said when he called the district attorney to report that he had put the gun in the store's safe about ten years before and then forgotten about it.[78]

This is how the story played out over the next weeks, as the news media went wild with continuing news reports, stories in *Newsweek*, *Time*, and *People*, features on *Nightline*, *Geraldo*, *Today*, and other programs. From portraying the Stuarts as the golden couple and poor aggrieved Chuck as the victim of an urban nightmare, the story turned 180 degrees to describe Bennett as an innocent victim and Stuart the sociopathic fiend who had killed his pregnant wife and unborn son for money.[79] At the same time, the story contributed to a political nightmare for the mayor and police by showing how they and the district attorney had so energetically gone after a black suspect based on Stuart's accusations, now shown to be false, rather than carefully investigating the case in the first place. It seemed a blatant case of biased justice, and various black groups and political activists quickly jumped on the case to support their political goals. Willie Bennett's lawyer at the time issued a statement that was highly critical of the police and prosecutors, noting among other things that Bennett had been made a scapegoat and his life had been ruined.[80] The rhetoric contributed to the political posturing and claims of racism that echoed after the case itself was seemingly resolved.

In hindsight, there were peculiar contradictions in Stuart's 911 call and his story from the hospital that suggested he was involved in plotting Carol's death—such as his failure to identify signs or other landmarks in the area or call out to any passersby for help, prolonging the search for his car. Also, Chuck's repeated questions about his wife in the hospital might have been to learn if she was dead.[81] There are also questions about Matthew's involvement that have not been answered. For example, although the hospital personnel, DA's office, and police have not released any details about Chuck's injury, a camera close-up of the wound, captured by the camera crew for *Rescue 911*, shows that the bullet entered his body low down on his right side, almost in the back, just above the kidney. That's why the doctors who examined him didn't suspect that he had shot himself; he would have to be something of a contortionist to do so.[82] The story that went out in the media and has been generally accepted after Chuck was found in the river is that he shot himself as a cover story after he shot Carol. But the question remains: Did he really do it? Was there a third person that night who shot him?

Did Chuck jump off the bridge himself to commit suicide? If so, why buy the new car? Why be so chipper and cheerful at 2 a.m. in the convenience store? The note left in the car talked of his pain and suffering but doesn't indicate his intention to actually kill himself. Was something else planned, like a disappearance out of the country? Perhaps his call from the hotel was to someone who was supposed to meet him to help him. Perhaps that person met him at the bridge and pushed him off. Or maybe Stuart did do the shooting and jumped off the bridge as the generally accepted story goes because he was accused as the killer and he couldn't face that revealed truth about himself.

We will probably never know, because after Stuart's death, the police and district attorney basically closed the investigation. The case had created political and racial havoc. No one wanted to pick at the wounds. As Englade writes at the end of his detailed examination of the case, because there was no further investigation or trial, "We don't know for sure if Chuck was guilty or if he committed suicide."[83] In fact, the case has been surrounded by a lack of official information, almost like a wall of silence has been built around it. There is none of the usual true crime story paper trail, such as court records, depositions, transcripts of interrogations, statements from investigators and prosecutors, police reports, public records, and so on. Even the autopsy report in the case was kept from the public.[84] There have been none of the usual leaks of someone willing to talk in a criminal case. The prosecutor, police, lawyer for the defendant—everyone shut up. Everyone involved hired a lawyer, helping preserve the silence.[85] As far the Boston media has been concerned, the case is an open-and-shut matter. "Chuck shot Carol, then himself, then he jumped off the Tobin Bridge. End of Story."[86]

THE CASE OF PAMELA SMART

Derry, Seabrook, and Hampton Beach, New Hampshire, 1990–91

Derry, New Hampshire, in 1990 was a kind of quiet New England town where people felt very safe and there was no serious crime. Derry was a town of about 32,000 people, located in Rockingham County near Hampton and Hampton Beach, a resort community at the edge of the Atlantic Ocean. The prestigious Winnacunnet High School there was known for its good education and special programs, and it was located in an area where people felt they knew each other and prided themselves on their traditional conservative values. Some might describe it as a bit of "middle America" in the heart of New England, where many residents lived in wooden single-family homes with neatly trimmed front lawns and clean streets. Parents sought to bring their children up as responsible citizens who followed a strict moral code. Winnacunnet High tried to instill those codes in its students.[87] One of the most baffling murders of the 1990s put quiet New Hampshire on the map, when Gregory Smart, a recently married and rising young insurance salesman, was killed.

At the time the murder happened, there was a growing national concern that the problems of the cities were creeping into the small towns of America, too. For example, crack and cocaine use had been spreading from the inner cities to the suburbs, making the national drug wars seem like a losing cause. Even Washington, D.C., Mayor Marion Barry Jr. was arrested for possession of crack that year after a sting in a Washington hotel room. In southern California, the longest, most expensive trial in U.S. history at the time against Peggy Buckey and her son, Ray Buckey (plus other preschool workers), for child molestation at the McMartin Preschool was just winding down with a not guilty verdict. In the movies, criminals, lawyers, and detectives were beginning what would become a 1990s reign of glory in films like Warren Beatty's *Dick Tracy*, *Goodfellas* about New York gangsters, and the courtroom drama *Presumed Innocent*. A number of celebrated fraud cases were in the news, such as when Michael Milken, known as the junk bond king, made at least $1 billion in his speculative ventures and was fined $600 million. In Boston, twelve works of art worth $100 million were stolen from the Isabella Sewart Gardner Museum, in what was then the world's largest art theft. In music, rap was just starting to catch on—and hard rock was becoming extremely popular, too.

The case began at 10 p.m. on Tuesday, May 1, 1990, when the Derry police got a 911 call from the son of Fred Lombardi. Lombardi had been hosting a holiday celebration for his son when he heard a woman screaming outside at a cluster of wooden townhouses that were mostly occupied by young working couples who generally kept to themselves and usually went to bed early during the week. Lombardi ran outside to learn what happened and encountered Pamela Smart, who was running quickly from the condo where she and her husband Gregory had been living for almost a year. Pam quickly told him what happened, "It's my husband. He's been killed! He's dead." At the time, Lombardi briefly wondered how the hysterically screaming Pam knew her husband was dead since the house lights weren't even on. Pushing the thought away and considering her to be in shock, he signaled for his son to call the police, which he did.

A few minutes later, investigators were on the scene, among them Derry Police Chief Edward Garone and Police Captain Loring Jackson. They even beat Greg's parents, William and Judith Smart, and his brother, who lived a block away. By the time the Smarts arrived, the officers had blocked off the scene.[88] Inside, they quickly found Greg's body, lying in the hallway with what later turned out to be a .38-caliber hollow-point slug (which fragments on impact) in his head. They also found his wallet without any money nearby on the floor, as well as a pile of stuffing from a pillow, compact discs strewn about, and a VCR upside down on the carpet. Upstairs, in the master bedroom, clothes were scattered about, and there were some pulled-out and overturned drawers. They found a small, tan, shaggy dog cowering in the basement.[89] The scene suggested there had been a burglary that resulted in a killing. The police weren't sure it really was a burglary, because it seemed more like someone wanted them to think it was—like a stage set.

The police proceeded as they usually did and collected whatever evidence they could find. The detective who later became the lead investigator on the case, Dan Pelletier, took videos of the interior and exterior of the condo, and others took still photos, made notes, and did an initial search of the area. Of particular interest was the unmown grassy hill beyond the condos that led through a field to a shopping plaza, which seemed like a possible getaway route, especially when one officer found a long carving knife stuck in the ground, which the police later learned came from the Smarts' kitchen. He also found nearby a white plastic jewelry box and two pieces of a cardboard jewelry box. Apparently someone had taken some jewelry and dumped the boxes after doing so.[90]

Meanwhile, two prosecutors from the state attorney's general's office—Cynthia White and Diane Nicolosi—arrived on the scene around 1 a.m. to supervise the investigation, which was standard policy in New Hampshire. The police still did most of the day-to-day investigation, the attorney general's office suggested holes in the case that might need further investigation.[91]

The police asked Pam to sign a consent form to search her home and the truck Greg had driven home that night, and she quickly agreed. "I'll do anything I can to help," she said, indicating she was quite willing to talk. About 2:30 a.m., the New Hampshire State Police Major Crimes Unit handled much of the detail work of carefully processing the crime scene, which including taking more photographs, gathering evidence, and dusting for fingerprints.[92] Meanwhile, Pelletier and another investigator, Detective Barry Charewicz, picked up Pam and took her to the Derry Police Department for a more detailed interview. That's when she told them how she worked as a media center director and had been at a school board meeting because several issues were up for a vote that related to her job.[93] It wasn't particularly necessary for her to be there; in fact, her supervisor had advised her not to interfere in what was going to be a routine administrative meeting to approve a request she had made to teach a media studies class for students at the high school. Pam had insisted she wanted to go. This subject came up for discussion at her trial.

In any event, Pam told the police that after she returned and saw her husband lying on the floor, a brass candlestick nearby, she thought he had been killed with this, and then she ran out screaming. She expressed some surprise that her dog, Halen, hadn't barked if strangers entered the house, alerting the neighbors; she speculated that the house might have been dark when Greg returned, because they usually didn't leave a light on. She added that she and Greg might have accidentally left the French doors in the back unlocked after they had a cookout there a few days earlier. As Pelletier finished the hour-long interview that night, he noted that everything Pam said seemed to fit with the notion that this had been a killing by a stranger who had committed a burglary. Yet something about her responses seemed strangely off. She seemed so much calmer than he would normally expect only a few hours after she had learned her husband was dead. She seemed very composed; she never cried; she seemed perhaps a little anxious as she glanced nervously around the room during the interview. Somehow, she didn't seem sad. Odd, he thought.[94] It was a perception that others developed about Pam, too—a strange reserve for someone supposed to be a grieving widow who had lost her husband after one short year.

The next morning, Captain Jackson, back at the crime scene, noticed this too when Pam, her family, and friends stopped by to get some personal items. Jackson wouldn't let them in until late in the afternoon. At the time, Pam was curious about how the investigation was going, and when Jackson spoke to her briefly in his car, asking her how she was holding up and some personal questions, such as whether Greg was having an affair or if they had money or drug problems, she simply said no very calmly. He wondered why she didn't cry more.[95] When he asked her not to release any details of the investigation to the press, he was surprised when she got defensive, describing herself as one of the media, too. In fact, she was really just on the fringes, developing materials and writing press releases for a school media center. For now, Jackson put it down to people showing their grief in odd ways, as some do.

As the crime scene investigation wound down in the early afternoon, there seemed little to go on. No one in the neighborhood had noticed anything especially out of the ordinary. About the only apparent thing was that whoever had committed the crime had come in through the French doors in the back or the door that led to the cellar, because both were unlocked and not forced open. It looked like the escape had been out the back, probably across the grass to the parking lot. The autopsy showed Smart had been shot once in the head (he wasn't killed by the candlestick), and it looked like the gun had been very close, though the shot had been unusually clean. There was no blood spatter on the walls, but perhaps a pillow or towel had been placed between the gun barrel and Greg's head to muffle the sound. There was a blue towel, apparently from the upstairs bathroom, found under Smart's head, covering most of the wound. Was this perhaps to keep the blood from spilling out, which might mess up the carpet? Were the two white paper towels near and under the body for that purpose, too? The neatness seemed to be an odd touch for a burglary. Though the place was obviously ransacked and a pillowcase apparently taken to cart away whatever the intruders stole, Smart's wedding ring with three diamonds was under his body, and his credit cards were still in his wallet. If the burglars were going to take things, why not take these items, too? A small-time thief would be unlikely to have a firearm, whereas a professional robber would almost certainly take the credit cards and diamond ring, knowing these items could quickly be turned into cash.[96]

There were a few other leads to check out. One friend said that Greg sometimes gambled, typically going to Atlantic City with his parents or friends. A few neighbors also speculated that perhaps he had been involved with drugs, since there had been a number of loud parties at their condo, and some of the people who came over had long hair and wore strange clothing. Police dogs found no evidence of narcotics anywhere around the condo; nor did the Smarts appear to be having any financial problems suggesting gambling or other debts. Could Pam be involved in some way, even though her alibi of being at the public meeting seemed airtight?

The police had suspicions early on for various reasons, although for the first few days and weeks, these were tentative. They began to look more closely. For one thing, they wondered about Pam Smart's comments when she told them, just like she told Greg's parents, that she thought he must have been killed by burglars who were robbing the place. Yet how could Pam be so sure? She had walked into the house after briefly turning on the light when she ran out screaming and saying her husband had been killed. How could she have known that burglars had even gone through the house ransacking it and taking anything?[97]

Burglaries were rare in Derry, and it was especially unusual for burglaries to occur in the early evening hours, when people were likely to be at home or notice a stranger nosing around a small housing complex. Burglary typically would occur during the day, when no one was likely to be home. Additionally, the police knew it was unusual for burglars to carry guns—generally, burglars didn't kill except in unusual circumstances. If they encountered someone in the house, they simply fled. So the police wondered what Greg might have done to provoke a burglar into killing him. They considered the execution-style killing with exploding bullets suspicious, too.[98]

Initially, there were no clues that pointed to anything other than a burglary gone bad. Pam had been documented as having been at a meeting from about 8:30 p.m. to when she left to return home shortly before 10 p.m. There were no fingerprints of any intruders, though the police carefully dusted the house, including Pam's white couch. None of the nearby neighbors in the condo complex had seen anyone breaking in or leaving the scene. The first indication of any problem was when they heard Pam screaming hysterically.

The police simply kept quiet about what they discovered and what they suspected, simply stating that Greg had been shot and killed in his house, but not much more.[99] Another reason they stopped talking, including to Pam Smart about the progress of her husband's investigation, is that she was soon sharing what she knew in interviews with the media. She began by calling Bill Spencer, a reporter for the Channel 9 news, telling him that the police were not informing the public about what really happened. She emphasized that the killing had nothing to do with drugs; she was certain Greg had interrupted a burglary, since the house had been ransacked, the stereo speaker placed by the door, and her jewelry was missing.[100] "I just want the truth to be known,"[101] she said. Yet it seemed like she was trying to manage the news. As she spoke to reporters from other media, it seemed like she was trying to draw attention to herself or even become a star. For example, although Jackson told her that releasing information about the crime could hinder the investigation, she continued to talk to reporters. A few days after the murder, she told several details about the crime scene, describing the overturned drawers and missing jewelry that convinced her it was a botched burglary.[102] Two days after the funeral, on May 6, she told a Nashua *Telegraph* writer about how she was determined to carry on, noting, "From this tragedy I'll learn to live life to its fullest. If there ever comes a time I'm at a crossroads in my life and there's something in my heart that I want to do, I'm going to go ahead and do it."[103]

To the police, her garrulousness seemed not only unseemly but suspicious. The released information threatened to damage the investigation by unduly alerting the public and the killer(s) about what the police knew. So they released as little information as they could to anyone, though they continued to ask Pam for more information. For example, during the wake and on the day after the funeral, Pelletier asked Pam for a list of everyone who had been at the condo during the last month so they could check their fingerprints against any others that turned up. Pam was glad to do so. She also provided them with various records, telephone bills, hair samples, and other answers to questions over the following weeks, whenever the police asked to know a little more. Yet they didn't provide her or anyone from the media with much information in return, limiting the news coverage of the crime. They hinted that they had some suspicions but couldn't say anything more. For example, two days after the murder, a story in the Nashua *Telegraph*, headlined "Derry Family Shattered by Murder," simply stated this from the Derry police: "Derry Police Cap. Loring Jackson said the crime probably wasn't a random attack or the result of a botched burglary. He would not comment on any possible motive or suspects."[104] In short, the police were engaged in a kind of quiet waiting game, saying nothing until they had more information to back up their suspicions.

The police strategy had the effect of making a few people in Derry and in nearby Seabrook, a working-class community, very nervous. A few other people start to become suspicious about what had really happened to Greg Smart. Among those who became suspicious were Greg's parents, Judith and William. They thought it was very strange that Pam didn't shed a single tear at the small family gathering the night that Greg died, while everyone else was weeping. Pam had also made what seemed an odd comment about the police investigation that first night when the police wouldn't let them in the house or tell them anything: "I wish they would tell me about my dog. I just want to know if he's all right."[105] They found it strange that she seemed more worried about the dog than her own dead husband. A few days later, on May 4, at the wake before the funeral service was held, Judith and William thought Pam seemed oddly removed; some relatives and friends thought so, too. She remained outside as friends and relatives passed by to say goodbye as Greg's body lay in a viewing room at the funeral home. She only entered after a funeral home employee closed the casket.[106]

Judith was also surprised when Pam, able to return to the condo on May 3, returned Greg's belongings packed in several black plastic garbage bags. When she went to visit Pam to share her sympathies, she was surprised that Pam didn't have a single picture of Greg up anywhere in the house.[107] The Smarts said nothing to anyone else, because they were so full of grief themselves. Perhaps some of Pam's odd behavior was due to shock.

Meanwhile, Pam was growing nervous as well. She worried about what the police knew. At the time of his death, Pam had been married to Greg for nearly one year; they were planning a party to celebrate their anniversary, and then take a trip to Florida, where Pam was from, since she loved being out in the sun.[108] They had met a few years after Pam's parents had moved to New Hampshire, looking for a small-town environment to raise their daughters. Pam had gone to a prestigious private high school in Derry, the Pinkerton Academy, and afterward went to Florida State University in Tallahassee, where she had majored in communications and specialized in broadcasting. She had developed a powerful interest in hard rock music, and even had her own weekly radio show called *Metal Madness,* where she played hard rock and heavy metal and called herself the "Maiden of Metal." On her trips home to New Hampshire, she dated Greg, whom she had met at a New Year's Party at the end of 1986. She was attracted because at that time, Greg loved going to parties and shared her love for rock music—in fact, he wore his hair long and played the guitar, thinking he might even play in a band. He moved to Florida while Pam finished her degree, and she accepted his marriage proposal. Everything seemed to be going well.

The Smarts began drifting apart after Greg decided to settle down and give up his footloose, hard-rock, partying ways. He wanted to become an insurance salesman like his father, and as Pam finished up her degree, he studied for and passed the agent exam. After she graduated, he persuaded her to return to New Hampshire, since he missed the snow and skiing. Pam agreed, and they moved into the rented condo in Derry. Although Pam was upset that Greg had turned into a straight-looking insurance sales trainee—no longer the long-haired free spirit who loved hard rock—she went ahead with the marriage. They said their vows on May 7, 1989.[109]

Soon after they got married, Greg turned into an extremely eager and aggressive apprentice salesman, which included long hours and frequent trips out of town. Pam got a job as the media services director with the school board in the town of Hampton, near the coast—about thirty miles from Derry. She was never a teacher, but she had an office in a building across the parking lot from Winnacunnet High School, and one of her jobs was producing and distributing educational videos for the school district.[110] She also volunteered as the adult facilitator of a local drug awareness program called Project Self-Esteem which high school freshmen were required to take. She had help running the program from several upper-class student facilitators who had been through the program.

That's where Pam met Billy Flynn, right around the time Greg was taking frequent business trips. On one of those trips, in December, Greg had met another woman and had a quick fling with her. It meant nothing, he told Pam when he confessed to her, feeling guilty about what he did. But the infidelity made Pam angry, and it contributed to what happened a few months after she met Billy. The affair with Billy had begun naturally. He had gotten involved in Project Self-Esteem at the beginning of his sophomore year, along with his two close friends, Vance "J.R." Lattime Jr. and Patrick "Pete" Randall. The three boys were so close that some students called them the "Three Musketeers."[111] Hanging out together gave them a feeling of belonging and increased self-esteem in a school where students from the more blue-collar town of Seabrook were regarded as lower down on the high school pecking order; some called them "Brookies" as a term of derision, a reminder of their lower class roots.

For Pam, Billy immediately stood out since he looked a little like a young Paul McCartney, with his blonde shoulder-length hair, large brown eyes, and his love of heavy rock music, especially Mötley Crüe.[112] Billy was almost immediately attracted to Pam, who looked younger than her twenty-two years. She shared his love of rock music, and she had a friendly, one-of-the-gang way about her, not like other adults. Even Cecelia Pierce, a slightly overweight, shy fifteen-year old who became Pam's student intern and soon a good friend, idolized Pam for her outgoing confidence and felt drawn to her friendly openness.[113]

It took several months for anything to develop beyond friendship. For a time, as they all worked together on the project, Pam began joining Cecelia, Billy, and sometimes J.R. at some of the teenage hangouts around the Hampton Coast, like shopping malls, clubs, and pizza parlors. Pam drove, since Billy and Cecelia were too young to drive. Meanwhile, Greg had his own friends, and he was spending more time with them, going hiking, skiing, or just hanging out.[114] Cecelia gave Pam a flyer about a national orange juice commercial contest, and Pam got Billy, Cecelia, and some of Billy's friends working on making a video. Billy told one of his friends, "I think I'm in love," but they just kidded him, noting that Pam was married and older. He should just forget it; nothing could come of his feelings.

One day in early February, when Billy was in her office because of some work he was doing on the orange juice commercial, Pam commented to him, "Do you ever think of me when I'm not around?" Nervously, he replied, "Yeah." Pam came back with the comment, "Well, I think about you all the time." Now Billy was hopeful, wanting Pam more than ever, though he was still a virgin. About a week later, their affair began.

It was February 15, the day after Valentine's Day. Greg was going to be out of town for an insurance meeting, so Pam invited Billy and Cecelia to come back to her condo after school. On the way, they picked up several movies at a video store, including *9 1/2 Weeks*, a steamy film featuring Mickey Rourke and Kim Basinger engaging in a kind of seductive game ending in passionate sex. In one scene, Rourke rubs some ice cubes over Basinger's body. After the three watched the video for a while, Pam invited Billy to come upstairs to help her with something, while Cecelia continued to watch the movie. After putting on a Van Halen album, Pam disappeared into the bathroom for a few minutes, put on a sexy blue negligee, and as the song "Black and Blue" boomed through the night, she undid her buttons. In moments Pam and Billy were locked in an embrace on the floor. As Billy would later describe it, they had sex "on the floor . . . on the bed . . . everywhere."[115] Briefly, Cecelia came upstairs after a couple of hours, saw them nude on the floor, and went back downstairs. It was Billy's first sexual encounter.

Over the following weeks, the passionate affair went on. Billy later described it to friends and at Pam's trial. They made love repeatedly, even several times a day, whenever they could—in Pam's car, in the woods, sometimes in her condo, in a camper outside J.R.'s house. Pam, however, suggested it happened only a few times—that first night and then a couple of times after that.

In any case, the affair was not something Pam wanted known. When the police asked her for names of people who had been in her condo in the first weeks after Greg's murder, one name she didn't give them was Billy's. When they asked about affairs, she never told them about her relationship with Billy.

This was information she desperately didn't want to get out. The news of her, a married woman of twenty-two, having sex with a fifteen-year-old student would certainly cause a scandal, at the very least cost her her job.

Detective Pelletier got a phone call on May 14, about two weeks after the murder, from a woman who claimed to know something. It's not clear exactly who this was, since she refused to give her name at first, saying she didn't want to get involved. Later, the police kept her name confidential. She said she had heard that "things were not as they may seem." She went on to say, "His wife planned to have him killed so she could collect from the insurance company. And he was killed at home and she came home and she put on a wonderful performance."[116] She went on to say she had the name of someone who knew a lot more—Cecilia Pierce. Supposedly, the caller went on to say, Pamela had already bought a new sports car with the insurance money, and she had been planning the crime for the last four or five weeks. Just before she hung up, she added, "I'm just trying to be helpful. I don't want to be involved." She gave a reason for calling: "There's been a murder committed here and I don't like the idea of that."[117]

The call was the beginning of a new investigative focus on Pam Smart. Though police officers had their suspicions before, these gut feelings were nothing they could pin down. Now there was a kind of confirmation and a new lead to pursue. Pelletier was determined to learn more about Cecelia Pierce, as well as check into what Pam was doing. Maybe that would help open some doors.

What *was* Pam doing? At the wake for Greg, a school guidance counselor brought Billy, Cecelia, and J.R. to pay their respects. Pam had greeted them nervously, surprised to see them, and then introduced them to a few of the mourners and other teenagers. After about ten or fifteen minutes, they left, and she was relieved to see them go.[118] A week after that, around May 10, Pam stopped by the Winnacunnet High School and spoke to Billy and J.R., noting that she was planning to leave her condo in Derry, move to the Hampton area nearer to the school, and go back to work. Within a few days, she was seeing Billy and Cecelia and a few other teens, including J.R. and Pete, as she had before Greg was killed. She even gave two Kenwood speakers that had belonged to Greg to J.R. In the beginning of June she moved into her rented condo in Hampton, which she furnished with her belongings from Derry, though she had replaced the couch and other pieces that had been damaged by the fingerprint dust. She used the insurance money from the policy where Greg worked to cover the expenses.[119] In all, she had gotten about $140,000 in insurance money, more than she had expected.

Life for Pam seemed to be smoothing out and going well again. She even did a third interview with TV reporter Bill Spencer and described how she felt frustrated because the police still hadn't made an arrest. "There's so many unanswered questions and there's so much speculation," she said. She told Spencer how she felt some fear because the killer was still out there, and she worried that it could happen to someone else.[120] Even so, Pam was moving on with her life. She didn't have any reminders of Greg in her new condo, as Spencer later noted with surprise when he talked about doing the interview. There wasn't even a simple tribute like flowers or candles. The house looked gorgeous, and so did Pam; she did the on-camera interview wearing a pink pullover sweater and jeans.[121]

Pam was settling into her life and picking up with Billy and Cecelia and her other teenage friends as she had before Greg's murder. But the odd phone call on May 14 had helped energize the investigation, which stumped the efforts of every investigator in the department. Up until this point, the investigation had hit a number of dead ends because of leads that didn't pay off. The interviews that had been conducted presented a picture of Greg and Pam as an ideal, happily married couple.[122] Pelletier and his partner, Detective Charewicz, decided to look more closely at Pam and, importantly, talk to Cecelia, who the detectives knew had also stayed at Pam's condo the week before Greg's murder. That was unusual, because it was rare for a student to become so friendly with a teacher. The phone call made Cecelia's role seem even more of interest.

On May 21, Charewicz went to talk to Cecelia, who was almost sixteen and living in her parents' condo in Seabrook. She acknowledged she had been friendly with Pam and stayed at her condo for a time while Greg was out of town, but she firmly assured Charewicz that she knew nothing about the murder.[123] A few days later, Charewicz also talked to Pam, who in turn expressed her surprised that Cecelia could have anything to do with Greg's death. Besides, she pointed out, Cecelia didn't even have a driver's license.[124]

Again, the investigation seemed stuck. But now Captain Jackson had an idea. He thought it might help to have someone close to Pam check into what she was doing and let the investigators know, just in case there was something to the various detectives' gut feelings and the May 14 call. Jackson decided to approach Greg's father in confidence, not knowing that Bill Smart was also beginning to wonder about Pam, since he was bothered by her oddly emotionless behavior after Greg's death.[125] Jackson told Bill that Pam was the prime suspect and asked for his help in monitoring her behavior—but Bill was to keep his participation in the strictest confidence, even from his wife. He readily agreed. Starting in June, Jackson decided to try an around-the-clock week-long surveillance on Pam. Gradually, more information started coming in—though as far as the press and public knew (and Pam as well), the police were completely stymied.

Perhaps to some extent they still were stumped, because even this new information only suggested that Pam was behaving oddly, running around with a bunch of teenagers, partying, going to clubs, and perhaps too quickly leaving mourning for her dead husband behind. But was she really involved in his murder? There was still no evidence of that.

On June 10 came the phone call that blew the whole case open. Apparently, a rumor had been spreading that Billy Flynn and some of his friends might have something to do with Greg's murder. No one had said anything to the police so far, but Ralph Welch, a teenager having trouble at home with a deeply impoverished family, heard the news. Ralph heard the rumor several months after he had moved in with J.R.'s family. He had been spending more time at their house, and J.R.'s parents, Diane and Vance, liked Ralph and wanted to help him out. When Ralph heard the rumor, he already knew that Billy was seeing Pam, since he not only bragged about it but Ralph had even seen them kissing. He once heard Billy joking about a week before Greg was killed that "We're gonna go do Greg." He hadn't taken the comment very seriously then; nor did he think that Billy or his friends could be involved after he heard that Greg had been murdered. He had put any suspicions aside, much like other teens who had heard the rumors and stories about various previous failed attempts or plots to murder someone, thinking the tales were just someone exaggerating or making up stories.

Ralph heard a tale from Danny Blake, twenty-year-old high school dropout, who heard his cousin Raymond Fowler talking about a murder for hire involving Pam Smart. Ray claimed he had driven to Derry with Billy, Pete, and J.R., and they had killed Greg. Ralph felt the story might be true.[126] Pete and J.R. denied their involvement, telling Ralph they would "never have something to do with anything like that . . . no way." After Ralph walked away, closing the door behind him, he quietly came back to the door to listen. At once he heard Pete and J.R. whisper, "Billy is gonna be pissed!" he heard one say. "Yeah, you know who's gonna be next," said the other.[127] Ralph burst into the room, accusing J.R. and Pete of lying to him. At this point, Pete told him the story of what happened the night of the murder, while J.R. occasionally added a detail, essentially confirming the story. As they described it, while J.R. and Raymond waited in the car, Pete had gone into the condo with Billy. They had ransacked the condo to make it look like a burglary and had put the dog in the cellar as Pam had requested. When Greg had returned, they confronted him and though he tried to escape and pleaded for mercy, Billy had finally shot him. Then they had fled.

Ralph wanted to know why they had done it. Because, Pete commented, Greg had not treated Pam very well, and he was "worth more dead than alive." Supposedly, Pam was going to pay each of them $500 out of the insurance money, and then J.R. pointed to Greg's speakers, explaining that that's why he had gotten these. Pete explained that he had originally planned to cut Greg's throat with a knife from the kitchen, but then Billy had killed him instead with a hollow-tip bullet in one of Pete's father's.38-caliber guns. On the way home, the group had been singing as they drove home, glad the mission was over.[128]

Ralph was noticeably disturbed that they could have done something like this, but Pete just brushed it off as something "they do in the army." Ralph was extremely bothered, surprised that his friends would talk about what they had done as just another scam, like stealing cars or fencing stolen property. Paradoxically, Pete and J.R. had decided to tell Ralph the whole story, thinking he would simply go along with them and share the secret. Instead, Ralph blew the whole story sky-high.

The next morning, Ralph told the Lattimes that Bill and Pete used Vance's gun to kill someone, and J.R. had driven them there. Immediately, Vance checked his drawer and found his .38 pistol, which was now unusually clean without a trace of gunpowder on it though he hadn't cleaned it himself after it had been fired some time before. Although Vance hated to believe his son had been involved in a murder, he wanted to know the truth. Around noon, he walked into the Seabrook police station, where he spoke to a sergeant in charge of the department's detective bureau.[129] She took the gun and called the Derry police.

Meanwhile, sure that the police would soon be after them, Pete and J.R. raced over to Pam's new condo in Hampton, where Billy was upstairs in bed with her, and told them the news. Shocked, Billy tracked down Ralph at his girlfriend's, and asked how he could do this. After finding that Ralph wouldn't believe his story that it was just a rumor, Billy asked Ralph to meet him somewhere, but Ralph refused, reluctant to possibly become the next victim.[130] Meanwhile, Raymond Fowler, who was supposed to meet J.R. and come to Pam's condo so the boys could come up with a mutually agreed-on explanation to tell the police, never showed up and left town.

Pam headed back to Seabrook with Billy, Pete, and J.R. in the car, and after few stops to look for J.R.'s parents, they learned that they were at the police station. Pam at first planned to drive Billy, Pete, and J.R. back to her place in Hampton so they could decide what to do. Just as they arrived, she ordered them out of the car and told them to stay away. Quickly, Pete and J.R. got their motorcycle out of Pam's garage, planning to get J.R.'s mother's car and return to pick up Billy. Meanwhile, Billy stopped to say goodbye to Pam and assure her that if arrested, he would never tell on her. "Well, don't worry," she told him in response. Because he and the other boys were juveniles, they could only be held until age eighteen.

After the Lattimes told their story, events moved quickly. That afternoon, Charewicz met with Vance and Diane Lattime, and after Captain Jackson joined them, they heard from Ralph too, taking his statement on videotape. He was especially broken up as he gave it, because he was violating a strong code of loyalty to tell on his buddies—the same code that had kept the silence for several weeks as the rumor spread—but he felt he had to tell the truth, even if it meant sending someone to prison. As Pelletier, Assistant Attorney General Diane Nicolosi, and others converged on Derry, Seabrook, and Hampton, the search for Billy, Pete, and J.R. went on.[131] Briefly, they made an effort to escape to North Grosvenor Dale, Connecticut, where Pete had relatives. J.R. called his parents and spoke to Diane, claiming they had only been joking with Ralph about the murder. About an hour later Pete called his father, who told him if he didn't have the car back by 9:30 he would call the Connecticut state police and have them arrested for theft. The great escape ended.

Pete, J.R., and Billy drove back, and soon after they returned at about 9 p.m., they were arrested. The Derry police made arrangements to put Ralph in protective custody. As for Raymond Fowler, he learned of the arrests and by 11 p.m. he and his mother turned up at the police station in Seabrook, where he said he was willing to talk and didn't need a lawyer. As a detective sat at the table with him, a tape recorder between them, he offered his version of events. He described how he and J.R. had waited in the car while Billy and Pete went inside, and afterward, they had picked them up. The four of them rushed back to Seabrook. Fowler insisted he was just along for the ride, the trip from Seabrook to Derry; he claimed he didn't know a killing was planned until Pete and Billy got back in the car saying they had done it.[132]

It was just a matter of time until the three boys were arrested. The rest of that Sunday and on Monday, Derry investigators spent time doing some more interviews with various relatives and friends of the three boys, include Pete's and J.R.'s girlfriends. One thing that became clear was that Billy Flynn's affair with Pam Smart was fairly common knowledge among many teens. Later that afternoon, the police had the ballistics results back from the lab. Vance Lattimes's .38-caliber revolver had indeed been the one that was used to shoot Greg Smart.[133]

Although it was clear the boys had done it, the one missing piece of the puzzle was Pam. Just what role did she play, if any? Did the boys decide to kill Greg on their own for some reason or had she been involved in asking them to kill?

Even as Pam tried to distance herself from Billy and his friends, the noose was tightening. Around 4 p.m. that day, Pelletier decided to try to talk to Cecelia and asked her mother to bring her to the Seabrook police department. Oddly, when she arrived, she brought Pam, who insisted on coming. As Pam waited outside the interview room, Pelletier and Charewicz spoke to Cecelia and her mother. Cecelia was determined not to say anything, insisting that she knew nothing about the murder or even that Pam had a relationship with Billy. Though the detectives could see she was lying and urged her to come clean, she resisted, and her mother jumped to her protection. Cecelia left without saying anything substantial.[134]

It was only a matter of time before Cecelia did say something important. About 10 p.m. that night, the three boys were arrested, initially charged with juvenile delinquency while the more formal charges against them as adults were being worked up. Flynn was later charged with first-degree murder, and Pete and J.R. were charged as accomplices.[135] A few days later, fearing she would be arrested for murder, Cecelia decided to speak up. She had tried to help the boys find a gun, unsuccessfully, for two earlier attempts on Greg's life that failed. She must have been sure the police knew she had lied. After telling a friend about her fears and telling her mother about Billy and Pam's affair and that she knew a lot more, her mother called the police. After they met with Jackson and a sergeant in the department at a local restaurant, Cecelia began describing what she knew—that Pam had asked Billy to kill her husband.[136] She had heard Pam asking them; Pam had run various ideas by her; she had heard them plotting.

It was only a question of getting some additional evidence to corroborate what Cecelia was saying. It began with a telephone tap at her apartment on June 19. Afterward, Cecelia agreed to wear a wire several times when she met with Pam. At the time, Pam was still treating Cecelia as a confidante and friend, someone she could talk to as she worried about what Billy and his friends might be saying to the police. This was a way to get Pam to talk about her role in the murder and get it on tape.

That's exactly what helped convict Pam Smart after she was eventually accused of three felonies: conspiracy to commit murder, accomplice to first-degree murder, and witness tampering. Her trial began in February 1991. She presented herself in court as the serious professional who had made a mistake of having an affair with a teenager. That's the reason she had lied to the police and others—because she didn't want the affair to come out, which would ruin her reputation and make her lose her job. To the jurors and the press, she tried to present herself as the victim of three teenage thrill killers who had betrayed her trust and killed her husband. Perhaps Billy was jealous of Greg after she told him their affair had to come to an end because she loved her husband and wanted to make things work out. Presumably they were all testifying against her because they had made a deal with the prosecution to get reduced sentences. The jury didn't believe her; for the most part, the press and the public didn't either. In fact, she soon gained the reputation in court as the "Ice Princess," because she seemed so calm and collected, so unmoved by her husband's death. She seemed mainly concerned about herself and her image, like she had been giving a performance.

What sealed the conviction against her were her own words, as she spoke to Cecelia on the phone and in several meetings immortalized on tape. It seemed she danced around some of the basic facts of the case, such as when Cecelia asked her in their first phone conversation, "What if they ask me again about you and Bill having an affair? Do you still want me to deny it?" Pam responded, "Well, we weren't." In a later conversation, Pam said, "Why would a twenty-two-year-old woman like me be having an affair with a sixteen-year-old high school student? That's just ridiculous and people will not believe that."[137]

In a July 12 conversation, Pam spoke even more damningly after she confronted Cecelia with what she had heard—that Cecelia was spreading rumors about the murder.[138] She commented in the course of their long, rambling conversation:

> Even if, say they have a note from Jenny or . . . one phone conversation or something with me and Bill, then I'd have to admit that yes, I was having an affair with Bill; I am never going to admit the fact that I asked, that I told him, that I hired them, 'cause I never paid them money . . . I never hired anybody. . . .
>
> But right now they [her lawyers] don't have to do anything unless I'm arrested, and if I get arrested, then they have to do shit. But if I get arrested the only way I would ever confess to the, um, affair would be if they had a note from Jenny . . .
>
> All I can say is that no matter what they try and make you talk about, if I were you I didn't know a damn thing . . .

> Well, you know, I'm just telling you that if you tell the truth, you're gonna be an accessory to murder . . .
>
> So if I were you, once you say no they leave you alone. . . . Once you say yes, they never leave you alone, you know?

Cecelia asked, "Don't you now, seeing what had happened, wouldn't you rather have just divorced Greg?" Pam gave this damning response: "Well, I don't know, you know. Nothing was going wrong until fucking they told Ralph. . . . It's their stupid-ass faults that they told Ralph, you know."[139]

Although in the end, Pam protested on the tape that the boys were old enough to make their own decisions, that she didn't force anybody to do anything, and importantly, that she didn't pay them and didn't know what happened in the house or who was there or waiting in the car. Her testimony and manner on the stand, combined with the confessions of the boys and Cecelia, were convincing. There was also some evidence that Pam had tried to hire a witness—a man whose mother was on her same cell block—to say that he had heard plotting about Pam's frame-up, though he quickly went to investigators and told them of the approach.[140]

The jury came back with guilty verdicts on all counts, announcing their verdict on March 22, 1991, after thirteen hours of deliberation. Afterward, the judge sentenced Pam to life in prison without possibility of parole on the accomplice to murder conviction. She was subsequently sentenced to a maximum of fifteen years on her conviction for conspiracy and seven years for witness tampering. As for Billy, Pete, and J.R., they were also sentenced to life, reduced to twenty-eight years in exchange for their cooperation. No charges were filed against Cecelia. Pam Smart is still in prison today. Like many convicted killers, she is still protesting her innocence.

THE MURDER OF TUPAC SHAKUR

Las Vegas, Nevada, 1996

Many people witnessed the shooting of rap and movie star Tupac Shakur on September 7, 1996, in a blast of gunfire about a mile from the Las Vegas Strip. It was a little before midnight and the night was lit up with the neon of the Strip. Dozens of people thronged the streets in cars or walking between clubs. A few hours earlier, thousands of fans had turned out for the Mike Tyson and Bruce Seldon boxing match at the MGM Grand, which drew big-name celebrities. After cruising along Las Vegas Boulevard, Suge Knight, Tupac's producer, who was driving, turned off the Strip onto Flamingo Road to go to a benefit party at the Club 662, a club Knight ran and where Tupac was scheduled to perform. As they drove, the sunroof of the car open, hip-hop music blaring from speaker, a small convoy of three other cars with friends and bodyguards followed.

As Suge stopped for a red light at a busy intersection of Koval Road, a light-colored late model Cadillac with three or four black men inside pulled up to the right. A moment later, a man in the back seat thrust the bore of a gun out of the left rear window, aimed, and shot at least thirteen rounds at the passenger side. At least four of them hit Tupac, and a fragment slightly grazed the back of Suge's head. Two of them blew out the BMW's two right side tires. Seconds later, as Tupac lay bleeding among fragments of shattered glass from the windows, the Cadillac roared away.[141]

At least six cars behind Suge tried to chase after the Caddy, but it got away. It seemed that whoever shot Tupac, who died six days later, would be quickly identified. But from that point on, the investigation ran into a series of dead ends and remains unsolved, although there were a series of tantalizing possibilities. Was it someone with whom Tupac and Suge had fought earlier that night after the Tyson fight—a man named Orlando Anderson, who was involved with the Crips gang in Compton. Tupac had allied himself with Suge, who was closely aligned with the Bloods, the Crips' longtime rivals. Was it engineered by some rival rappers—Biggie Smalls and the CEO of Bad Boy Entertainment, Sean "Puffy" Combs—whom Tupac had accused in a recent album release of setting him up for a 1994 shooting in New York? Could it have even been Suge himself who had recently taken out a million-dollar policy on Tupac's life?

Tupac's life was certainly one that bred enemies, since he had grown up on the mean streets of New York and then Marin City and Oakland in northern California before finally tasting success. He had a heritage of gangster connections that was as real as the thug life he sang about—his mother was Afeni Shakur, who had been an important member of the national Black Panthers Party based in New York, along with his biological father, Billy Garland. Tupac had been born a month after Afeni got out of jail after being acquitted on charges of conspiracy for blowing up department stores and police stations; Mutulu Shakur, the man his mother married when he was a toddler, went underground when Tupac was a teenager for masterminding a 1981 Brinks truck robbery in which two security guards were killed. Mutulu went to prison after his capture in 1986; Afeni's lover Legs, who became Tupac's de facto father, was jailed for credit card fraud and died there from a heart attack due to crack use.[142] Tupac drifted into the gang life, telling a minister at age ten that he wanted to be a "revolutionary" when he grew up, since he had never known anything else.[143] The one thing that enabled him to pull away from his gang roots was his talent, which led him to start writing hip-hop and rap songs and earned record deals and then movie deals. His talent turned him into a pop icon and a millionaire with a bad-boy-from-the-streets image. Street life was never far away as Tupac found himself involved in a series of brushes with the law starting in 1992, including fifteen days in jail for a beating up a man in 1993 and eighteen months on Riker's Island for a rape charge in 1994. Suge Knight provided bail money to get him out, and that led him to Death Row Records.

Investigators have not been able to find out all the connections and potential parts in Shakur's death—in part because no one's talking and in part because police tactics and mistakes screwed up the investigation early on, making this a case with many hints, but little solid evidence. It's a mystery that investigators believe has roots in Shakur's past.

The problems with the investigation began almost immediately. Right after the shooting, the Cadillac quickly escaped, and despite all of the witnesses, no one observed or reported its license plate number. Maybe it didn't have one. None of the bystanders or nearby drivers said they could identify the shooter—with one exception: Yafeu Fula, a rapper from the Outlaw Immortalz group who toured with Tupac. He was in a car with another rapper and a bodyguard behind Suge's BMW. When initially questioned he told police that he had seen the shooting and thought he could identify the shooter. The police didn't immediately take him in or hold him for questioning; when they tried to contact him later, he was back in New York. Two weeks later he was killed. Was it just a random shooting, or was he killed to keep him quiet? It was one of the odd turns that continued to beset the investigation of the Tupac murder.

A second major problem was that Suge's BMW, even with two flat tires, didn't stay at the original crime scene. There was a hospital—the Desert Springs Hospital—very near Club 662, where they were headed, and Knight was quite familiar with the Las Vegas area. He had gone to college at the University of Nevada in Las Vegas for two years.[144] Suge had a cell phone with him in the front of the car, though he didn't use it to try to call the police or a hospital. Instead of either driving on or staying put, Suge made a U-turn and headed back to the Strip, presumably to get to a hospital.

In any case, two Metro Police bike patrol officers heard the shots from the nearby parking garage and approached the scene. About ten other cars also made U-turns and followed Knight.[145] So did the two bike cops, although one of them should have stayed at the crime scene to secure it. Because of this, much evidence was lost, trampled, or driven over in the confusion. Perhaps it wasn't clear to the police that anyone had been hit by the shots; for about twenty minutes, the crime scene was left open until some officers finally came to secure it.

Whatever the reason, as the bike cops followed, several of the cars that had turned to follow the BMW peeled off, presumably because they saw the police behind them. The bike cops didn't get their license numbers either. These were potential witnesses who simply got away. After two more tires on the BMW blew out, the car came to a rest in the middle of the Las Vegas Strip, about a mile from the original shooting, with three cars from the shooting scene still behind it. These included the various friends and bodyguards from the convoy, including Yafeu Fula.

At this point, once the BMW came to a halt, dozens of police cars, ambulances, and a fire department truck poured onto the scene. Instead of treating the members of Tupac's entourage as victims or witnesses, the cops acted like they were criminals. Only the gravely wounded Tupac was treated like a victim.

As he lay conscious but breathing heavily and painfully in the car, the cops approached the cars with guns drawn and ordered everyone in them, including Suge, to lie face down on the street while the police determined what was going on. As the ambulance arrived with paramedics, the police permitted the members of the group to get up one by one and sit on the sidewalk while they waited for detectives from homicide to arrive.[146] Perhaps this was reasonable patrol procedure, but it also contributed to a deep hostility toward the police that made potential witnesses unwilling to talk. These rappers and their associates with gang backgrounds were already suspicious of the police to begin with. Everyone the police questioned in the entourage said they hadn't seen or didn't know anything. Only Fula indicated that he was willing to talk.

The problem was that the victim, his entourage, and the many fans and other witnesses were very much part of the gangsta rap culture and the thug world of the streets. They already had a deep suspicion of the police and resistance to talking to them, so from the beginning, witnesses didn't want to cooperate. As one close observer of the scene writing for the *Las Vegas Sun*, Cathy Scott noted, "The detectives were frustrated from the very beginning, stunned by the number of witnesses who claimed not to have seen the assailants, or anything else for that matter." The general response was, "I didn't see nothing. I didn't know nobody. I wasn't even there."[147] Even Tupac's paid bodyguards, who were supposed to protect him, and Suge claimed they had no detailed information—not even an accurate description of the car with the killers.[148]

The police tried hard, but it was an uphill battle to get any information from anyone, and Fula was one of the few cooperative eyewitnesses. When the homicide detectives interviewed him briefly on the street near where the car had stopped, he said he could possibly ID the gunman, whose face wasn't covered, and said he would "probably be able to pick out the shooter from a photo lineup of suspects."[149] Unfortunately, the police didn't get to him soon enough. Though they might have detained him as a material witness, they let him go. Within a few days, Fula had a lawyer, David Kenner, who represented Death Row Records. The Las Vegas detectives tried to set up a meeting with Fula, but they were continually disappointed by unkept promises and meetings that didn't happen. Two months later, Fula was killed in New Jersey. He was shot in the face on November 13 in the hallway of a housing project, where he had gone to visit his girlfriend. Ironically, he was shot a few hours after another Tyson fight in Las Vegas.[150] Was it a random gang shooting or an effort to silence the one person who had told the police he knew who shot Tupac? Las Vegas detectives and many others suspect the latter; no one has any proof, however.

In the six days he lingered in the hospital after the shooting, Tupac wasn't able to provide any information either. He was brought to the hospital in conscious but critical condition. After surgery, which included removing a lung, he was put on a ventilator and respirator; on the following day, still hooked up to this equipment, he was put in a drug-induced coma. Members of his family, friends, and fans waited at the hospital every day in a twenty-four-hour vigil.

Tupac never woke up, and six days after he was shot, he died Friday, September 13.[151]

Without much to go on, the police pursued a few possible theories. One that seemed the most promising was that a fight earlier that night at the MGM with Orlando Anderson had something to do with Tupac's murder a few hours later. The police hadn't even made a crime report of the fight at the time, because no one lodged a complaint; with no victim for a misdemeanor scuffle, there was no crime. Initially the police didn't even know who was involved in the fight, but later, when Anderson was identified from a video taken at the time, the argument seemed of greater significance, since Orlando was active in the Crips and Suge and Death Row Records was strongly aligned with the Bloods.

As detectives learned, the fight occurred soon after the boxing match ended, as Tupac was walking through the MGM casino with Suge and other associates to get their cars. On the way, they ran into Anderson and began fighting. There were rumors that this fight might have been a continuation of an earlier dispute that occurred before the match when Tupac, Suge, and their entourage appeared and found Anderson and his friends in their front-row seats. No one knows for sure exactly what the fight was about. Whatever the problem, after a few punches and shoves back and forth, the hotel security guards quickly intervened and stopped the fight. Tupac and the rest of his group rushed away, while an MGM security guard called the Las Vegas Police. However, when they asked Anderson if he wanted to fill out a police incident report and sign a complaint, he said he was fine and didn't want to press charges. As a result, because the police felt he seemed uninjured, they simply let him go without taking his name. Under Nevada law, there was no crime; therefore, there was no reason to pursue the matter. Without the victim's willingness to cooperate, including filing a complaint and being willing to testify, there was nothing to prosecute.

After Tupac was killed, homicide detectives, led by Detective Brent Becker and Mike Franks, looked at the matter more closely. For one thing, the MGM security tape showed more than just a minor scuffle. Tupac, Suge, and five or six other members of their party jumped Anderson, threw him on the casino floor, and began beating and kicking him before security intervened. He was actually beaten fairly badly, but he was able to walk away. Afterward the MGM security staff and police made no effort to stop Tupac and his party for any questioning, perhaps because of their celebrity.

In any case, detectives wanted to find out who this person was and question him. They began by contacting the Las Vegas Police officers who responded that night. Fortunately, one of them recalled that the man's first name was Orlando, and that was enough for them to learn who he was from the Compton police.[152] Though it's not clear exactly what led them to Compton—perhaps they might have tried contacting a number of police departments in the Los Angeles area to check on gang ties—the contact produced Anderson's name because he was well known to the police as a member of the L.A. Southside

Crips gang. Immediately, the Compton police sent a mug shot of Anderson from a previous arrest to the Las Vegas Police. After the police and security officers on the scene saw it, they positively identified Anderson as the man in the video.

Once they had done this, they received several tips that Anderson was connected to the killing. These came from several unnamed informants who, according to a Compton police affidavit of September 25, told the police that "the Southside Crips were responsible for the Las Vegas shooting." The informants explained that there was an "ongoing feud between Tupac Shakur and the Bloods-related Death Row Records with rapper Biggie Smalls and the East Coast's Bad Boy Entertainment, which employed Southside Crips gang members as security."[153] In fact, the feud was widely known. Tupac even sang about it, at one point accusing Biggie Smalls and Puffy Combs of having been behind his 1994 shooting. Did the informants know something about Anderson, or was this just helpful speculation?

In any event, a spokesperson for Bad Boy Entertainment quickly denied that the company hired Crips, stating it hired full-time security personnel and off-duty police officers for its security. An attorney representing Orlando Anderson admitted that Anderson was the subject of the MGM assault, but he denied involvement in the killing of Tupac in any way. Later, Anderson himself firmly denied any connection, though the Compton police believed a Blood-Crips feud led to Tupac's murder.[154]

The police lacked any additional proof, though they certainly tried to find it. In mid-September, they began organizing a major sweep of the Bloods and Crips neighborhoods in Compton, which included a search warrant at Anderson's house. A key factor that led to the raids was that there were twelve shootings, resulting in three deaths, the week after Tupac was killed. The Compton police believed these might have occurred to retaliate for Tupac's murder, as Compton Police Captain Steven Roller told a reporter. In fact, the Compton police invited lead Las Vegas detectives Becker and Franks to come to Los Angeles and be present at the raids so they could question Anderson.

On October 2, the raid went down. Around 300 police and federal agents from the area swooped in wearing masks, helmets, and heavy vests. They raided thirty-seven homes, including Anderson's. As they did, Becker talked to Anderson outside the house, focusing on the fight at the MGM Grand. Whether Becker asked about Tupac's murder or not—which the Las Vegas Police later denied, perhaps because there wasn't enough evidence to make Anderson an actual suspect in this case and he would have to read him his Miranda rights before asking such questions—Anderson clearly thought the questioning was related. In a CNN interview shortly after the raid, Anderson said that Becker and the Las Vegas Police had told him he was a suspect, and he wanted to set the record straight by saying, "I didn't do it." He accused the Las Vegas officers of trying to make him a scapegoat, and his lawyer spoke darkly about how Anderson felt like a prisoner who has to be "very careful" when he goes out.[155] Afterward, with no one talking and Anderson denying any involvement, the Las Vegas

Police didn't have enough evidence against Anderson to charge him with Tupac's murder. The Compton police briefly held him in connection with another gang-related murder, but they didn't have enough evidence and also let him go. Though the police may still think he was involved, it was one of those tantalizing leads that went nowhere. In the gangster world, no one was talking, and there was no proof.

Another avenue investigators looked into was the feud between the East Coast and West Coast rappers. Tupac had East Coast ties going back to his childhood. He got his start in 1990 on the West Coast as a dancer and then a rapper for the Digital Underground. He lived something of a dual life, writing songs and performing on the one hand, struggling for a living, and hustling and selling drugs on the other hand.[156]

His songs expressed his spirit of rebellion against the drug-drenched life of the streets, but they began to echo the rivalries that developed as hip-hop and rap were discovered in the early 1990s and began to make the rappers, producers, and their associates rich. This attitude and propensity to violence helped make these rivalries more bitter—and perhaps led to murder, though much of the evidence was only circumstantial. For example, in his first solo album, released in November 1991, *2Pacalypse Now*, which went gold and launched his career, Tupac began to write about this deep rage of the streets. His words were an early premonition of his death.

Around the same time, Tupac was drawn back to the East Coast when he filmed the first of his movies—*Juice*, which was released in January 1992. It was a story about the kind of hip-hop, gangster life Tupac was already living, and it was set and filmed in Harlem.[157] Tupac's role, the character of Bishop, was drawn to robbing to get ahead. He repeated again and again the lines from his hit song, "I don't give a fuck . . . I don't give a fuck!"[158] Showing his commitment to this life of the streets, Tupac even had the words *Thug Life* tattooed across his stomach—the first of many such words Tupac tattooed on his body to express his attitude of rebellion and toughness.[159] This attitude started to get him in serious trouble with the law, as well as other rappers, especially on the East Coast.

The serious trouble started in March 1993, when Tupac got into a fight with a limo driver who accused him of using drugs in his car. Tupac was arrested, but the charges were eventually dropped. In April 1993, he was arrested for swinging a baseball bat at a local rapper during a concert, and he was sentenced to ten days in prison. In October 1993, he was arrested for shooting at two off-duty Atlanta police officers, claiming they were harassing black motorists, though these charges were then dropped. In a more serious charge that led to some jail time, Tupac was accused of sexual assault by a nineteen-year-old woman after he invited three buddies to strip her and have sex with her in his hotel room in Manhattan. He had sex with her the night before and she had returned to the hotel to pick up some of her clothes. He got into a fight with director Allen Hughes, after Hughes dropped him from the motion picture *Men-*

ace II Society due to Tupac's growing reputation for violence. That led to a fifteen-day-prison sentence in March 1994.

While Tupac's sexual assault trial was going on, he was shot five times and robbed of about $50,000 in jewels and cash when he entered the Quad Recording Studios in Times Square. This was the day before the trial ended, and he was found guilty of sexual abuse, though other charges of sodomy and weapons ended with an acquittal. He began serving his sentence (eighteen months to four and a half years) at Riker's Island on February 14, 1995.[160]

Tupac began singing about these brushes with the law in albums like *Me Against the World*, which debuted mid-March 1995 while he still in prison. Significantly, he began singing and talking about his belief that the robbery was a set-up, engineered by Biggie Smalls and Puffy Combs because of the rivalry between East Coast and West Coast labels. Initially, perhaps, the East Coast/West Coast rivalry had sprouted as a promotional ploy to sell records as hip-hop and rap grew in popularity. When Tupac appeared in court on the last day of his trial in a wheelchair after three hours of surgery the previous night, he was determined to settle the score. While he was in jail, feeling left out of the rap scene for the eight months he served, his anger against Biggie and Puffy grew even stronger.[161]

As a result, several months after Suge Knight bailed him out of jail for $1.4 million in October 1995, Tupac began his revenge. He allegedly had an affair with Biggie's wife, Faith Evans, though Faith denied the widespread stories that began in February 1996. In his *All Eyez On Me* double album, released in February 1996, which he began working on as soon as he got out of prison, Tupac began his lyrical campaign against Biggie and Puffy. He hinted at revenge in his song "No More Pain," which concluded with the words, "Retaliation is a must."[162] Even more directly, in "Heartz of Men," he sang about "friends vs. enemies."[163] By May 1996, he was even more explicit when he released "Two of Americaz Most Wanted" with Snoop Doggy Dogg, and in a video featured caricatures of Biggie and Puffy.

Financially, these records of anger and retaliation did fantastically well. *Me Against the World* went double platinum in 7 months; *All Eyez on Me*, rap's first double CD, went quintuple platinum in a little over two months.[164] They were also perhaps setting the stage for retaliation, especially when Death Row released the "Hit 'Em Up" single in June 1996, in which Tupac even more directly struck back against Biggie and Puffy, after Biggie himself had released a mocking song titled "Who Shot Ya?" to Tupac's earlier charges they were involved.[165] Tupac riposted back angrily: It was like an audacious challenge to "come get me" that hit the airwaves about three months before Tupac was killed. Tupac tried to downplay the rivalry in an interview with *Vibe*, stating in a June 1996 interview that "there was never a beef, only a difference of opinion,"[166] Suge Knight tried to downplay any problems in August, commenting, "There's nothing between Death Row and Bad Boy, or me and Puffy. Death Row sells volume—so how could Puffy be a threat to me, or Bad Boy be a threat to Death

Row?" In fact, there were still stories going around about "Suge and Tupac pulling guns on Puffy and Biggie or whatever," to quote a *Vibe* interviewer in the days before Tupac was killed.[167]

As tantalizing as these stories were, the police were never able to pursue them, because no one was talking. They were not too hopeful that anyone ever would. Could the East Coast/West Coast rivalry have led to murder if it wasn't the Crips-Bloods rivalry that did so? The police didn't know this either.

Perhaps those in the know were simply taking care of the matter privately. On Sunday, March 9, 1997, Biggie Smalls was killed in Los Angeles under circumstances that looked mysteriously like Tupac's murder. Biggie came to L.A. to celebrate the Eleventh Annual Soul Train Music Awards. He had already been in town for about two weeks, doing interviews, and then he canceled a flight to Europe to go to the Soul Train celebration. Supposedly, the afterparty, held at the Peterson Automotive Museum, was supposed to be private, but about 2,000 people turned up. Soon after midnight, a fire marshal broke up the party because the crowd was so big. Biggie and his three-car entourage headed off. At the intersection of Fairfax and Wilshire, a dark-colored car pulled up on the passenger side and the driver stuck a nine-millimeter gun out of the window and began shooting, hitting Biggie seven times in the chest and abdomen. Within moments, he lost consciousness and died.[168]

When the police began an investigation, the parallels with Tupac's shooting were haunting. Not only were their backgrounds in gangster culture and music similar, but the circumstances of the shooting were very much the same. Like Tupac, Biggie also had off-duty cops guarding him the night he was killed; right after the shooting, Puffy Combs told his bodyguard to leave the scene and drive right to a hospital; in both cases, hundreds of people saw the shooting, but no one took down the license plates of the fleeing cars. Again, it was a case where no one wanted to talk. While the Los Angeles police were sure the killing was a targeted, gang-related hit and might have been payback for Tupac's death, they had no proof of anything. They advised the Las Vegas homicide investigators of their own progress in working on Biggie's murder, but that didn't help much either. There was nothing much they could do. As one L.A. homicide detective told the media at a press conference after Biggie's death, "People are afraid and don't want to talk to us. People (rappers) have careers to look after."[169]

The other theory police investigators explored is whether Suge Knight was behind the killings. Although he was hit in the back of the head in Las Vegas, it was a superficial wound. Some of his actions after the shooting had been curious, such as driving away from the scene to find a hospital as he told investigators, although he knew Las Vegas well and a hospital was very near the club where he was headed. There was more. On the surface, Suge appeared tight with Tupac. He had bailed him out of prison in October 1995, putting up $1.4 million so he could get out during the appeals process. Suge signed him to a recording contract, and Tupac had become Death Row Records' biggest star. It made Death Row the biggest rap label, and at the time of his death, Tupac's motion picture career was off to a great start. To many there was the sense that Tupac had sold his soul to Suge and Death Row.[170] For one thing, with more attention on Death Row Records after the shooting, a shady picture began to emerge about Suge's record for intimidation, running the company as if he was a kind of mob boss, using intimidation and fear to maintain control. Some compared signing with Death Row to "taking a blood oath."[171] Perhaps as Tupac gained more success, he might have started feeling restless, especially with his movie career rising; perhaps Suge started to sense his pulling away.

There were rumors that after Tupac signed with Death Row, Suge took out a $4 million insurance policy on him, naming Death Row as the beneficiary. Perhaps Tupac was starting to become worth more dead. For one thing, he was leading a lavish lifestyle and often got in trouble; Suge frequently had to help him out of one mess or another. Shortly before his death, Tupac was reportedly looking around for a new record company to produce his albums after he had completed his three-album contract with Death Row. He even sent the attorney representing him and Death Row, David Kenner, a letter dismissing him.[172] There were some growing problems around money. Death Row claimed that Tupac owed the company $4.9 million at the time of his death, which included the money to bail him out of jail. Tupac had started questioning what had happened to all the money his albums were making and had never received a repeatedly requested accounting.

With Tupac raising hard questions and making noises about leaving Death Row, there could be a benefit if he could be stopped in his tracks, especially since he had already recorded about 200 unreleased songs, worth millions to Death Row. If he died, these songs might do even better—as in fact they did. His posthumously released record *Don Killuminati: The Seven Day Theory*, released under a recently adopted pseudonym, Makaveli, sold over 650,000 copies the first weeks it was released; 2.5 million copies by the following April.[173] With all of the changes of plans after the Tyson fight, only Suge knew exactly when and where the entourage would be going that night.[174]

It was an intriguing theory, although detectives questioned whether Suge would take the risk of being shot by a semi-automatic gun spraying bullets or agree to take a bullet in the head to make it appear he was not involved in Tupac's murder. He even had a bullet-proof vest on that night. There certainly were some major benefits that might have led Suge to want Tupac conveniently out of the way.

For all their suspicions, Suge Knight's life and Death Row Records certainly did not benefit from Tupac's death. Despite the immediate burst of sales of Tupac's records, everything began to unravel. For one thing, the attention to the case, particularly to the videotape of the beating of Orlando Anderson, brought renewed attention to Suge, who was on probation after pleading no contest in 1995 for assaulting rappers at a recording studio in Hollywood. On October 18, 1996, a warrant for his arrest was issued because he failed to submit to periodic drug testing. Soon after, he surrendered for violating probation and was jailed without bail while awaiting a hearing. He was also charged with violating probation because of his involvement in the MGM scuffle. Eventually, after his November 5 hearing, Anderson testified against Suge, and the judge sentenced him to nine years in state prison.[175] The Justice Department and federal investigators began a stepped-up investigation into Death Row Records and its links to street gangs, drug traffickers, and organized crime, and whether it was launched with drug or organized crime money.[176] After the furor over Tupac's death, Time Warner, which had distributed Death Row Records, ended its distribution deal with the label. Afeni Shakur sued the label itself—first in December 1996 for infringement for selling items with Tupac's name or image on it without her permission, and later for not giving her any money from her son's estate after his death (Death Row countersued for $7 million in advances and expenses to Tupac).[177] In any event, since the murder, the survival of Death Row has become uncertain. Suge certainly didn't benefit from Tupac's death—just the opposite. The police haven't seriously continued to pursue the theory that Suge was behind the shooting.

So who did it? Though the Crips-Blood feud or East Coast/West Coast feud seem the most promising, there is still the possibility of some kind of independent hit by rival gang members or rappers who happened to see the Tupac caravan at the intersection and took advantage of the opportunity. Whatever the motive and whoever did it, the case remains unsolved. Much of the evidence was destroyed at the scene. No one wants to talk. Many of the people who might have known something are dead. There remain only a number of tantalizing theories.

Notes

CHAPTER 1

1. Roger Lane, *Murder in America* (Columbus: Ohio State University Press, 1997), pp. 269, 272.
2. Ibid., p. 268.
3. Ibid., p. 273.
4. Ibid., p. 272.
5. Shaila Dewan and Ariel Hart, "Ex-Klansman Guilty of Manslaughter in 1964 Deaths," *New York Times*, June 22, 2005, p. A1.
6. Lane, *Murder in America*, pp. 274–75.
7. Ibid., pp. 275–76.
8. Ibid., p. 278.
9. Ibid., pp. 278–80.
10. Ibid., pp. 280–82.
11. Ronald M. Holmes and Stephen T. Holmes, *Murder in America* (Thousand Oaks, CA: Sage, 1994), p. 98.
12. Lane, *Murder in America*, pp. 289–90.
13. Ibid., p. 290.
14. Ibid., p. 294.
15. Ibid., pp. 294–95.
16. Ibid., pp. 298–99.
17. Ibid., p. 299.
18. Colin Wilson and Damon Wilson, *The Killers Among Us Book I: Motives Behind Their Madness* (New York: Warner Books, 1995), p. 2.
19. Ibid., p. 2.
20. Ibid., p. 4.
21. Ibid., p. 11.

22. Ibid., p. 12.
23. Ibid., p. 13.
24. Ibid.
25. Ibid.
26. Ibid., p. 16.
27. Colin Wilson and Damon Wilson, *Written in Blood: Detectives and Detection* (New York: Warner Books, 1989), pp. 236–37.
28. Ibid., pp. 136–38.
29. Wilson and Wilson, *Written in Blood*, pp. 191–95.
30. Brian Marriner, *On Death's Bloody Trail: Murder and the Art of Forensic Science* (New York: St. Martin's, 1991), pp. 273–78.
31. John Gilmore, *Cold-Blooded* (Portland, OR: Feral House, 1996), p. 9.
32. Ibid.
33. Ibid., p. 20.
34. Ibid., pp. 14–15.
35. Ibid., p. 24.
36. Ibid., p. 25.
37. Ibid., p. 26.
38. Ibid.
39. "Three Jailed in Arizona 'Sex Club' Killing," *New York Times*, November 17, 1965, p. 2:3.
40. Gilmore, *Cold-Blooded,* p. 27.
41. Ibid.
42. Ibid., p. 29.
43. Ibid., pp. 29–30.
44. Ibid., pp. 31–32.
45. Ibid., p. 33.
46. Ibid., p. 35.
47. Ibid., pp. 35–38.
48. Ibid., p. 40.
49. Ibid.
50. Ibid.
51. Ibid., pp. 41–42.
52. Ibid., p. 42.
53. Ibid., p. 44.
54. Ibid., p. 46.
55. Ibid., pp. 46–47.
56. Ibid., p. 50.
57. Ibid., p. 51.
58. Ibid.
59. Ibid., p. 53.
60. Ibid., p. 55.
61. Ibid., p. 58.
62. "Secrets in the Sand," *Time*, November 26, 1965, p. 26.
63. Gilmore, *Cold-Blooded,* p. 83.
64. Ibid., p. 88.
65. Ibid., p. 101.
66. Ibid., pp. 103–4.

67. Ibid., p. 110.
68. Ibid., p. 116.
69. Ann Rule, *Lust Killer* (New York: Signet Books, 1983), pp. 9–11.
70. Ibid., p. 71.
71. Ibid., p. 73.
72. Ibid., p. 80.
73. Ibid., pp. 90–91.
74. Ibid., p. 92; Wilson and Wilson, *The Killers among Us, Book I*, p. 90.
75. Rule, *Lust Killer,* pp. 102–3.
76. Ibid., p. 195.
77. Wilson and Wilson, *The Killers among Us, Book I*, p. 92.
78. Ibid., p. 92.
79. Ibid., p. 94.
80. Rule, *Lust Killer*, p. 43.
81. Wilson and Wilson, *The Killers among Us, Book I*, pp. 96–97.

CHAPTER 2

1. Roger Lane, *Murder in America* (Columbus: Ohio State University Press, 1997), p. 301.
2. Ibid., p. 303.
3. Ibid.
4. Ibid., pp. 307–9.
5. Ibid., p. 311.
6. Ibid., p. 313.
7. Ibid., p. 314.
8. Ibid., p. 316.
9. Ibid., p. 318.
10. Ibid., p. 317.
11. Ibid., p. 318.
12. Ibid., pp. 319–20.
13. Ibid., p. 319.
14. Ibid., pp. 319–20.
15. Colin Wilson and Damon Wilson, *The Killers among Us, Book I: Motives Behind Their Madness* (New York: Warner Books, 1995), pp. 196–200.
16. Wilson and Wilson, *The Killers among Us,* p. 147.
17. Steven A. Egger, *Serial Murder: An Elusive Phenomenon* (New York: Praeger, 1990), p. 20.
18. Wilson and Wilson, *Killers among Us, Book I*, pp. 147–48.
19. Egger, *Serial Murder*, p. 166.
20. Ibid.
21. Ibid., p. 167.
22. Ibid.
23. Brian Marriner, *On Death's Bloody Trail: Murder and the Art of Forensic Science* (New York, St. Martin's, 1991), p. 278.
24. John Douglas, *Mind Hunter* (New York: Pocket Books, 1996), pp. 80–81.
25. Marriner, *On Death's Bloody Trail*, p. 279.

26. Ibid.

27. Colin Wilson and Damon Wilson, *Written in Blood: Detectives and Detection* (New York: Warner Books, 1989), p. 284.

28. Marriner, *On Death's Bloody Trail,* p. 232.

29. Ibid., pp. 231–33.

30. Margaret Cheney, *The Co-ed Killer* (New York: Walker, 1976), pp. 48–49.

31. Ibid., p. 50.

32. Ibid., pp. 54–55.

33. Ibid., p. 3.

34. Ibid., p. 5.

35. Ibid., p. 60.

36. Jay Robert Nash, *Bloodletters and Badmen* (New York: M. Evans, 1995), p. 249.

37. Ibid., pp. 248–49.

38. Ibid., p. 450.

39. Cheney, *The Co-ed Killer*, pp. 60–61.

40. Ibid., pp. 58–59.

41. Ibid., p. 57.

42. Ibid..

43. Ibid., p. 66.

44. Ibid., p. 67.

45. Ibid., pp. 132–37.

46. Ibid., pp. 137–40.

47. Ibid., pp. 75–76.

48. Ibid., p. 84.

49. Ibid., pp. 87–90.

50. Ibid., p. 94.

51. Ibid., p. 105.

52. Ibid., pp. 106–108.

53. Ibid., p. 109.

54. Ibid., p. 113; Elliott Leyton, "A Demonstration to the Authorities," in *Compulsive Killers: The Story of Modern Multiple Murder* (New York: New York University Press, 1986), pp. 41–42.

55. Cheney, *The Co-ed Killer*, p. 130.

56. Ibid., p. xiii.

57. Ibid., p. 10.

58. Ibid., p. 9.

59. Ibid.

60. Ibid., p. 15.

61. "Why Boy Went on Rampage," *San Francisco Chronicle*, August 29, 1964, p. 5:1.

62. Cheney, *The Co-ed Killer*, pp. 28–29.

63. Ibid., p. 29.

64. Ibid., pp. 173–75.

65. Ibid., p. 179.

66. Ibid., p. 131.

67. Ibid., p. 187.

68. Ibid., p. 193.

69. Ed Cray and Richard Hawk, *Burden of Proof* (New York: Macmillan, 1973), p. 15.

70. Ibid., p. 7.

71. Ibid., pp. 13–15.

72. Ibid., pp. 15–16.

73. Ibid., p. 17.

74. Ibid., p. 22.

75. Ibid., pp. 24–25.

76. Ibid., pp. 26–27.

77. Ibid., p. 31.

78. Ibid., p. 70.

79. Ibid., p. 75.

80. Tracy Kidder, *The Road to Yuba City* (Garden City, NY: Doubleday, 1974), p. 57.

81. Ibid., p. 58.

82. Ibid.

83. Ibid., p. 59.

84. Ibid., pp. 59–60.

85. Ibid., p. 68.

86. Ibid., p. 65.

87. Cray and Hawk, *Burden of Proof*, p. 167.

88. Ibid., p. 200.

89. Kidder, *Road to Yuba City*, pp. 94–95.

90. Ibid., p. 106.

91. Ibid., pp. 117–18.

92. Ibid., p. 121.

93. Ibid., p. 133.

94. Ibid., p. 137.

95. Ibid., p. 130.

96. Ibid., p. 194.

97. Ibid.

98. Ibid., p. 163.

99. Ibid., p. 187.

100. Ibid., p. 229.

101. Ibid., p. 252.

102. David Abrahamsen, *Confessions of Son of Sam* (New York: Columbia University Press, 1985), p. 2.

103. Elliott Leyton, "The Demons Were Turning Me into a Soldier," in *Compulsive Killers: The Story of Modern Multiple Murder* (New York: New York University Press, 1986), p. 155.

104. Ibid., p. 156.

105. Abrahamsen, *Confessions*, p. 3.

106. Lawrence Klausner, *Son of Sam* (New York: McGraw-Hill, 1981), pp. 141–42.

107. Ibid.

108. Abrahamsen, *Confessions*, p. 4.

109. Klausner, *Son of Sam*, pp. 179, 185.

110. Richard Glyn Jones, "1977. David Berkowitz. Son of Sam," in *The Mammoth Book of Murder* (New York: Carroll and Graf, 1990), pp. 553–554.

111. Leyton, "Demons Were Turning," p. 158.
112. Abrahamsen, *Confessions*, p. 6.
113. Ibid., p. 8.
114. Ibid., p. 12.
115. Ibid.
116. Ibid.
117. Ibid., p. 30.
118. Ibid., p. 35.
119. Ibid., p. 36.
120. Ibid., p. 24.
121. Ibid., p. 25.
122. Ibid., p. 65.
123. Ibid., p. 78.
124. Ibid., p. 83.
125. Ibid., p. 87.
126. Ibid.
127. Ibid., p. 89.
128. Ibid., p. 93.
129. Ibid., p. 94.
130. Ibid., p. 99.
131. Ibid., p. 103.
132. Ibid.
133. Ibid., p. 108.
134. Ibid., pp. 145–46.
135. Ibid., pp. 158–61.
136. Ibid., pp. 191–98.

CHAPTER 3

1. Roger Lane, *Murder in America* (Columbus: Ohio State University Press, 1997), p. 308.
2. Ibid., p. 339.
3. Philip Jenkins, *Using Murder: The Social Construction of Serial Homicide* (New York: Aldine de Gruyter, 1994), p. 8.
4. Ibid., p. 9.
5. Ibid., p. 10.
6. Brian Marriner, *On Death's Bloody Trail: Murder and the Art of Forensic Science* (New York: St. Martin's, 1991), p. 253.
7. Jenkins, *Using Murder*, pp. 11–12.
8. Ibid., pp. 12–13.
9. Ibid., p. 14.
10. Ibid., p. 29.
11. Ibid., p. 16.
12. Ibid., p. 21.
13. Ibid., p. 31.
14. Ibid., pp. 40–41.
15. Ibid., p. 45.

16. Ibid., p. 50.
17. Ibid., p. 52.
18. Ibid., p. 51.
19. Ibid., p. 55.
20. Ibid., pp. 55–56.
21. Ibid., pp. 56–57.
22. Ibid., p. 57.
23. Ibid., pp. 57–58.
24. Ibid., p. 59.
25. Ibid., p. 63.
26. Ibid., pp. 63–65.
27. Ibid., p. 67.
28. Ibid., pp. 70–71.
29. Ibid., p. 96.
30. Ibid., pp. 98.
31. Marriner, *On Death's Bloody Trail*, pp. 92–93.
32. Ibid., p. 93.
33. Ibid., pp. 93–94.
34. Ibid., pp. 94–95.
35. Ibid., pp. 96–97.
36. Jenkins, *Using Murder*, pp. 98–99.
37. Marriner, *On Death's Bloody Trail*, p. 154.
38. Ibid., pp. 154–55.
39. Ibid., p. 155.
40. Ibid.
41. Ibid., pp. 212–13.
42. Ibid.
43. Ibid., pp. 231–33.
44. Ibid., pp. 213.
45. Ibid., pp. 213–14.
46. Ibid., p. 235.
47. Ibid., pp. 279–80.
48. Ibid., p. 281.
49. Ibid.
50. Clifford L. Linedecker, *Thrill Killers* (New York: Paperjacks, 1987), p. 163.
51. Ibid., p. 166.
52. Ibid.
53. Ibid., p. 163; John Douglas and Mark Olshaker, *Mind Hunter* (New York: Pocket, 1995), p. 198.
54. Douglas and Olshaker, *Mind Hunter*, p. 199.
55. Ibid.; Linedecker, *Thrill Killers*, p. 163.
56. Linedecker, *Thrill Killers*, p. 164.
57. Ibid.
58. Ibid.
59. Ibid., pp. 166.
60. Ibid., pp. 167–68.
61. Ibid., p. 168.
62. Ibid., p. 169.

63. Douglas and Olshaker, *Mind Hunter*, p. 200.

64. Arthur Lyons and Marcello Truzzi, *The Blue Sense* (New York: Mysterious Press/Warner Books, 1991), p. 225.

65. Linedecker, *Thrill Killers*, p. 171.

66. Douglas and Olshaker, *Mind Hunter*, p. 201.

67. Ibid.

68. Ibid.

69. Ibid., p. 202.

70. Ibid., pp. 202–3.

71. Ibid., p. 203

72. Ibid., pp. 203–4.

73. Ibid., p. 204.

74. Ibid.

75. Ibid.

76. Ibid., pp. 205–8.

77. Ibid., p. 208.

78. Ibid., pp. 208–9.

79. Ibid., p. 210.

80. Lyons and Truzzi, *Blue Sense*, p. 226.

81. Douglas and Olshaker, *Mind Hunter*, p. 211.

82. Linedecker, *Thrill Killers*, p. 172.

83. Douglas and Olshaker, *Mind Hunter*, p. 212.

84. Linedecker, *Thrill Killers*, p. 175.

85. Ibid., pp. 175–76.

86. Ibid., pp. 178–79; Douglas and Olshaker, *Mind Hunter*, p. 213.

87. Douglas and Olshaker, *Mind Hunter*, p. 213.

88. Ibid.

89. Ibid., p. 214.

90. Linedecker, *Thrill Killers*, p. 179.

91. Douglas and Olshaker, *Mind Hunter*, p. 217.

92. Ibid., p. 217; Linedecker, *Thrill Killers,* p. 180.

93. Douglas and Olshaker, *Mind Hunter*, p. 217.

94. Ibid., pp. 217–218.

95. Linedecker, *Thrill Killers*, p. 180.

96. Douglas and Olshaker, *Mind Hunter*, p. 222.

97. Ibid., p. 222.

98. Linedecker, *Thrill Killers*, p. 181.

99. Douglas and Olshaker, *Mind Hunter*, p. 223.

100. Carla Norton, *Disturbed Ground* (New York: William Morrow, 1994), p. 24.

101. Ibid., pp. 25–26.

102. Ibid., p. 25.

103. Ibid., p. 33.

104. Ibid., p. 35.

105. Ibid., pp. 36–37.

106. Ibid., pp. 41–43.

107. Ibid., p. 45.

108. Ibid., pp. 49–50.

109. Ibid., pp. 58–60.
110. Ibid., pp. 65–66.
111. Ibid., pp. 66–67.
112. Ibid., p. 69.
113. Ibid., p. 70.
114. Ibid., pp. 72–73.
115. Ibid., pp. 74–75.
116. Ibid., pp. 80–81.
117. Ibid., p. 85.
118. William P. Wood, *The Bone Garden* (New York: Pocket Books, 1994), p. 25.
119. Ibid., p. 17.
120. Ibid., p. 18.
121. Ibid., p. 26.
122. Daniel J. Blackburn, *Human Harvest* (New York: Knightsville, 1990), p. 11.
123. Ibid., p. 13.
124. Wood, *Bone Garden*, p. 28.
125. Ibid., p. 32, Norton, *Disturbed Ground*, p. 89.
126. Norton, *Disturbed Ground*, pp. 91–93.
127. Ibid., pp. 92–93.
128. Wood, *Bone Garden*, p. 40.
129. Norton, *Disturbed Ground*, pp. 113–14.
130. Ibid., p. 116.
131. Ibid., p. 117.
132. Ibid., p. 121.
133. Ibid., p. 123.
134. Ibid., pp. 123–24.
135. Ibid., p. 122.
136. Ibid., p. 221–23.
137. Ibid., p. 122.
138. Ibid., pp. 126–27.
139. Ibid., pp. 127–28.
140. Ibid., pp. 126–31.
141. Ibid., pp. 132–33.
142. Ibid., pp. 13–15, Wood, *Bone Garden*, pp. 162–67.
143. Wood, *Bone Garden*, pp. 273–74.
144. Ibid., pp. 274–75.
145. Ibid., pp. 275–76.
146. Ibid., p. 275.
147. Ibid., p. 302.
148. Ibid.
149. Ibid., p. 303.
150. Ibid., p. 305.
151. Ann Rule, *If You Really Loved Me* (New York: Simon & Schuster, 1991), p. 22.
152. Ibid., p. 23.
153. Ibid., p. 27.
154. Ibid., p. 30.

155. Ibid., p. 33.

156. Ibid., pp. 34–35; Marvin J. Wolf and Katherine Mader, *Perfect Crimes* (New York: Ballantine Books, 1995), pp. 149.

157. Rule, *If You Really Loved Me*, pp. 36–38; Wolf and Mader, *Perfect Crimes*, p. 150.

158. Wolf and Mader, *Perfect Crimes*, p. 151.

159. Rule, *If You Really Loved Me*, p. 41.

160. Ibid., p. 47; Wolf and Mader, *Perfect Crimes*, p. 152.

161. Rule, *If You Really Loved Me*, p. 51.

162. Ibid., p. 53; Wolf and Mader, *Perfect Crimes*, p. 153.

163. Wolf and Mader, *Perfect Crimes*, p. 153.

164. Rule, *If You Really Loved Me*, pp. 57–58; Wolf and Mader, *Perfect Crimes*, pp. 153–54.

165. Wolf and Mader, *Perfect Crimes*, p. 154.

166. Rule, *If You Really Loved Me*, p. 58.

167. Wolf and Mader, *Perfect Crimes*, p. 156.

168. Rule, *If You Really Loved Me*, p. 79.

169. Wolf and Mader, *Perfect Crimes*, p. 156.

170. Rule, *If You Really Loved Me*, p. 82.

171. Ibid., p. 90.

172. Wolf and Mader, *Perfect Crimes*, pp. 158–59.

173. Ibid., p. 159.

174. Ibid., p. 160.

175. Ibid., p. 162.

176. Rule, *If You Really Loved Me*, pp. 114–15.

177. Ibid., p. 115.

178. Ibid., pp. 126–27.

179. Ibid., p. 132.

180. Wolf and Mader, *Perfect Crimes*, p. 163.

181. Rule, *If You Really Loved Me*, p. 137.

182. Ibid., pp. 140–41.

183. Ibid., p. 145.

184. Ibid., pp. 146–47.

185. Ibid., p. 149.

186. Ibid., pp. 159–63.

187. Ibid., pp. 169–71.

188. Ibid., p. 170.

189. Ibid.

190. Ibid., pp. 171–173.

191. Wolf and Mader, *Perfect Crimes*, p. 165.

192. Ibid., pp. 164–166.

193. Rule, *If You Really Loved Me*, p. 189.

194. Ibid., p. 191.

195. Ibid., pp. 193–4.

196. Ibid., pp. 196–97; Wolf and Mader, *Perfect Crimes*, pp. 166–67.

197. Rule, *If You Really Loved Me*, p. 199, Wolf and Mader, *Perfect Crimes*, p. 167.

198. Rule, *If You Really Loved Me*, pp. 199–200; Wolf and Mader, *Perfect Crimes*, pp. 167–68.

199. Wolf and Mader, *Perfect Crimes*, p. 168.

200. Rule, *If You Really Loved Me*, p. 210; Wolf and Mader, *Perfect Crimes*, pp. 168–69.

201. Rule, *If You Really Loved Me*, p. 214, Wolf and Mader, *Perfect Crimes*, p. 169.

202. Wolf and Mader, *Perfect Crimes*, p. 171.

203. Ibid., p. 172.

204. Ibid., p. 173.

205. Ibid.

206. Ibid.

207. Ibid., p. 175.

208. Ibid.

209. Rule, *If You Really Loved Me*, pp. 358–59.

210. Wolf and Mader, *Perfect Crimes*, p. 182.

CHAPTER 4

1. Roger Lane, *Murder in America* (Columbus: Ohio State University Press, 1997), p. 353.

2. Ronald M. Holmes and Stephen T. Holmes, *Murder in America* (Thousand Oaks, CA: Sage, 1994), p. 94.

3. Lane, *Murder in America*, pp. 351–52.

4. Gerald Sheindlin, *Blood Trail* (New York: Ballantine, 1996), p. 63.

5. Ibid., pp. 70–84.

6. Ibid., pp. 97–98.

7. Ibid., p. 99.

8. Robert D. Keppel, *Signature Killers* (New York: Pocket Books, 1997), p. 291.

9. Ibid., pp. 291–92.

10. Ibid., pp. 296–97.

11. Holmes and Holmes, *Murder in America,* pp. 107–11.

12. Philip Jenkins, *Using Murder: The Social Construction of Serial Homicide* (New York: Aldine de Gruyter, 1994), pp. 56–57.

13. Author interview with police officer Lt. Paul Berlin, 1995, in Oakland.

14. Ken Englade, *Murder in Boston* (New York: St. Martin's, 1990), p. 12.

15. Ibid., p. 13.

16. Ibid., p. 24.

17. Ibid., p. 27.

18. Ibid., pp. 21–23.

19. Ibid., p. 23.

20. Ibid., pp. 23–24.

21. Ibid., pp. 25–26.

22. Ibid., p. 30.

23. Ibid., p. 33.

24. Ibid., p. 34.

25. Ibid., pp. 33–45.
26. Ibid., pp. 44–47.
27. Ibid., pp. 47–48.
28. Drew Mackenzie, "Presumed Innocent," in *Sunday Bloody Sunday* (London: Blake, 192), p. 110.
29. Ibid.
30. Ibid., pp. 109–10.
31. Englade, *Murder in Boston*, p. 54.
32. Ibid., pp. 55–56.
33. Ibid., p. 56.
34. Ibid., p. 57.
35. Ibid., p. 58.
36. Ibid., pp. 61–62.
37. Ibid., pp. 63–64.
38. Ibid., pp. 64–65.
39. Ibid., pp. 65–66.
40. Ibid., p. 64.
41. Ibid., pp. 66–67.
42. Ibid..
43. Ibid., p. 68.
44. Ibid., pp. 68–69.
45. Ibid., pp. 68–70.
46. Ibid., p. 71.
47. Ibid., pp. 71–72.
48. Ibid., pp. 73–75.
49. Ibid., p. 83.
50. Ibid., p. 77.
51. Ibid., pp. 77–78.
52. Ibid., pp. 78–79.
53. Ibid., p. 81.
54. Ibid., p. 82.
55. Ibid., pp. 82–83.
56. Ibid., pp. 83–84.
57. Ibid., pp. 86–87.
58. Ibid., p. 87.
59. Ibid., pp. 88–89.
60. Ibid., p. 90.
61. Ibid., p. 91.
62. Ibid., p. 93.
63. Ibid., p. 94.
64. Ibid., p. 98.
65. Ibid., pp. 100–101.
66. Ibid., pp. 102–3.
67. Ibid., pp. 103–4.
68. Ibid., pp. 104–5.
69. Ibid., pp. 105–6.
70. Ibid., p. 95.
71. Ibid., p. 109.

72. Ibid., pp. 110–11.
73. Ibid., pp. 111–13.
74. Ibid., p. 113.
75. Ibid., p. 114.
76. Ibid., pp. 116–17.
77. Ibid., pp. 118–19.
78. Ibid., p. 125.
79. Ibid., pp. 125–29.
80. Ibid., pp. 130–31.
81. MacKenzie, "Presumed Innocent," p. 111.
82. Englade, *Murder in Boston*, p. 249.
83. Ibid., p. 253.
84. Ibid., p. 255.
85. Ibid., p. 254.
86. Ibid., p. 257.
87. Wensley Clarkson, *Hell Hath No Fury: True Stories of Women Who Kill* (London: Blake, 1991), p. 60–61.
88. Ken Englade, *Deadly Lessons* (New York: St. Martin's, 1991), pp. 10–11.
89. Stephen Sawicki, *Teach Me to Kill* (New York: Avon, 1991), p. 9.
90. Ibid., pp. 12–13.
91. Ibid., pp. 13–14.
92. Ibid., pp. 14–15.
93. Ibid., p. 15.
94. Ibid., p. 16.
95. Ibid., p. 17.
96. Ibid., pp. 20–21.
97. Englade, *Deadly Lessons*, p. 13.
98. Ibid., pp. 13–14.
99. Ibid., p. 20.
100. Sawicki, *Teach Me to Kill*, p. 24.
101. Ibid.
102. Ibid., pp. 60–61.
103. Ibid., p. 62.
104. Englade, *Deadly Lessons*, p. 20.
105. Ibid., p. 16.
106. Ibid., pp. 15–16.
107. Ibid., p. 19.
108. Ibid., p. 13.
109. Ibid., pp. 25–34.
110. Ibid., pp. 34–35.
111. Ibid., pp. 38–39.
112. Ibid., p. 38.
113. Ibid., p. 42.
114. Ibid., p. 44.
115. Ibid., pp. 44–47.
116. Sawicki, *Teach Me to Kill*, p. 70.
117. Ibid., p. 71.
118. Ibid., p. 147.

119. Ibid., ppp. 149–51.
120. Ibid., pp. 151–52.
121. Ibid., p. 152.
122. Ibid., p. 144.
123. Ibid., p. 145.
124. Ibid., pp. 145–46.
125. Ibid., p. 146.
126. Ibid., pp. 154–55.
127. Ibid., p. 155.
128. Ibid., pp. 155–56.
129. Ibid., p. 159.
130. Ibid., pp. 159–61.
131. Ibid., pp. 163–64.
132. Ibid., pp. 166–67.
133. Ibid., pp. 168–71.
134. Ibid., pp. 171–74.
135. Ibid., p. 176.
136. Ibid., p. 182.
137. Ibid., pp. 185–88.
138. Ibid., p. 201.
139. Ibid., pp. 201–10.
140. Englade, *Deadly Lessons*, pp. 269–70.
141. Cathy Scott, *The Killing of Tupac Shakur* (Las Vegas: Huntington Press, 1997), pp. 1–10.
142. Ibid., pp. 61–66.
143. Ibid., p. 67.
144. Ibid., p. 95.
145. Ibid., p. 8.
146. Ibid., p. 10.
147. Ibid., pp. 36–37.
148. Ibid., pp. 38–39.
149. Ibid., p. 45.
150. Ibid., p. 112.
151. Ibid., p. 14.
152. Ibid., pp. 27–29.
153. Ibid., p. 30.
154. Ibid., p. 30–31.
155. Ibid., pp. 31–32.
156. Armond White, *Rebel for the Hell of It: The Life of Tupac Shakur* (New York: Thunder's Mouth Press), p. 36.
157. Ibid., pp. 69–76.
158. Ibid., p. 75.
159. Ibid., pp. 82, 91.
160. Ibid., pp. 214–16.
161. Ibid., pp. 128–31, 138.
162. Ibid., p. 157.
163. Ibid.
164. Ibid., p. 216–17.

165. Ibid., p. 180.
166. *Vibe, Tupac Amaru Shakur: 1971–1996* (New York: Crown, 1997), p. 101.
167. Ibid., p. 103.
168. Scott, *The Killing of Tupac Shakur*, pp. 117–19.
169. Ibid., pp. 122–23.
170. Ibid., pp. 83–87.
171. Ibid., p. 102.
172. Ibid., pp. 159–60.
173. Ibid., pp. 161–62.
174. Ibid., pp. 157, 161.
175. Ibid., p. 33–34.
176. Ibid., pp. 101, 136.
177. Ibid., pp. 162–64.

Selected Bibliography

Abrahamsen, David. *Confessions of Son of Sam*. New York: Columbia University Press, 1985.

Blackburn, Daniel J. *Human Harvest*. New York: Knightsville, 1990.

Cheney, Margaret. *The Co-ed Killer*. New York: Walker, 1976.

Clarkson, Wensley. *Hell Hath No Fury: True Stories of Women Who Kill*. London: Blake, 1991.

Cray, Ed, and Richard Hawk. *Burden of Proof*. New York: Macmillan., 1973.

Douglas, John, and Mark Olshaker. *Mind Hunter*. New York: Pocket, 1995.

Egger, Steven A. *Serial Murder: An Elusive Phenomenon*. New York: Praeger, 1990.

Englade, Ken. *Murder in Boston*. New York: St. Martin's, 1990.

Englade, Ken. *Deadly Lessons*. New York: St. Martin's, 1991.

Gilmore, John. *Cold-Blooded*. Portland, OR: Feral House, 1996.

Holmes, Ronald M., and Stephen T. Holmes. *Murder in America*. Thousand Oaks, CA: Sage, 1994.

Jenkins, Philip. *Using Murder: The Social Construction of Serial Homicide*. New York: Aldine de Gruyter, 1994.

Jones, Richard Glyn. "1977. David Berkowitz. Son of Sam," in *The Mammoth Book of Murder*. New York: Carroll and Graf, 1990.

Keppel, Robert D. *Signature Killers*. New York: Pocket Books, 1997.

Kidder, Tracy. *The Road to Yuba City*. Garden City, NY: Doubleday, 1974.

Klausner, Lawrence. *Son of Sam*. New York: McGraw-Hill, 1981.

Lane, Roger. *Murder in America*. Columbus: Ohio State University Press, 1997.

Leyton, Elliott. *Compulsive Killers: The Story of Modern Multiple Murder*. New York: New York University Press, 1986.

Linedecker, Clifford L. *Thrill Killers*. New York: Paperjacks, 1987.

Lyons, Arthur and Truzzi, Marcello. *The Blue Sense*. New York: Mysterious Press/Warner Books, 1991.

Mackenzie, Drew. *Sunday Bloody Sunday*. London: Blake Paperbacks, 1992.

Marriner, Brian. *On Death's Bloody Trail: Murder and the Art of Forensic Science*. New York: St. Martin's, 1991.

Nash, Jay Robert. *Crime Chronology: A Worldwide Record: 1900–1983*. New York: Facts on File, 1984.

Nash, Jay Robert. *Bloodletters and Badmen*. New York: M. Evans, 1995.

Norton, Carla. *Disturbed Ground*. New York: William Morrow, 1994.

Rule, Ann. *Lust Killer*. New York: Signet Books, 1983.

Rule, Ann. *If You Really Loved Me*. New York: Simon & Schuster, 1991.

Sawicki, Stephen. *Teach Me to Kill*. New York: Avon, 1991.

Scott, Cathy. *The Killing of Tupac Shakur*. Las Vegas: Huntington Press, 1997.

Sheindlin, Gerald. *Blood Trail*. New York: Ballantine, 1996.

Vibe. Tupac Amaru Shakur: 1971–1996. New York: Crown, 1997.

White, Armond. *Rebel for the Hell of It: The Life of Tupac Shakur*. New York: Thunder's Mouth Press, 1997.

Wilson, Colin, and Damon Wilson. *Written in Blood: Detectives and Detection*. New York: Warner Books, 1989.

Wilson, Colin, and Damon Wilson. *The Killers Among Us, Book I: The Motives Behind Their Madness*. New York: Warner Books, 1995.

Wolf, Marvin J., and Katherine Mader. *Perfect Crimes*. New York: Ballantine Books, 1995.

Wood, William P. *The Bone Garden*. New York: Pocket Books, 1994.

Index

Abrahamsen, David (Dr.), 74, 78, 79, 80, 81, 82
African Americans, 1–2
The Agony and the Ecstasy (Stone), 51
"A Hard Day's Night" (Beatles), 12
Allen, Debbie, 161, 166
Allen, William, 46
All Eyez On Me, 189
Allison, Dorothy, 104
Altamont concert, 4
American Academy of Forensic Sciences, 10
American Law Enforcement Assistance Administration, 45–46
America's Most Wanted, 91, 152
Anderson, Orlando, 183, 186, 187
Anderson, Seatwright (Dr.), 135
Andrews, Gloria, 21
Animal House, 41
Annie Hall, 41
anthropologists, 123, 125
Appeal-Democrat, 61
archaeologists, 96
Arizona, 12–25
Arizona Daily Star, 22
Atascadero State Hospital, 58
ATKID, 104–5
Atlanta Constitution, 108
Atlanta Journal, 108
The A to Z Encyclopedia of Serial Killers (Schechter and Everitt), 148
Attica Prison, 83

Baclaan, Aguinalbo, 66
Bad Boy Entertainment, 183, 187
Bailey, Ethel, 138
Bailey, F. Lee, 6, 24, 68
Bailey, Patti, 130
Bakker, Jim (Rev.), 114
Ballenger, Mildred, 116
ballistics: advances during the 1960s, 10; during the 1990s, 180
Baltazar, Patrick, 108
Barnett, E. G., 2
Barry, Marion Jr. (Mayor), 168
Basinger, Kim, 175
Baumann, Edward, 148
Beame, Abraham (Mayor), 73
Beatles, 12
Beatty, Warren, 168
Beaver, Ninette, 46
Becker, Brent, 186
behavior, rules of, 12
Bell, Camille, 100

Bell, Yusef, 99–100
Belushi, John, 41
Bennett, Willie, 159
Berkowitz, David (Son of Sam), 43, 44, 45, 47–48, 71–83, 85, 88, 90
Beverly Hills Cop, 86
Bianchi, Kenneth (Hillside Strangler), 47, 90
Billionaire Boys Club, 98
Binder, Al, 112
"Black and Blue," 175
Black Muslims, 3
Black Panthers, 2, 3, 10, 11, 39, 183
Blake, Danny, 178
Bloodletters and Badmen (Nash), 148
Bloods, 183
blood typing: during the 1970s, 70
Boesky, Ivan, 86, 114
bombs, 11. *See also* Kaczynski, Ted
Bond, James, 12
Bonin, William (Freeway Killer), 47
Boogie Nights, 41
Borrelli, Joseph (Captain), 73
Boston Globe, 154, 158, 160
Boston Strangler, 6, 11
Botkin, Cordelia, ix
Brady, William (Dr.), 30
Brando, Marlon, 41
Breslin, Jimmy, 74–75
Bridgewater State Hospital, 6
Brimage, David, 160
Brook, Peter, 12
Brown, Arthur, 139
Brown, Brenda, 134
Brown, Cinnamon, 128, 130
Brown, David, 98, 128–45, 131
Brown, Jerry (Governor), 113
Brown, Krystal, 131
Brown, Lee (Public Safety Commissioner), 99, 102, 110
Brown, Linda, 128
Brown, Terry, 120
Brucker, Edward, 25
Brudos, Darcie, 34, 36, 38, 89
Brudos, Jerry, 5, 25–38
Bruns, Richard, 14, 16
Brussel, James (Dr.), 11, 45
BSU. *See* Federal Bureau of Investigation, Behavioral Sciences Unit
Buckey, Peggy, 168
Buckey, Ray, 168
Bugliosi, Vincent, 46
Bundy, Carol, 98
Bundy, Ted, 42–43, 44, 47, 88, 89
Bundy: The Deliberate Stranger (Larsen), 90
Buono, Angelo (Hillside Strangler), 47, 90
Burr, Sheriff, 24–25

Cabrera, John (Detective), 119, 120, 126
Cahners Publishing, 157
California, 43, 48–59, 59–71, 113–28, 128–45
California Department of Highways, 56
California Youth Authority, 58
Campbell, Bob, 110
The Cannibal (Heimer), 46
Cannibal Killer. *See* Dahmer, Jeffrey
Capital Journal, 28
Capote, viii
Capote, Truman, vii–viii
Car 54, Where Are You?, 112
Caril (Beaver), 46
Carpenter, Leona, 128
Carr, Sam, 76
Carter, Anthony "Tony," 102
Carter, Jimmy (President), 86
Casebook of a Criminal Psychiatrist (Brussel), 11
Casey, Patty, 116
Cater, Nathaniel, 110, 111
CBS, 126
Chaney, James, 2, 58
Channel 9, 172
Charewicz, Barry (Detective), 170, 177, 180
Chase, Richard (the Dracula Killer), 43
Chávez, César, 61
Cheney, Margaret, 46, 52, 55–56, 57
children, murder of, 90; in Atlanta, 98; during the 1980s, 91
cities: during the 1970s, 39–40
civil rights: during the 1960s, 12

Clark, Douglas (Sunset Killer), 98
Clay, Cassius. *See* Muhammad Ali
Cleckley, Hervey M., 43–44
A Clockwork Orange (Kubrick), 41
Close, Glenn, 87
Clutter, Herb, viii
Clymo, Kevin, 127
Codd, Michael J. (Police Commissioner), 73
Co-Ed Killer. *See* Kemper, Ed
The Co-ed Killer (Cheney), 46
Coleman, Olie (Sergeant), 61
Collins, John, 5
Collins, John Norman, 46
The Color of Money, 87
Combs, Sean "Puffy," 183, 187, 189
Committee to Stop Children's Murders, 100–101
communes, 4
Con Edison, 11
Congress of Racial Equality, 2
Connoly, Thomas P. Jr. (Dr.), 60
Copeland, Faye, 98
Copeland, Raymond, 98
Coppola, Francis Ford, 41
Coppolino, Carl (Dr.), 11, 24
Corll, Dean, 43, 46, 91
Corning Glass Works, 10
Corona, Juan V., 43, 45, 46, 48, 59–71
Corona, Natividad, 61
Costner, Kevin, 87
counterculture: during the 1960s, 3–4, 26
Courtesy Outreach Program, 115
Court TV, 147, 150
Cox, Robert C., 95–96
Cray, Ed, 66
crime: interest in, 40–41; pattern of, vii
Criminal Personality Research Project. *See* Federal Bureau of Investigation, Criminal Personality Research Project
The Criminal Personality (Yochelson and Samenow), 43
Crips gang, 183
Cronin, Jerome, 165
CSI, 150
culture: during the 1970s, 58, 74; during the 1980s, 86. *See also* lifestyles
Dahmer, Jeffrey (Cannibal Killer), 98, 148
Daily News (New York), 74–75
Dallas, 86
Dalmane (flurazepam), 125
Darvocet-N, 130
Dateline, 147
Daugherty, Gene (Lt.), 31
Davis, Cacilia, 76
Davis, Don, 148
Davis, Sammy Jr., 103
Dawley, John T., 165
Dean, James, 12
Death Row Records, 185, 186, 187, 189, 190–91, 192
DeLong, Roy, 63
DeMasi, Donna, 72
Democratic National Headquarters, 40–41
Denaro, Carl, 72
dental records, 95
Department of Motor Vehicles, 137
Depue, Roger, 91
DeSalvo, Albert, 5, 6
Dick Tracy, 168
Die Hard, 86
Diel, John, 72
The Die Song (Lunde and Morgan), 90
Digital Underground, 188
Ding-Dong, Avon-Calling killer. *See* Frazier, John Linley
Dixon, Jeane, 107–8
DNA: anlysis during the 1990s, viii; during the 1970s, 46; during the 1980s, 92–93; as evidence during the 1990s, 149–50
DNA Task Force, 150
Dogg, Snoop Doggy, 189
Don Killuminati: The Seven Day Theory, 191
Douglas, John, 45, 90, 92, 103, 104–5, 106, 148, 150–51
Douglas, Michael, 87
Dowd, Timothy J. (Inspector), 74
Dracula Killer. *See* Chase, Richard
drugs, 4, 125; during the 1960s, 4–5; during the 1970s, 39–40
Dukakis, Michael S. (Governor), 158

Duke, David, 103
Duncan, Eddie, 109
Duron, Ray, 62, 66, 69
Dyazide, 130

Edward Gein (Gollmar), 90
Eftimiades, Maria, 148
Elisa, Louis, 158
The Encyclopedia of Serial Killers (Lane and Gregg), 148
Englade, Ken, 158
Engleman, Glennon, 47
Esau, Alexander, 73
Evans, Alfred, 99
Evans, Faith, 189
Everitt, David, 148
Evers, Medgar, 1
Ewing, Richard, 118
executions, 88

Falco, Betty, 78
Family Dog, 4
The Family (Sanders), 46
Fatal Attraction, 86–87
FBI. *See* Federal Bureau of Investigation
Federal Bureau of Investigation (FBI), 2, 16, 42, 49, 101, 103, 109; Behavioral Sciences Unit (BSU), viii, 45, 85, 89, 90, 104–5, 150–51, 152; Criminal Personality and Research Project, 90; National Crime Information Center, 91; profilers, viii, 103; Uniform Crime Reports, 39, 40
Federal Bureau of Narcotics, 61
Fernandez, Raymond, 97
Ferry, Robert, 10
Field of Dreams, 87
Fifth Amendment (U.S. Constitution), 5
fingerprints: during the 1960s, 14; during the 1970s, 51, 60, 65, 68; during the 1980s, 92, 93, 107, 131; during the 1990s, 150; latent, 107
Fink, Benjamin, 119, 121, 128
First Blood, Part II, 129
Fish, Albert, 25, 46, 73
Fitzgerald, Robert (Judge), 136
flurazepam (Dalmane), 125
Flynn, Billy, 174, 177
Flynn, Mayor, 158
Flynn, Raymond, 156
forensics, during the 1980s, 95, 122, 123, 125
Forgette, Al, 135
Fort, Joel (Dr.), 55, 58–59
48 Hours, viii
Foster, Jodie, 89
Fourth Amendment (U.S. Constitution), 5
Fowler, Raymond, 179–80
Franklin, Joseph Paul, 47
Franks, Mike, 186
Frawley, Tim, 123
Frazier, Jerry (Detective), 31
Frazier, John Linley, 43, 47, 50, 51, 59
Frederickson, Dick, 139
Freeway Killer. *See* Bonin, William; Kraft, Randy
French, Mary, 13–25, 23
French, Pamela, 133
The French Connection, 41
Freund, Christine, 72
Friedkin, William, 41
Fritz, Gretchen, 16–17
Fugate, Caril, 46
Fula, Yafeu, 184

Gacy, John Wayne, 43, 44–45, 89, 90, 91
Gaddis, Thomas, 46
Galante, Carmine, 74
Gammons, John (Range Deputy), 19
gangs: during the 1990s, 183, 187
Garcia, Ernesto, 62
Garden of Graves (Eftimiades), 148
Isabella Sewart Gardner Museum, 168–69
Garland, Billy, 183
Garone, Edward (Police Chief), 169
Gates, Bill, 87
Gecht, Robin, 97–98
Gein, Edward, 8, 25, 90
Gentry, Curt, 46
Georgia, 98–113
Georgia State Crime Lab, 111
Geraldo, 166
Gere, Richard, 86
Gideon v. Wainright, 5
Gillmouth, Everson, 127
Gilmore, Jack, 12

Glass, Darron, 104
Glassman, Craig, 76–77
The Godfather, 41
Goetz, Bernhard, 86
Golding, William, 12
Goldman, Ronald, 148
Gollmar, Robert H., 90
Goodfellas, 168
Goodman, Andrew, 2
Goodwin, John, 46–47
Google, 152
Grabowski, Daniel (Sergeant), 153–54
Graff, Paul, 17
Graham, Bill, 4
Graham, Gwendolyn, 98
Graham, Louis (Police Chief), 113
Green River Killer, 98
Greenwood, Vaughan Orrin, 47
Gregg, Wilfred, 148
Gregory, Detective, 61
Gregory, Dick, 101
Gunness, Belle, 8, 124
gun shot residue test, 134
Gurwell, John, 46
Guy, Ruth (Dr.), 70

Hallett, Sally, 53
Halligan, Darrow (Patrol Officer), 129–30
Halloween, 92
Hampton, Fred, 3, 10
Harlem (New York), 12
Harris, Thomas, 89
Harvey, Donald, 98
Harvey, Milton, 100, 103, 909
Hawk, Richard, 65, 66, 67
Hazelwood, Roy, 92, 104–5, 106
Hearst, Patty, 41
"Heartz of Men," 189
Heck, Robert, 91, 92
Hee Haw, 65
Heglar, Rodger (Dr.), 123
Heimer, Mel, 46
Helig, William, 19
Heller, Mark, 78
Hells Angels, 4
Helms, Chet, 4
"Help!" (Beatles), 12
Helter Skelter (Bugliosi and Gentry), 46
Herald Tribune (New York), 11
Hibernia National Bank, 41
Hill, George Roy, 41
Hill, Timothy, 109
Hillside Strangler. *See* Bianchi, Kenneth; Buono, Angelo
"The Hillside Strangler," 43
The Hillside Strangler (Schwarz), 90
Hill Street Blues, 86
hip-hop music, 182
hippies, 3–4, 26
Hodge, Nancy, 93
Holmes, Ronald M., 149
Holmes, Stephen T., 149
homicide: during the 1960s, 1–38; during the 1970s, 39–83; during the 1980s, 85–145, 95; during the 1990s, 147–92; lower income killers, 6; mortality statistics, 40; murder rates, 40
Homicide Task Force, 74, 109
homosexuality, 43, 44, 61, 62, 68–69, 71, 98, 112
Hoover, J. Edgar, 45, 91. *See also* Federal Bureau of Investigation
Houston Police Department, 44
Howard, Clark, 90
Howard, Mary Ellen, 116
Hughes, Allen, 188–89
Hughes, Howard, 41
Hunt, Joe, 98

If I Did It (Simpson), 148
In Cold Blood (Capote), vii–viii
Infamous, viii
interferon, 101
Internet, 152
Irises (Van Gogh), 87
Irving, Clifford, 41

Jackson, Aaron, 104
Jackson, Calvin, 47
Jackson, Derek, 159–60, 161
Jackson, Loring, 169, 173
Jackson, Maynard (Mayor), 99, 102, 104
Jackson, Michael, 87
Jackson, Tony, 159–60
Jack the Ripper, 8, 97–98
Jeffreys, Alec (Dr.), 92, 93

Jenkins, Philip, 87–88
Johnson, Bill, 117
Johnson, Lyndon (President), 2, 87
Jones, Clifford, 104
Jones, Genene, 98
Jones, Jim, 41
Juice, 188
Jultak, Ira, 78
Jury Room, 52, 53
"Just Say No!" campaign, 88, 114
Justus, James (Detective), 77
Juvenile Justice Subcommittee in the Senate, 91

Kaczynski, Ted (the Unabomber), 41–42, 82, 148
Kagehiro, Goro, 59–60
Kakas & Sons, 156
Karr, John Mark, 148
Kearney, Patrick Wayne (Trash Bag Killer), 47
Kearns, John P. (Police Chief), 125
Keaton, Diane, 41
Keenan, Rosemary, 72
Kemper, E. E. Jr., 57
Kemper, Ed (Co-Ed Killer), 43, 45, 46, 48–59, 74, 78, 85, 88
Kendall, Elizabeth, 90
Kennedy, John F. (President), 1, 12
Kennedy, Robert F. (Senator), 3
Kenner, David, 185, 191
Keppel, Robert D., 148, 151
Keyes, Edward, 46
Keystone Kops, 112
Kidder, Tracy, 46, 67
"Kids Don't Go With Strangers" campaign, 103
Killen, Edgar Ray, 2
Killer (Gaddis and Long), 46
killers: characteristics and differences between different types of, 42; serial, 42–43, 89, 149
King, Martin Luther Jr. (Dr.), 3
King of Pop. *See* Jackson, Michael
Kirk, Darlene, 17, 22
Kitchens, Jim, 112
Klausner, Lawrence, 90
Knight, Frank (District Attorney), 30
Knight, Suge, 182–83, 189, 191
Koo, Aiko, 49, 51, 56
Kraft, Randy (Freeway Killer), 98
KRCA-TV, 126
Kubrick, Stanley, 41
Ku Klux Klan, 2, 102, 104

La Associacion de los Charros, 65
La Bianca, Rosemary, 4
Lance, Judge, 150
Lane, Brian, 148
Lane, Roger, 1, 2–3, 7, 40, 41–42, 147
Larry King Live, 147
Larsen, Richard, 90
Last Tango in Paris, 41
Las Vegas Police, 186
Las Vegas Sun, 185
LA Times, 89
Lattime, Vance "J.R." Jr., 174, 180
Lauria, Donna, 71–72, 74
Law, Bernard (Cardinal), 158
Law Enforcement Assistance Administration, 87
Leary, Timothy, 4
Lecter, Hannibal, 89
Lee, Harper, viii
legislation: during the 1960s, 6; during the 1970s, 50; during the 1980s, 91
Lenair, Angel, 100
lifestyles: during the 1960s, 4–5. *See also* culture
Linedecker, Clifford, 90, 108
Liston, Sonny, 12
literature: during the 1970s, 46–47; during the 1980s, 89, 90; during the 1990s, 148
Live Oak Police Department, 60
Lombardi, Fred, 169
Lomino, Joanne, 72
London, Sondra, 148, 149
Long, James O., 46
Lord of the Flies (Golding), 12
LSD, 4, 51
Lucas, Henry Lee, 92
Luchessa, Anita, 48, 51, 55
Lui, Alice, 56–57
Lunde, Donalt T., 46, 90
Lupo, Sal, 74
Lynch, Neil (Judge), 162

MacDonell, Herbert Leon, 10–11
Maczak, Joseph, 66
Mad Bomber, 45
Madonna, 114
Major Case 30, 104–5
The Making of a Serial Killer (Rolling and London), 148, 149
Malcolm X, 3
Manson, Charles, 4–5, 9, 45, 46, 50, 148
The Man Who Killed Boys (Linedecker), 90
The Man with the Candy (Olsen), 46
Mapp v. Ohio, 5
marijuana, 4
Marinelli, Nick, 113
Marriner, Brian, 94–95, 96
Martin, Jack, 113
Mary Poppins, 12
Marysville Police Department, 61
Mason, Roger (Deputy Sheriff), 60
Massachusetts, 153–68
Massachusetts State Police, 153
mass murderers, 60; during the 1960s, 5; during the 1970s, 73
Mass Murder in Houston (Gurwell), 46
Mathis, Jefferey, 100
McCauley John, 123
McFall, Russel A. (Dr.), 125
McIntosh, Michael, 109
McLaughlin, Gary, 153–54
McLean, Fred, 128, 130
McMahon, John "Jack," 163
Me Against the World, 189
media: during the 1970s, 72, 74; during the 1980s, 89, 100–101; during the 1990s, 154, 156
Menace II Society, 188–89
Mental Hygiene for New York State, 11
Merrill, David, 90
Metal Madness, 173
Mexico, 64
MGM Grand, 182
Michelangelo, 51
The Michigan Murders (Keyes), 46
Microsoft, 87
Middlebrook, Eric, 101
Milken, Michael, 168
Miller, Dorothy, 128
Miller, Gordon, 112, 113
The Milwaukee Murders (Davis), 148
Minnesota Multi-Phasic Indicator, 129
Miranda rights, 133
Miranda v. Arizona, 5
Missing Children's Act (1982), 91
Missing Persons, 26, 119
Mississippi, 2
Mitchell, Artie, 94
Mitchell, Jim, 94
modus operandi, 112
Moise, Judy, 115
Monroe, Ruth, 124, 127
Montoya, Bert, 115, 123–24, 126
Moran, Gary, 153–54
Morgan, Jefferson, 90
Moskowitz, Stacy, 75–76
Mötley Crüe, 174
movies: during the 1970s, 41; during the 1980s, 86–87, 90, 92, 114, 129; during the 1990s, 168, 188
Muhammad Ali (Cassius Clay), 12, 102–3
Mullany, Pat, 45
Mullen, Mary, 6
Mullin, Herbert, 43, 46, 50, 51, 52, 59, 90
Murder and Madness (Lunde), 46
Murder in America (Lane), 40
Murder in Boston (Englade), 158
The Murdering Mind (Abrahamsen), 78
Murder USA (Goodwin), 46–47
Murphy, Eddie, 86
mushrooms, 4
music, 4; awards, 190; during the 1980s, 87; during the 1990s, 175, 182, 189, 191; hip-hop, 182; rap, 183
My Fair Lady, 12
MySpace, 152
The Mysterious Deaths at Ann Arbor (Wilcox), 46

NAACP, 158
Nash, Jay Robert, 148
National Association of Criminal Defense Lawyers, 150
National Center for the Analysis of Violent Crime (NCAVC), 91, 152

National Crime Information Center. *See* Federal Bureau of Investigation, National Crime Information Center
National Institute of Justice, 90
National Research Council, 150
Native Americans, 42
NCAVC. *See* National Center for the Analysis of Violent Crime
Nelson, Earle, 8, 97
Neufeld, Peter, 150
Nevada, 182–92
Newell, Jay, 128, 134, 136
New Hampshire, 168–92
New Hampshire State Police Major Crimes Unit, 170
Newman, Paul, 87
Newsweek, 92, 155, 166
New York City Police, 76
New York Police Department, 44
New York Post, 108
New York Psychiatric Center, 83
New York (state), 43, 71–83
New York Times, viii, 89
Nicholson, Jack, 41
Nicklous, Reba, 127
Nicolosi, Diane, 169
Nightline, 166
Night Stalker. *See* Ramirez, Richard
9 1/2 Weeks, 175
Nixon, Richard (President), 40–41
"No More Pain," 189
Norris, Joel, 97

Obregon, Michel, 118, 119
An Officer and a Gentleman, 86
Of Men and Monsters: Jeffrey Dahmer and the Construction of the Serial Killer (Tithecott), 148
Ohta, Victor (Dr.), 47, 50–51, 61
Olsen, Jack, 47
Olshaker, Mark, 148
O'Malley, Peter (Detective), 159
O'Mara, John, 127–28
One Flew Over the Cuckoo's Nest, 41
150 Commonly Prescribed Drugs, 124
Oregon, 12, 25–38
Ossining Correctional Facility, 83
Oswald, Lee Harvey, 3
outlaw as hero, 12
Outlaw Immortalz, 184

paleopathologists, 96
Panzram, Carl, 46
Payne, Jimmy Ray, 109, 111
Pelletier, Dan (Detective), 169, 170, 176, 180
People, 155, 166
Peoples Temple, 41
People v. Castro, 150
Pesce, Mary Ann, 48, 51, 53, 55
Peterson Automotive Museum, 190
The Phantom Prince (Kendall), 90
Phil Donahue, 104
Pied Piper of Tucson. *See* Schmid, Charles
Pierce, Cecelia, 174–75, 176
Placido, Judy, 74
Polanski, Roman, 4
police: during the 1960s, 12–13; during the 1980s, 100; homicide departments, 44
pop culture, 74; during the 1970s, 58
Portland Police Department, 26
poverty: during the 1970s, 39–40
Presley, Elvis, 18
Presumed Innocent, 168
Price, John, 15–16, 22
Project Self-Esteem, 174
psychics, 104, 107–8
psychologists, during the 1970s, 47–48
PTL Club, 114
Pue, Terry, 107
Puente, Dorothea, 98, 113–28
Purcell, John (Detective Sgt.), 61, 62

Quantico, 90, 96, 97. *See also* Federal Bureau of Investigation
Quinn, Anthony, 12

race, riots during the 1960s, 12
radio, during the 1990s, 173
Rambo, 129
Rambo: First Blood Part II, 86
Rambo films, 86, 129
Ramirez, Richard (Night Stalker), 97
Ramsey, JonBenét, 148

Randall, Patrick "Pete," 174
rape, 52
Ray, James Earl, 3
Reagan, Nancy, 88, 114
Reagan, Ronald: as Governor, 50; as President, 85, 86
Reams, Charles, 30
Rees, Melvin, 8
Rescue 911, 154, 155, 167
Ressler, Robert, 90, 92, 103, 150–51
Richardson, Christopher, 101
Rifkin, Joel, 148
The Right Stuff (Wolfe), 86
riots, during the 1960s, 12
Roache, Francis "Mickey," 156
The Road to Yuba City (Kidder), 46
Robinson, Jeoff, 143
Robles, Detective, 23
Rock, Wayne (Officer), 154
Rodriguez, Carlos, 141
Rogers, Dayton Leroy, 47
Roller, Steven, 187
Rolling, Danny, 148, 149
Rolling Stones, 4
Rourke, Mickey, 175
Rowe, Alleen, 17
Rowe, Norma, 15, 19
Roxbury, Roy, 10
Rule, Ann, 90, 137, 145
Ruthless People, 114

Sacramento, 116, 117
Sacramento Bee, 126
Sacrifice Unto Me (West), 46
Saia, Police Superintendent, 158
Salee, Linda Dawn, 29, 30, 34, 37–38
Salem Statesman, 28
Samenow, Stanton E., 43
Sanders, Ed, 46
Sanders, Steve, 132
San Francisco Chronicle, 65
Saturday Night Fever, 41
Saunders, John, 13–25, 23, 24
Schall, Cindy, 56
Schechter, Harold, 148
Scheck, Barry, 150
Scherer, Charles (Lt.), 54
Schmid, Charles, 5, 12–25
Schmid, Diane, 25
Schwarz, Ted, 90
Schwerner, Michael, 2
Scorsese, Martin, 41
Scott, Cathy, 185
Seldon, Bruce, 182
serial killers, 89; during the 1960s, 5; during the 1970s, 42–43; during the 1990s, 149
Serial Killers (Norris), 97
Seventh Amendment (U.S. Constitution), 5
Seventh Day Adventists, 47
sex crimes, 8
Shakur, Afeni, 183, 192
Shakur, Mutulu, 183
Shakur, Tupac, viii–ix, 182–92
Sharp, John, 118–19
Sheindlin, Gerald (Judge), 149–50
Sheppard, Marilyn, 5–6
Sheppard, Sam, 5–6
Signature Killers (Keppel), 148, 151
The Silence of the Lambs (Harris), 89
Silver, Gene, 126
Simpson, Nicole Brown, 148
Simpson, O. J., viii, 61, 93, 148, 150
Sinatra, Frank, 4, 103
Sirhan, Sirhan, 3
60 Minutes, viii
Sizelove, Steve (Deputy Sheriff), 60
Slawson, Linda, 25–26, 33, 37
Smalls, Biggie, 183, 187, 189
Smart, Gregory, 169
Smart, Judith, 169, 173
Smart, Pamela, 168–82, 178
Smart, William, 169, 173
Smith, Edward Hope, 99
Smith, Robert, 8
Smith, William French (U.S. Attorney General), 91
Smitty. *See* Schmid, Charles
social environment, during the 1970s, 41
Son of Sam. *See* Berkowitz, David
Son of Sam (Klausner), 90
South Chicago Community Hospital, 6–7
South Dakota, 42
Southside Crips, 187
Speck, Richard, 6–7, 45

Spencer, Bill, 172, 176
sports, during the 1990s, 182
"spree killings," 89
Spring, Polly, 116
Sprinker, Karen, 27–28, 31, 37, 38
Stallone, Sylvester, 86, 129
Starkweather, Charlie, 46
Starkweather (Allen), 46
State Police Communications Center (Massachusetts), 153
Stehens, Charles, 104
Step Into My Parlor: The Chilling Story of Serial Killer Jeffrey Dahmer (Baumann), 148
Stern, Leon, 78
Stine, Paul, 9
The Sting (Hill), 41
stockmarket, crash of 1989, 87
Stone, Irving, 51
Stonewall Club, 61
STOP. *See* Stop Children's Murders
Stop Children's Murders (STOP), 103
Stovall, Jim (Detective), 27, 28, 29, 30, 31
Stranberg, Clarnell, 56
The Stranger Beside Me (Rule), 90
Stuart, Carol, 153–68
Stuart, Charles, 153–68
Stuart, Mark, 162
Stuart, Matthew, 157
Stuart, Michael, 157, 162
suicide, 166
Sullivan, J. L., 62
Sullivan, Jack, 68
Sullivan, Mary, 6
Summer of Love (1967), 4
Sunset Killer. *See* Clark, Douglas
Suriani, Valentina, 73

Task Force on Missing and Murdered Children, 103
Task Force on Violent Crime, 91
Tate, Sharon, 4
Taxi Driver (Scorsese), 41
technology, during the 1990s, 147
Ted Bundy: The Killer Next Door (Winn and Merrill), 90
Teja, Dave, 62–63
Telegraph, 172, 173
television: during the 1980s, 86, 91, 104, 112, 126; during the 1990s, 147, 150, 152
Terms of Endearment, 86
Terrell, Earl, 103
terrorism, during the 1970s, 42
Terry, Maury, 83
Teten, Howard, 45
Texas, 86, 92
Thorpe, Rosalind, 56–57
Thriller, 87
Thug Life, 188
Tickle Me, 18
Time, 13, 23, 92, 155, 166
Time Warner, 192
Tinney, William, 23
Tinning, Marybeth, 98
Tithecott, Richard, 148
Today, 166
Trash Bag Killer. *See* Kearney, Patrick Wayne
Travolta, John, 41
"Trial of the Century," 6–7
Trujillo, Brenda, 120
Tucson American, 24
Tucson Police Department, 23
20/20, 147
Twin Cities Mortuary, 60
"Two of Americaz Most Wanted," 189
2Pacalypse Now, 188
Tyler, Mary, 17
Tyson, Mike, 182

The Ultimate Evil (Terry), 83
Unabomber. *See* Kaczynski, Ted
Unabomber: The Trail of America's Most Wanted Serial Killer (Douglas and Olshaker), 148
unemployment, during the 1970s, 39–40
United States: during the 1960s, 1–38; during the 1970s, 39–83; during the 1980s, 85–145; during the 1990s, 147–92; stockmarket crash of 1989, 87; World War II, 12, 57
"Unsung Heroes," 116
U.S. Centers for Disease Control, 101, 103

U.S. Department of Justice, 2, 88–89; Criminal Identification and Investigation division, 6565; Latent Prints Section, 65
U.S. Supreme Court, 5, 7

Vacaville Medical Facility, 71
Valdosta Correctional Institution, 113
Valenti, Jody, 71–72
Valentine, Beth, 115
Vanezis, Peter (Dr.), 96
Van Gogh, Vincent, 87, 114
Ventura School for Girls, 129
veterinarians, 95
Vibe, 189, 190
VICAP. *See* Violent Criminal Apprehension Programm
victims, 90
video identification, 96
Vietnam, 2, 39, 58
Vilcko, Stephanie, 27
Violante, Bobby, 75–76
Violent Criminal Apprehension Programm (VICAP), 91, 92, 96–97, 152
VOA. *See* Volunteers of America
Volunteers of America (VOA), 115
Voskerichian, Virginia, 72–73

Walker, Curtis, 108
Wall Street, 114, 887
Walpole State Prison, 6
War on Poverty, 87
Warren Commission (1964), 3
Watergate, 40–41
Watson, Tex, 4
Weatherman, 42
Webster, William, 106
Welch, Ralph, 178
Welcome, Mary, 112
West, Don, 46
White, Cynthia, 169–70
White, Robert (State Police Lieutenant), 27
Whiteaker, Roy (Sheriff), 60, 61
White House, 104, 107
Whites, 2
Whitney, Eric, 159, 160, 161
Whitney, Jan, 26–27, 37
"Who Shot Ya?," 189
Wilcox, Robert, 46, 62
Wilhelm, Robert (Sergeant), 15, 16, 22
Willgues, Charles, 125–26
Williams, Bart, 70
Williams, Faye, 109
Williams, Homer, 109
Williams, Wayne B., 98–113, 109, 110, 113
Willis, Bruce, 86
Wilson, Colin, 7–8, 43
Wilson, Damon, 7–8, 43
Wilson, Jim, 120, 121
Wilson, LaTonya, 101, 104, 106
Winn, Steven, 90
Winnacunnet High School, 168
Wolfe, Tom, 86
Wolfgang, Marvin, 40
women: and their killers, 43; as victims, 90
Wood, Catherine, 98
Wood, Sharon, 34
Woodstock, 4
World War II, 12, 57
Wyche, Aaron, 102

Yahoo, 152
Yochelson, Samuel, 43
Arthur Young Company, 156
YouTube, 152
yuppies, 86, 157

Zebra (Howard), 90
Zebra murders, 90
Zeller, Sharon, 46
Zellers, 95
Zodiac killer, 5, 9–10, 89
Zorba the Greek, 12

ABOUT THE AUTHOR

GINI GRAHAM SCOTT is a professional writer with over 40 books to her credit including *Homicide by the Rich and Famous: A Century of Prominent Killers* (Praeger, 2005), *Disagreements, Disputes, and All Out War*, and *A Survival Guide for Working with Humans*, among others.